BLACK&DECKER®

THE COMPLETE GUIDE TO

A GREEN HOME

The Good Citizen's Guide to Earth-friendly Remodeling & Home Maintenance

by Philip Schmidt

Creative Publishing
international

MINNEAPOLIS, MINNESOTA
www.creativepub.com

Creative Publishing international

Copyright © 2008
Creative Publishing international, Inc.
400 First Avenue North, Suite 300
Minneapolis, Minnesota 55401
1-800-328-0590
www.creativepub.com
All rights reserved

Printed at R.R. Donnelly

10 9 8 7 6 5 4 3 2 1

Library of Congress Cataloging-in-Publication Data

The complete guide to the green home : the good citizen's guide to Earth-friendly remodeling & home maintenance.
    p. cm.
  At head of title: Black & Decker.
  Summary: "Features popular home remodeling projects and maintenance information from an approach that's 100% green"--Provided by publisher.
  Includes bibliographical references and index.
  ISBN-13: 978-1-58923-379-9 (soft cover : alk. paper)
  ISBN-10: 1-58923-379-4 (soft cover : alk. paper)
  1. Ecological houses--Design and construction. 2. Dwellings--Maintenance and repair. 3. Environmental protection--Citizen participation. I. Title.

  TH4860.C66 2008
  643'.7--dc22

2008003772

President/CEO: Ken Fund
VP for Sales & Marketing: Kevin Hamric

Home Improvement Group

Publisher: Bryan Trandem
Managing Editor: Tracy Stanley
Senior Editor: Mark Johanson
Editor: Jennifer Gehlhar

Creative Director: Michele Lanci-Altomare
Senior Design Managers: Jon Simpson, Brad Springer
Design Managers: Sara Holle, James Kegley

Lead Photographer: Steve Galvin
Photo Coordinator: Joanne Wawra
Shop Manager: Bryan McLain
Shop Assistant: Cesar Fernandez Rodriguez

Production Managers: Linda Halls, Laura Hokkanen

Page Layout Artist: Danielle Smith
Illustration: Accurate Art, Inc.
Photographer: Andrea Rugg
Shop Help: Scott Boyd, Dave Hartley

The Complete Guide to A Green Home
Created by: The Editors of Creative Publishing international, Inc., in cooperation with Black & Decker.
Black & Decker® is a trademark of The Black & Decker Corporation and is used under license.

Contents

The Complete Guide to A Green Home

Going Green— an Introduction

What does it mean to go green? It depends on who you ask. For some, it means filling their homes with natural, non-toxic materials and furnishings to ensure safe, high-quality indoor air. For others, it's carefully choosing products made from sustainable and renewable sources. And to a great many others, going green is mostly about conservation: saving energy and water in an effort to reduce pollution and help protect our natural resources for future generations. But perhaps most likely of all, the incentive for going green is some combination of these goals.

Whatever you hope to achieve by going green, the good news is that you don't necessarily have to sell your house and build an earth-sheltered hut on the outskirts of civilization. There are so many ways to make an ordinary home greener that we couldn't possibly include all of them in this book (although we've tried to touch on most of them). You can make these changes as they seem necessary or perhaps start by tackling a short list of items that are most important to meeting your green goals.

This chapter gets you started with a brief introduction to thinking green and will help you recognize what makes some products and materials greener than others. From there, the book takes you on a room-by-room tour of a green home, followed by an in-depth look at each of a home's primary systems. Along the way, you'll find dozens of step-by-step projects that show how easy it is for one home—your home—to make a difference.

In this chapter:

- The Principles of Green
- Choosing Materials

The Principles of Green

In the big picture, the green movement encompasses all aspects of building design and construction, as well as the operation of a building or home throughout its life. It also considers the destruction of old buildings and the disposal or recycling of used building materials. "Green" means different things to different people, but here are the basic principles common among most green home initiatives:

1. *Energy efficiency*
   Reducing energy demands through everyday conservation; energy-efficient appliances; and an airtight, well-insulated thermal envelope.

2. *Water conservation*
   Planning drought-tolerant, low-maintenance landscapes and gardens; using low-flow fixtures and water-saving appliances throughout the house.

3. *Smart materials*
   Choosing construction and finish materials for their low environmental impact, sustainable production, low toxicity, durability, and recyclability.

4. *High air quality and minimal pollution*
   Ensuring healthy indoor air with non-toxic materials and effective ventilation; minimizing outdoor environmental pollution from fertilizers, pesticides, and landscape equipment.

5. *Natural systems*
   Increasing reliance on the sun, wind, and plants for electricity, lighting, heating, cooling, and air quality.

All of these principles can be applied by homeowners in any type—or age—of home and in all climates. For those planning to build a new home or expand an existing one, additional design considerations can be followed to minimize site disturbance during excavation and to reduce waste through efficient construction techniques and building materials. At the highest level of green home building, city planners and residential developers can plan communities that allow residents to walk, cycle, or take public transportation instead of driving to their everyday destinations. Housing projects can also be designed to minimize the destruction of prime land and to preserve natural areas for everyone to enjoy.

The furnishings and decorative finishes we choose for our homes can have a significant impact on the quality of our indoor air. Natural materials and easy-to-clean surfaces reduce airborne pollutants and help limit hiding places for mold and other allergens.

Meeting all of these goals may sound idealistic, but it's happening in countless communities and cities throughout the world. And it's easy to see why, because the more you start to think green, the more you realize that it's simply a better way to do what we're already doing. A green home isn't just easier on the environment, it's more comfortable and more pleasant to live in—and it costs less to run, every day of every year.

Landscapes, and how we maintain them, play an important role in creating green homes and communities. Low-maintenance ground covers and drought-tolerant grasses consume much less in the long run than sprawling turf lawns.

Building science has made enormous strides in recent decades, making high-tech and high-performance home products such as solar energy panels more accessible and affordable.

The Paradox of Green

Going green always makes sense, but that's not to say it's always simple. One of the inherent challenges of making responsible decisions is getting to the bottom line. In other words, what is the net effect (or final benefit) of doing something green? For example, let's say you have a fairly old but well-functioning refrigerator that uses 40% more electricity to run than a new Energy Star model. You crunch some numbers and determine that the new fridge will save you $100 a year in energy costs, meaning the upgrade will pay for itself within a few years.

Of course, saving electricity yields clear environmental benefits, but what about the environmental costs of producing the new appliance and shipping it to your local store? And then there's the matter of disposing of your old fridge—if you don't recycle it through a reputable vendor, it could end up in the landfill, or, worse, become damaged and release ozone-depleting Freon gas into the atmosphere. Keeping your old unit merely postpones the inevitability of replacement, but doesn't it also slow the pace of consumption and the industrial processes that are so taxing to the environment?

Here's another example of a green paradox: You're remodeling your kitchen and are committed to using as many green products as possible. One of them is a fabulous new countertop material made with recycled glass and non-toxic, petroleum-free binders. However, this product is currently made only in Oregon, and you live in Atlanta. On the upside, this product promotes the reuse of discarded materials and supports low-impact production methods. On the downside, it has to be shipped thousands of miles on a gas-guzzling, heavily polluting truck.

In the end, it's up to you to make the call on whether something is—ultimately—green or not. In the first example, maybe you'd decide to keep the old fridge and focus your energy-saving efforts elsewhere, perhaps replacing a couple of dozen lightbulbs with compact fluorescent lamps. In the second example, maybe you'll look a little harder for a locally made countertop that's also eco-friendly. Or you might decide to go with your original inclination on both counts.

But regardless of which route you take, one undeniable net benefit remains: By using your purchasing power to support eco-minded businesses and high-quality, efficient product design, you're helping to promote a marketplace and a business community that's committed to positive change. In our market economy, nothing speaks louder than the consumer dollar. It's a simple equation: green begets green.

Closing the loop: Choosing products made with recyclables and alternative materials makes sustainable systems stronger.

Room for (Home) Improvement ▸

The home building and remodeling industry deserves some credit for many efficiencies and improvements made over the years. Homes today are far better insulated and more airtight than they were 50 years ago. Engineered products like plywood and oriented strandboard (OSB) use much less wood than traditional solid lumber. Advances in windows, appliances, and heating and cooling equipment also have played a big role in reducing energy waste.

But at the same time, our homes continue to grow in size, and these larger spaces must be heated and cooled around the clock. We also have a lot more gadgets that require electricity, like computers, extra TVs, hot tubs, and multiple refrigerators (fortunately, waterbeds and their hoggish heaters went out of style decades ago).

It's easy to ignore the environmental effects of our homes because most of the damage is done remotely; that is, at the power plants and mines where most of our energy comes from. In light of that, here are a few statistics (just a few) that can help put the role of housing into perspective:

- In 1950, the average single-family American home was about 1,000 sq. ft., or about 290 sq. ft. per family member.
- In 2004, the average home size was 2,340 sq. ft., about 900 sq. ft. per family member.
- Building the average single-family home produces 7,000 to 12,000 pounds of construction waste.
- The typical family in the U.S. spends $1,300 a year on home energy bills.
- Measured in the year 2000, residences accounted for 20% of the total energy-related carbon dioxide emissions in the U.S. and consumed 35% of all electricity produced in the nation.
- Carbon dioxide is one of the primary greenhouse gasses believed to be causing global warming, among other environmental problems.
- Constructing homes and commercial buildings, along with heating and cooling these buildings, accounts for about half of the total greenhouse gas emissions in the U.S.

As average home sizes have risen, so has average energy consumption. As a result, high-voltage power lines have become standard fare in most neighborhoods.

Choosing Materials

You've probably noticed that product manufacturers are increasingly catching on to the marketability of all things "green." You see packaging everywhere featuring little, green tree emblems and buzzwords like healthy, earth, and eco. These marketing symbols should prompt you to look closely at the ingredients list or product description so you really know what you're getting. But when it comes to larger purchases of building materials, like lumber and paint, and finish elements, like flooring and cabinets, choosing green products is more complicated.

The following is an overview of the many criteria that determine a product's relative greenness ("relative" because purchasing decisions often involve some compromise, as you'll see). In general,

there are four factors that you should consider when choosing a product:

- Embodied energy
- Sustainability and resource efficiency
- Toxicity
- Durability

Any of these factors may influence your decision to use one material over another. Considering all of them in addition to what happens with the material at the end of its useful life is a concept often referred to as life-cycle assessment. Simply put, a material that scores well on all of the four main factors *and* can be recycled or reused at the end of its life is about as green as it gets.

Assessing the environmental impact of a product starts with a look at the energy and other resources used in cultivating or extracting its raw materials. For example, try to choose lumber species that are native to your area to reduce the energy needed for transportation.

Embodied Energy

Embodied energy is a measure of the total energy required to manufacture, transport, and install a product or material. This includes all of the energy used in harvesting or extracting the raw materials, fabricating the finished product, shipping it to your local store or job site, and applying it to your house.

As an example, goods made with recycled raw materials typically have lower embodied energy than those made with virgin materials. Using recycled paper,

for instance, means you don't have to grow trees, cut them down, and ship them for initial processing. Similarly, stone cut from a local quarry has lower embodied energy than stone trucked in from another state.

Embodied energy is something that you'll probably never find listed on product labels, but experts in the building sciences frequently use it as a factor of greenness, and you'll see it mentioned in numerous green building sources (including this book).

Sustainability & Resource Efficiency

Sustainability, or sustainable production, relates to the environmental impact of producing or harvesting a material. Generally speaking, a renewable resource, such as wood, is more sustainable than a finite resource, such as marble or a petroleum-based product. Rate of renewal is another factor to consider. For example, many types of bamboo can be harvested every three to five years, while hardwood products may come from trees that are 25 years old or older. But when it's harvested from properly managed forests, wood can be a highly sustainable material; see Forest Stewardship Council, on page 13.

Resource-efficient products are those that make the most with the least amount of resource material. Good examples are engineered wood products, like plywood and particleboard. These are made with small, fast-growing trees or with wood chips or pulp that may or may not be recycled. Reclaiming or salvaging used materials is ideal in terms of resource efficiency because it means an existing material is getting a second life, obviating the manufacture of a new product (see Resource Revival, on page 12).

Cork, used to make these floor tiles, is a sustainable material because it's taken from trees every 10 years or so without harming the tree.

Toxicity

Many common building products contain chemicals and pollutants that can seriously compromise the quality of the air in a home. Paints, stains, and other finishes, as well as caulks and adhesives, often are made with agents that release volatile organic compounds (VOCs) as they dry and for extended periods afterward. Composite wood materials, such as particleboard used for cabinet boxes and bookshelves, may contain toxic binders that offgas into the home, while carpeting, furniture, and textiles may be treated with harmful flame retardants and pesticides. For all of these products and materials, there are low-toxicity and non-toxic alternatives available, many at competitive prices.

Adhesives, spray products, paints, and other finishes with low emissions of toxic fumes are becoming commonplace on retail store shelves. Many are clearly labeled as *green* or *low-VOC*.

Durability

Quality, highly durable materials can be green simply because they last longer and require less maintenance than lower-quality goods. Postponing or preventing replacement means fewer resources are used in producing new goods. In some cases, durability is considered a tradeoff with the inherent greenness of a product. For example, aluminum comes with a high price tag of embodied energy. However, it's a very durable material and essentially rustproof, so it outlasts many other products and requires very little maintenance.

A green product on many counts, wood composite decking is made with post-consumer recycled plastic and wood fibers. It doesn't need toxic finishes for protection, and it outlasts solid-wood decking by a long shot.

Resource Revival

Finding new uses for old materials is one of the best ways to go green. It not only saves on the production of new goods, it often means you get unusual products of a quality or variety that are no longer available. Old building materials may come from a number of sources. Wood elements can be reclaimed from all kinds of buildings being torn down. Salvaged timber may come from urban trees that are felled by city maintenance crews and from "sinker logs" dredged up from river bottoms, where they sank during the old days when timber was transported down waterways.

Reclaimed timbers and lumber can be machine-milled for a variety of applications or may be sold with a hand-hewn finish or in "as-is" condition, retaining all of its original character marks. Other materials that can be had on the salvage market include brick, stone, metal construction members, and all sorts of finish materials, like tile, trimwork, and plaster details.

If you're looking for one-of-a-kind interior elements or period details, architectural salvage dealers have it all—windows, doors, fireplace mantels, stair parts, light fixtures, sinks, bathtubs, cabinetry, and so on. Some of these same treasures can also be found at antique shops and through building materials recyclers.

In addition to buying reclaimed products, you might approach the salvage market from the supply side: If you're planning a major renovation, consider deconstruction instead of demolition. An increasing number of companies and contractors are making a business out of taking apart homes and other buildings and selling the salvageable materials. Or, you can do your own deconstructing and sell the materials to a recycler to help offset your construction costs (and do a good turn for the environment to boot).

To find salvage and used materials retailers in your area, look in the phone book under *Building Materials—Used, Salvage, Junk Dealers* or under the names of specific building materials. Sources for reclaimed lumber and wood products can be found by searching online using keywords like *reclaimed lumber, recycled lumber,* and *salvaged wood.*

Before you head out on the salvage trail, here are a few words of warning about reusing materials:

- Check for lead on any old painted stuff. There are several ways to deal with lead paint and effectively eliminate its health risks; for more information, visit the EPA's web page at www.epa.gov/lead.
- Select kiln-dried reclaimed lumber and timbers; this is the best way to ensure the wood is bug-free.
- Have an expert inspect any materials you plan to use for structural applications.
- Don't use old windows and toilets for their original purposes; they're too wasteful.

Commonly available forms of reclaimed lumber include structural beams and columns, flooring, paneling, and custom-milled trimwork.

Post-Consumer & Post-Industrial Recycling

POST-CONSUMER RECYCLED PAPER

Take a look on the back of an ordinary recycled paper product and you're likely to see a note like this: *Printed on 85% post-consumer recycled paper.* Manufacturers' literature and green products directories may include a similar statement about a specific product, but they might also provide the percentage of the product's *post-industrial* content. What's the difference?

Post-consumer means the source materials were taken from consumers' garbage, or, rather, their recycling bins. This is stuff that would end up in the landfill if it weren't claimed for use in a new product. Post-industrial means the material comes from manufacturing waste—the trimmings that fall to the factory floor or the sawdust created at the mill. Both types of recycled content represent a good use of material that would otherwise go to waste. But post-consumer offers the advantage of creating a break (if only a partial break) in the waste stream and therefore yields a greater environmental benefit than post-industrial content.

Tip: FSC-Certified Wood ▶

The Forest Stewardship Council (FSC) is an international nonprofit group that certifies forests and wood products based on established standards of responsible forest management. Products bearing the FSC stamp have been monitored by third-party officials from the raw material stage in the forest through processing, manufacturing, and distribution— what the FSC refers to as part of their "chain of custody" standards. FSC certification is the best way to ensure that wood products and materials come from sustainable, renewable sources, just like all wood should. For more information, visit www.fsc.org.

Pre-consumer and post-consumer waste paper are primary ingredients in the slurry that is hardened to produce this innovative new countertop material. Individual sections of countertop can be sawed, sanded, and then fastened together by gluing, screwing, or nailing. The appearance is similar to solid surfacing, but the product is made without the plastic resins and chemical binders used in the manufacture of solid surfaces.

Who Are The Green Experts? ▸

As a grassroots movement, green building has been defined and promoted by a variety of groups and individuals, including state and local governments, industry organizations, building design and construction professionals, manufacturers, and homeowners. The federal government has also weighed in, with programs like Energy Star and other initiatives that establish standards of energy efficiency and promote advancement in building technologies. However, there is currently no set of nationally recognized codes or standards for green home building and remodeling.

The following is a partial list of experts and organizations that are working to define what a green home should be. Many of them have extensive websites and/or publications full of information for both homeowners and professionals interested in going green.

U.S. GREEN BUILDING COUNCIL—USGBC

www.usgbc.org

The USGBC, a nonprofit group of industry professionals and government experts, has been a leading national authority on green building for many years. The Council's LEED program (Leadership in Energy and Environmental Design) is the most widely recognized certification program for green commercial and residential buildings.

U.S. ENVIRONMENTAL PROTECTION AGENCY—EPA

www.epa.gov

The EPA's website is a good source of information for a variety of home-health issues, such as mold, lead, radon, asbestos, and indoor air quality.

NATIONAL ASSOCIATION OF HOME BUILDERS—NAHB

www.nahb.org

The nation's leading organization of professional home builders educates members and consumers on a broad range of green building issues. The NAHB's *Model Green Home Building Guidelines* is a comprehensive guide for mainstream home builders to follow when designing and building a green home. The complete *Guidelines* document is available for free download on the association's website.

U.S. DEPARTMENT OF ENERGY—DOE

www.eere.energy.gov
www.energystar.gov

The Department of Energy sponsors two extensive programs for educating consumers on energy efficiency and other home energy-related topics:

- The Energy Efficiency and Renewable Energy website offers detailed, user-friendly information on everything from home appliances to solar panels.
- The Energy Star program awards the Energy Star label (see page 21) to the most energy-efficient home products. The Energy Star website is a great consumer resource for finding products and manufacturers, as well as tips and tools for saving energy around the home.

PARTNERSHIP FOR ADVANCING HOUSING TECHNOLOGY—PATH

www.pathnet.org

PATH is a public-private organization overseen by the Department of Housing and Urban Development (HUD). Its main goal is to promote innovation in residential technology to make ordinary homes more durable, efficient, and affordable. PATH's *Top 10 Technologies* is an annually compiled list of cutting-edge products and techniques, many of them ideally suited to a green home.

STATE & MUNICIPAL ENERGY OFFICES

Your state or local energy authority may be a good resource for information on green policies and green professionals in your area.

BUILDINGGREEN, INC.

www.buildinggreen.com
BuildingGreen is a publisher of print and electronic resources for green building professionals. Its *GreenSpec* product directory is widely used in the industry, while the companion reference, *Green Building Materials,* is a good resource for homeowners seeking green products and manufacturers.

AMERICAN INSTITUTE OF ARCHITECTS—AIA

www.aia.org
The leading national organization of professional architects is supporting a challenge to reduce the carbon emissions of all new and renovated buildings by 50% by 2010 and a longer-term goal of carbon neutral buildings by 2030. As part of this initiative, the AIA publishes a list of 50 principles of sustainable design (called 50to50) on its website. Local architects who specialize in green building also can be a good source of information.

Keeping Pace with Green Technology ▸

With the recent explosion of interest in green technology for the home, the number of new green products available to consumers is growing faster than most of us can track. From building materials to appliances to diagnostic equipment, it takes some effort to keep pace with what's new. If you do a bit of exploring, you'll find a wealth of e-newsletters, periodicals, and websites that are dedicated to reporting on the latest eco-friendly products.

As the green demand continues to grow, however, staying up-to-date will only get easier. In what was formerly a niche market, even larger manufacturers have begun bringing green-oriented products to market in the types of stores most do-it-yourselfers are accustomed to visiting. For example, the power-monitoring device seen here is one of a new class of products from Black & Decker. The idea is fairly simple. A wireless transmitter is strapped to an electric meter. It wirelessly sends information to a small cordless display monitor (shown in hand in picture) that you keep in a central household location. Once you program the display unit with your electricity rate (from your utility bill), it tells you minute-by-minute energy usage, in both dollars and kW/Hr readings. This creates the ability for you to gauge exactly how much energy each appliance or other load is consuming simply by watching the output readings change when the load is turned on. This tool even has a month-to-date feature so you can track your energy costs and a predictive tool that gives you an estimate of your bill weeks before you receive it.

As green home products move from niche markets into the mainstream, devices such as this electronic energy-monitoring device are becoming easier to locate and more affordable.

Green Kitchens

In the evolution of home design, the kitchen has steadily gained prominence for several decades now. Compared to plans of the 1950s, today's kitchens are more open, brighter, and better integrated with the rest of the house. They're also more visible and play a much larger role in the home's overall decorative scheme. So what better place than the kitchen to start making green improvements. Besides, shopping for beautiful, eco-friendly cabinets is a lot more fun than comparing performance ratings on attic insulation (but we'll get to that later).

Greening up your kitchen doesn't have to be an exercise in restraint. All that's required is clever design and attention to detail. In today's marketplace, you'll find that restricting yourself to kitchen products and materials that promote efficiency, healthfulness, and sustainability is anything but restrictive.

In this chapter:

- What Makes a Kitchen Green?
- Green Kitchen Appliances
- Replacing a Dishwasher
- Water for Drinking & Recycling
- Carbon Water Filtration Systems
- Reverse Osmosis Water Filtration Systems
- Kitchen Lighting
- Under-Cabinet Fluorescent Task Lighting
- Cabinets & Countertops
- Laminate Countertops
- Flooring

What Makes a Kitchen Green?

In many ways, a green kitchen is just like any well-designed kitchen. There are windows for natural lighting and air circulation. Surfaces are durable, hygienic, and low-maintenance. The room is well lighted, with overhead fixtures and plenty of task lighting. And the overall plan is designed for maximum work efficiency and tailored to the way the homeowners use the kitchen on a daily basis. In terms of aesthetics, a green kitchen can be just as beautiful, if not more so, than a conventional kitchen.

So what's different about a green kitchen? For starters, it has highly efficient appliances, particularly the refrigerator. It contains sustainable and non-toxic materials, like formaldehyde-free cabinet cases and linoleum flooring. It's also ready to deal with the variety of waste products surrounding food preparation, including organic garbage, recyclable materials, and gray water.

Many green kitchens are further defined by what they don't have: trendy upgrades and extras that do little to improve anyone's daily experience in the kitchen. Depending on the type of cooking you do, you might get a lot of use out of special features, like a pot filler faucet, an extra prep sink, warming drawers, or a commercial-style range. But in reality, most cooks don't get full value from these pricey additions, which always take up space and are often over-engineered and energy-inefficient (not to mention the environmental impact of producing them).

Whether you're planning a major kitchen remodel or simply replacing an item or two, here are some of the main elements you should consider for making the space more useful, healthful, and resource-efficient.

Efficiency and common sense are two of the hallmarks of any green room, but this is especially true in the kitchen. Keep the appliances as small as you can and look for natural materials, like this butcherblock countertop made from maple cutoffs.

Portrait of a Green Kitchen

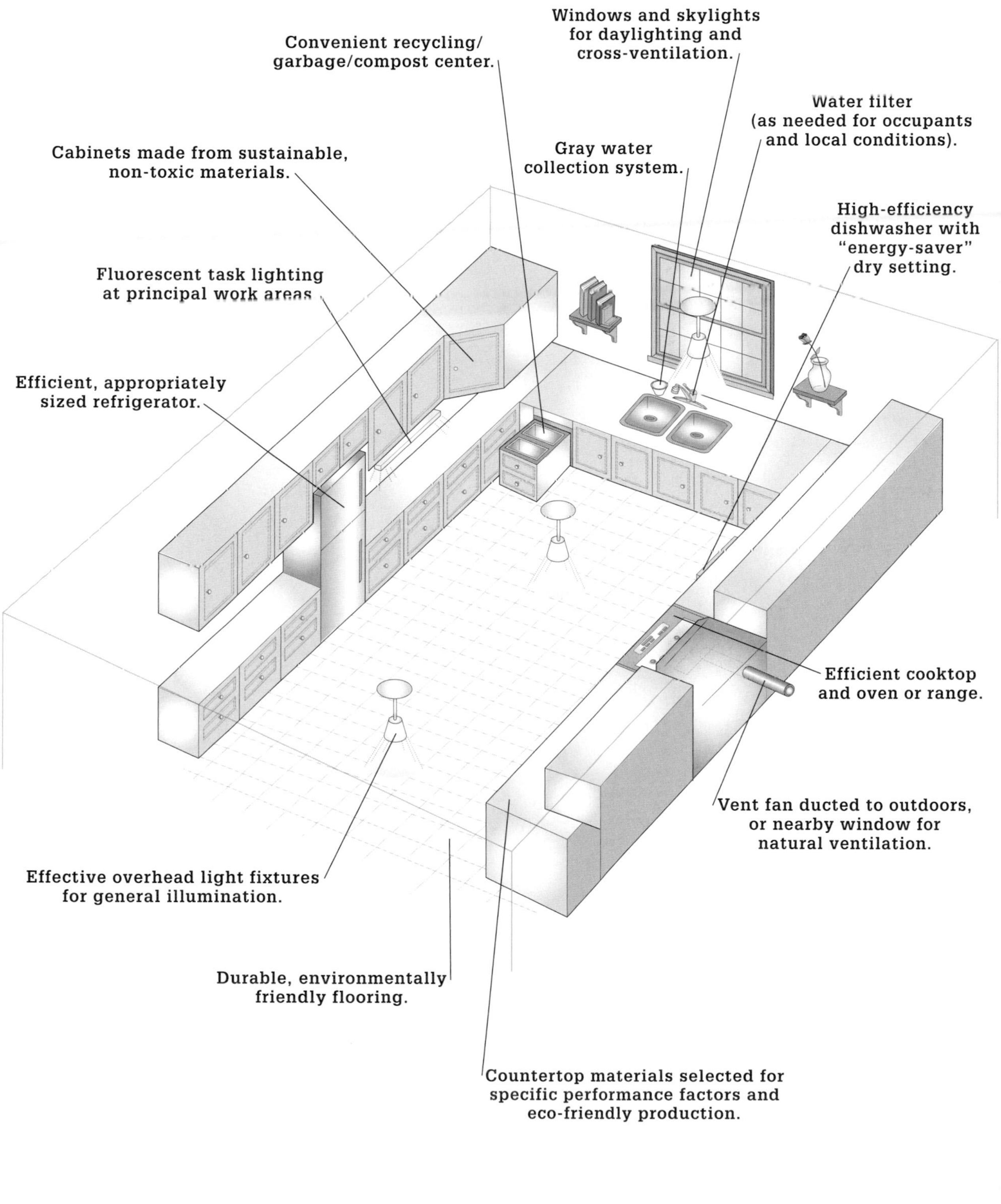

Convenient recycling/
garbage/compost center.

Windows and skylights
for daylighting and
cross-ventilation.

Water filter
(as needed for occupants
and local conditions).

Cabinets made from sustainable,
non-toxic materials.

Gray water
collection system.

High-efficiency
dishwasher with
"energy-saver"
dry setting.

Fluorescent task lighting
at principal work areas

Efficient, appropriately
sized refrigerator.

Efficient cooktop
and oven or range.

Effective overhead light fixtures
for general illumination.

Vent fan ducted to outdoors,
or nearby window for
natural ventilation.

Durable, environmentally
friendly flooring.

Countertop materials selected for
specific performance factors and
eco-friendly production.

Green Kitchen Appliances

Because it's full of hardworking appliances, the kitchen uses more energy than any other room in the house. Upgrading your old machines with more efficient models is one of the simplest ways to help make your kitchen green. Refrigerators are the big users, accounting for up to 15% of the average home's total electricity usage. Fortunately, you don't have to sacrifice quality or style to save energy. Highly efficient appliances, like many other machines, are simply better designed and better built than their hoggish counterparts. And you can't tell a miserly model by its looks.

Lots of do-it-yourselfers install their own appliances; see pages 30 to 33 for steps on installing a high-efficiency dishwasher. A refrigerator is the easiest to install: Just plug it in, slide it in place, and level it. If yours has an icemaker (a not-so-green option), you'll have to connect a small water line in the back of the unit (and check it for leaks in the beginning).

If you're replacing an existing appliance, first find out where you can recycle the old unit.

Appliances are a major source of recyclable steel and other materials, and besides, dumping an operable machine in the landfill just to make room for a new one isn't a very green move. Appliances that still work can find a great home through a local charity organization (this means an old, inefficient appliance is still in circulation, but it postpones the production of a new product, and it helps out those in need). To scrap an ailing or dead appliance, contact your local recycling authority or Earth 911, online at www.earth911.org.

Whatever you do, don't keep your old refrigerator and move it into the garage for backup storage. If you need that much space, you're either drinking too much beer (or maybe not enough) or you're a freezer-hoarder (if you've recently discovered a frost-covered parcel labeled "Thanksgiving stuffing 1997," your problem is the latter). Keeping a second fridge plugged in will undo all energy-saving efforts from your kitchen upgrades many times over.

European sized refrigerators are becoming increasing popular as a way to control energy usage. A typical model like the one above has a refrigerator compartment of 7-to-8 cubic feet in capacity, with a freezer that's 3 to 4 cu. ft.

Scale is important and many kitchen appliance manufacturers have begun marketing to this. Narrow dishwashers with smaller compartments offer ample space for some users, and they do their job with much less water and energy.

Energy Star & Energyguide Labels ▸

If you're in the market for a new appliance, it's time to start paying attention to those yellow-and-black ENERGYGUIDE labels you see pasted to the front of many new products. The labels, required by the Federal Trade Commission, help consumers quickly compare models for their energy efficiency. The box in the middle of each label provides the "energy use" of all models in a given class, with an arrow showing where that particular model falls within the range. The label also gives you an estimated annual operating cost for the appliance.

Energy Star is the Department of Energy's wide-reaching program that awards Energy Star status to the most efficient products in a given class. The program applies to major appliances, windows, doors, HVAC systems, and other household items. In general, Energy Star products exceed the federal government's energy-efficiency standards and perform within the top 25% of their category.

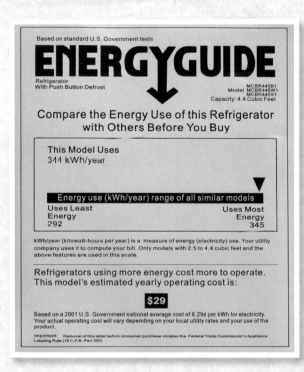

Additional Resources for Choosing & Using Kitchen Appliances ▸

- U.S. Department of Energy (DOE): www.eere.energy.gov
- Energy Star: www.energystar.gov
- Consumer Reports, for unbiased analysis of appliance performance and other shopping considerations, online at www.consumerreports.org
- American Council for an Energy-Efficient Economy: www.aceee.org

- Your local utility provider
- Your state's energy authority; some states offer rebates on high-efficiency appliances
- Association of Home Appliance Manufacturers: www.aham.org
- The Green Guide: www.thegreenguide.com

Refrigerators

Thanks to stricter federal standards, today's refrigerators are about three times more efficient than those of a few decades ago. However, your fridge still accounts for a good chunk of your electric bill, mostly because it's one of the only appliances that runs constantly. So it pays to shop carefully when buying a new one.

First, decide what size is right for the household. If you go too big, you'll be paying to cool empty space for the next 10 to 15 years. Go too small and you might be forced to get a second unit, which is the least-green way to refrigerate. Next, consider type and features. Units with freezers on top tend to be the most efficient, while side-by-side units are the least. Icemakers also reduce efficiency, as do through-the-door ice and water dispensers. Manual defrost on a freezer tends to add efficiency. However, if you're like most people and won't defrost regularly, you'll lose the extra energy savings due to frost buildup. Energy Star refrigerators are commonly 10 to 20 percent more efficient than conventional new models.

Efficient Refrigeration Tips ▸

- Set refrigerator temperature at 36° to 38° F; set freezer at 0° to 3° F. These are standard storage temperatures, not "conservation" settings.
- If possible, locate refrigerator out of direct sunlight and away from the stove and other heat sources.
- Allow adequate space for air circulation around the unit's condenser coils.
- Use power-saving mode, if available.
- Cover food for storage (to reduce condensation inside the units), and let hot foods cool before refrigerating or freezing.
- Keep fridge and freezer full but not stuffed; food retains cold better than air, but the units must have air circulation to work efficiently.

A standard-size (18 to 21 c. ft.) top-freezer refrigerator offers excellent energy performance.

Dishwashers

Washing dishes is one of the few things that are greener to do mechanically than manually. Studies have shown (yes, this has actually been researched by science) that hand-washing dishes uses two to four times more water than washing in a dishwasher. Today's full-size dishwashers use only around seven to 10 gallons of water per load, but therein lies their greatest energy consumption: heating the water.

Up to 80% of a dishwasher's energy use comes from heating the water at your water heater. So when shopping for a new unit, be sure to compare models for their water usage, among other factors. Many newer dishwashers have internal heaters that boost the incoming water temperature from the standard 120° up to 140° or higher for optimal cleaning. This prevents you from having to turn up your water heater (and heating all of its 40 to 75 gallons of water the extra 20°, 24 hours a day) to get the same performance.

Other features affecting consumption are load settings, such as "light/china," "normal," and "pots and pans." To compare the relative efficiency among models, you'll have to obtain the water and energy usage data for the various settings from the salesperson or manufacturer. Be aware that soil-sensing features (which automatically set water use and cycle duration by how dirty the dishes are) can significantly affect efficiency, and manufacturers may base their data on ideal rather than realistic conditions. Most models also have an "energy-saver" or "no-heat" dry option, which uses air rather than heat to dry the dishes. In general, an Energy Star rating often means 25% greater efficiency over comparable non-Energy Star models.

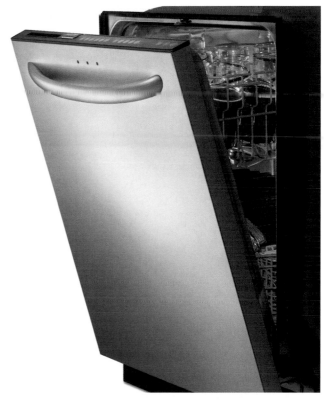

The most efficient dishwashers use less water, since most of this appliance's energy goes toward water heating.

Efficient Dishwashing Tips ▸

- Wash full loads only.
- Don't pre-rinse dishes in the sink (if you have a good dishwasher); just scrape off the solids into a compost or trash container and go straight to the dishwasher. If you find rinsing is necessary, don't run the tap while you rinse. Instead, stop the sink or use a plastic tub and reuse the same water for all rinsing; the dishes won't be clean, but even a lousy dishwasher can take it from there.
- Install a booster heater on an older dishwasher instead of turning up your home's water heater. It makes sense to heat 10 or so gallons for each dish load rather than an entire tank-full at all times.
- Use air-dry option whenever practical. In dry climates, turning off the dishwasher and pulling out the racks is usually faster than mechanical drying.
- Wash dishes during off-peak hours (typically 9 pm to 7 am) if your utility company offers a reduced rate for off-peak usage.

Cooking Appliances

Cooktops, ovens, ranges, microwaves, and other cooking devices generally don't consume a lot of energy in the average household. Typically, cooking habits have a far greater effect on efficiency than choosing one brand or model of appliance over another. If you're looking to replace an appliance, cooking performance will most likely outweigh energy efficiency. As for the kitchen on the whole, providing ventilation is an important element to ensure health and comfort. But for the record, here's a quick breakdown of energy performance:

- Cooktop/Stove: Induction cooktops are the most energy efficient (about 90% energy efficiency), followed by electric (60%) and gas (50%).
- Oven: Gas ovens are cheaper to operate than electric (at current average rates). Convection ovens can be the most efficient because they require less cooking time than conventional types.
- Microwaves, crockpots, and toaster ovens can be far more efficient than full-size electric ovens because they are smaller and/or faster.

Induction cooktops are at the high end of the price scale but are the lowest in terms of energy use, and they add the least amount of ambient heat to the kitchen.

Efficient Cooking Tips ▸

- Use small appliances, like toaster ovens and crockpots, instead of the regular oven whenever possible.
- Keep appliances clean, particularly ovens, microwaves, toasters, and the metal burner pans under electric coil stove burners.
- Don't preheat the oven unless it's really necessary (pastry and other baked goods usually require preheating)
- Make sure gas burners are burning efficiently—a blue flame is good and an orange flame is bad.

Induction cooktops are getting a lot of press in the green building world for a couple of reasons: They're 30% to 40% more efficient than conventional electric and gas ranges, and they add less ambient heat to your kitchen. Induction elements send electromagnetic energy directly to the pan. This energy is then converted to heat, which is absorbed by the pan. Once you take the pan away, the cooktop has almost no residual heat. Also, there's no spillover heat like you get with gas flames going beyond the outsides of a pan or when an electric burner is larger than the pan's surface. This means less wasted energy.

Other advantages of induction technology are that it responds quickly to temperature changes (much like gas burners), it's easy to clean (like ceramic-topped electric models), and it's good at maintaining very low temperatures. Induction's main drawbacks are that it works only with ferrous-metal pans (iron, some stainless steel, and others)—not with aluminum pans—and it's expensive (but that's sure to change if the technology catches on).

And Now for a Commercial Break ▶

Kitchens have always been important, but today more than ever we have become passionate about our cooking appliances. Even though most of us actually cook at home less frequently than cooks of past generations, we own much more fancy, specialized kitchen equipment. Case in point: the commercial-style range. Arguably, many owners of these super-sized cooking devices aren't getting the most from the high Btu outputs and acreage of burner space. And from a green perspective, commercial-style ranges simply don't pass the test. First, they're loaded with extras, like extra stainless steel, iron, and chrome; producing these materials comes with very high embodied energy. Second, because the cooking surface is so large, you need an oversized vent hood (more stainless steel) and a high-powered fan (more electricity, more noise, and potential backdrafting in the house). So if you want a green kitchen, seriously consider taking a break from commercials.

Large commercial-grade appliances have tremendous appeal to many of us, but from a green point of view they fail on all levels.

Kitchen Ventilation

Effective ventilation is important for ridding your kitchen of cooking odors, excess moisture (think: mold), smoke, and exhaust fumes from gas burners. If you don't already have a good vent system in place, you should consider installing one to improve your indoor air quality. Recirculating vent fans—those without a duct running outside—also should be replaced, since all they really do is pretend to filter the air before blowing it right back into the kitchen.

The two main types of mechanical ventilation are overhead hoods and downdraft (or cooktop) fans. Overhead systems include the basic under-cabinet types and the higher-end suspended styles with exposed ducting extending from the ceiling. Overheads are more effective and require less suction than downdraft vents, primarily because they work with nature rather than against it: Hot air rises, so all that steam, grease, and fragrant cooking air is easy to capture inside a hood and get it outdoors. Downdraft fans have to work much harder in reversing the natural flow of air and vapor. Also, many downdraft systems tend to draw heat away from burners (especially gas burners), so your pans don't heat as evenly when the fan is on.

Sizing is important with hood systems. The hood should be at least as wide as, but preferably up to 6" wider than, the cooktop and at least 20" deep. The power, or capacity, of the fan is another critical factor. Expert recommendations vary. Some say a standard hood fan should move 40 cfm (cubic feet per minute) for every 12" of cooktop width; for example, a 30"-wide cooktop gets a 100 cfm fan, which is the minimum required under many building codes. The National Kitchen & Bath Association (www.nkba.org) recommends 150 cfm as a minimum for hood fans. The manufacturer of your range or cooktop may have its own recommendations. Undersizing a fan results in inadequate ventilation, but oversizing it could potentially lead to a dangerous backdrafting into the home.

Backdrafting is caused by negative pressure: When you run an exhaust fan, air is sucked out of the house. That air must be replaced by outdoor air—often through tiny breaches in the building envelope, under doors, and other draft-producing places. But when the home is airtight (as most green homes are), the makeup air might be drawn downward through appliance chimneys, such as that for a gas furnace or boiler. This means the poisonous exhaust (particularly carbon monoxide) from the appliance enters the home instead of going up the chimney. If your vent fan is so strong that it throws off your home's pressure balance, you'll have to install a makeup air duct somewhere; consult an HVAC professional. An energy auditor (energy rater) can test for pressure imbalances in your home.

Ventilation is a green concept as it relates to healthfulness more than to energy conservation. Ridding your kitchen of odors is an added convenience, but the real benefit of installing an adequately powered kitchen vent or draft hood is to draw moisture out of the room and help discourage the growth of mold and mildew.

Three Types of Kitchen Ventilation

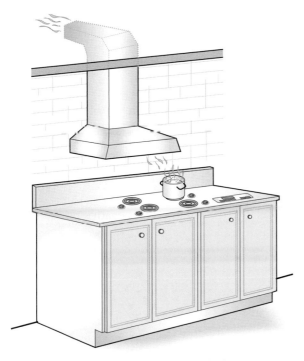

Vent hood. Overhead vent hoods are the best all-around performers.

Downdraft vent. Downdraft systems have no hood to capture rising exhaust and must pull the hot air down to evacuate it.

Windows. Windows are a low-tech option. They can introduce cross breezes but are less effective than fan systems at eliminating cooking exhaust.

Replacing a Dishwasher

A dishwasher that's past its prime may be inefficient in more ways than one. If it's an old model, it probably wasn't designed to be very efficient to begin with. But more significantly, if it no longer cleans effectively, you're probably spending a lot of time and hot water pre-rinsing the dishes. This alone can consume more energy and water than a complete wash cycle on a newer machine. So even if your old dishwasher still runs, replacing it with an efficient new model can be a good green upgrade.

In terms of sizing and utility hookups, dishwashers are generally quite standard. If your old machine is a built-in and your countertops and cabinets are standard sizes, most full-size dishwashers will fit right in. Of course, you should always measure the dimensions of the old unit before shopping for a new one, to avoid an unpleasant surprise at installation time. Also be sure to review the manufacturer's instructions before starting any work.

Tools & Materials ▸

Screwdrivers
Adjustable wrench
2-ft. level
⅝" automotive heater hose
Teflon tape

Cable connector
4"-length of ½"
　　copper tubing
Hose clamps
Wire connectors

Replacing an old, inefficient dishwasher is a straightforward project that usually takes just a few hours. The energy savings begin with the first load of dishes and continue with every load thereafter.

Efficient Loading ▸

To get the best circulation of water for effective *wash action,* follow these tips when loading dishes:

- Make sure dishes are loaded so water can reach all of the soiled surfaces.
- Be sure that larger items are not blocking smaller items from the wash action.
- Place all items in both racks so that they are separated and face the center of the dishwasher. This will help to ensure that water reaches all soiled surfaces.
- Place glasses with the open end facing downward to allow proper washing action.
- Do not place glasses over the tines, but between them. This will allow the glasses to lean toward the spray arm and will improve washing. It also promotes drying by reducing the amount of water remaining on the top of the glass after the wash cycle is complete.
- Do not allow flatware to "nest." This prevents proper water distribution between the surfaces.
- Load flatware, except knives, with some handles up and some down to prevent nesting. For safety, knives should always be loaded handles up.

How to Replace an Inefficient Dishwasher

1

Start by shutting off the electrical power to the dishwasher circuit at the service panel. Also, turn off the water supply at the shutoff valve, usually located directly under the floor.

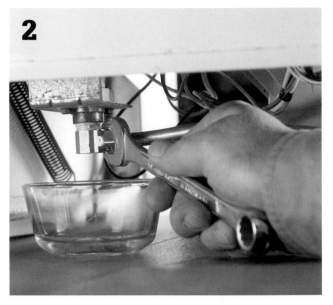

2

Remove the old unit. First unscrew the front access panel. Once the access panel is removed, disconnect the water supply line from the L-fitting on the bottom of the unit. This is usually a brass compression fitting, so just turning the compression nut counterclockwise with an adjustable wrench should do the trick. Use a bowl to catch any water that might leak out when the nut is removed.

3

The dishwasher has an integral electrical box at the front of the unit where the power cable is attached to the dishwasher's fixture wires. Take off the box cover and remove the wire connectors that join the wires together.

4

The discharge hose from the dishwasher is usually connected to the dishwasher port on the side of the garbage disposer. To remove it, just loosen the screw on the hose clamp and pull it off. You may need to push this hose back through a hole in the cabinet wall and into the dishwasher compartment so it won't get caught when you pull out the dishwasher.

5

The last thing that needs to be done before you can pull out the unit is to remove the screws that hold the brackets to the underside of the countertop. Then put a piece of cardboard or old carpet under the front legs to protect the floor from getting scratched, and pull out the dishwasher.

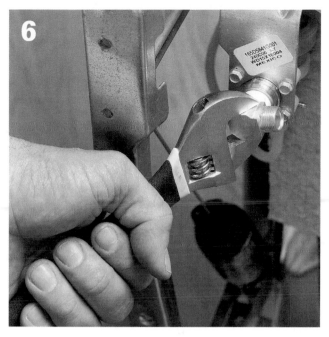

6

Tip the new dishwasher on its back and install the new L-fitting into the threaded port on the solenoid. Apply some Teflon tape or pipe sealant to the fitting threads before tightening it in place to prevent possible leaks.

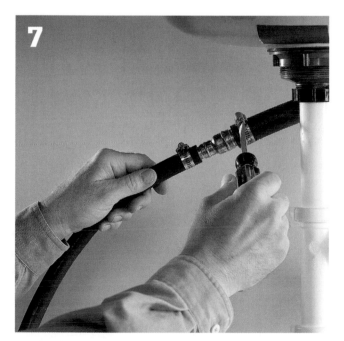

7

Attach a length of new automotive heater hose, usually ⅝" diameter, to the end of the dishwasher's discharge hose nipple with a hose clamp. The new hose you are adding should be long enough to reach from the discharge nipple to the port on the side of the kitchen sink garbage disposer.

8

Like the old dishwasher, the new one will have an integral electrical box for making the wiring connections. To gain access to the box, just remove the box cover. Then install a cable connector on the back of the box and bring the power cable from the service panel through this connector.

(continued)

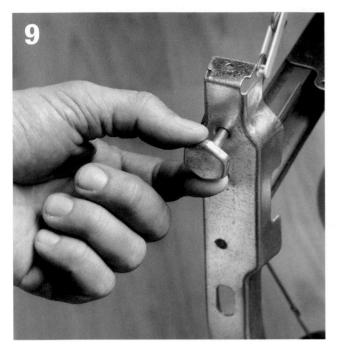

While the new dishwasher is still on its back, install a leveling leg at each of the four corners. Just turn these legs into the threaded holes designed for them. Leave about ½" of each leg projecting from the bottom of the unit. These will have to be adjusted later to keep the appliance level. Tip the appliance up onto these feet and push it into the opening. Check for level in both directions and adjust these feet as required.

Once the dishwasher is level, attach the brackets to the underside of the countertop to keep the appliance from moving. Then pull the discharge hose into the sink cabinet and install it so there's a loop that is attached with a bracket to the underside of the countertop. This loop prevents waste water from flowing from the disposer back into the dishwasher.

Lengthening a Discharge Hose ▸

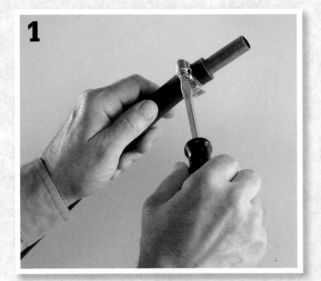

If the discharge hose has to be modified to fit onto the disposer port, first insert a 4"-long piece of ½" copper tubing into the hose and hold it in place with a hose clamp. This provides a nipple for the rubber adapter that fits onto the disposer.

Clamp the rubber disposer adapter to the end of the copper tubing nipple. Then tighten the hose clamp securely.

Push the adapter over the disposer's discharge nipple and tighten it in place with a hose clamp. If you don't have a disposer, this discharge hose can be clamped directly to a modified sink tailpiece that's installed below a standard sink strainer.

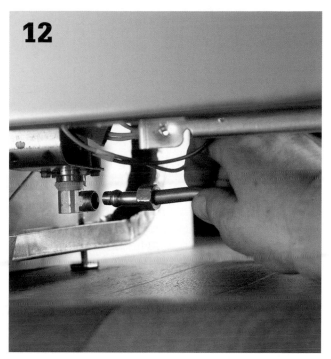

Adjust the L-fitting on the dishwasher's water inlet valve until it points directly toward the water supply tubing. Then lubricate the threads slightly with a drop of dishwashing liquid and tighten the tubing's compression nut onto the fitting. Use an adjustable wrench and turn the nut clockwise.

Complete the electrical connections by tightening the connector's clamp on the cable. Then join the power wires to the fixture wires with wire connectors, attach the ground wire (or wires) to the grounding screw on the box, and replace the cover.

Install the access panel, usually by hooking it on a couple of prongs just below the dishwasher's door. Install the screws that hold it in place and turn on the water and power supplies. Replace the toe-kick panel at the bottom of the dishwasher.

Water for Drinking & Recycling

In a green home, water is an important consideration for both health and conservation. The kitchen is where we go for most of our drinking water, and it's second only to the bathroom in terms of total water consumption inside the home. This makes the kitchen a prime location for water-related upgrades.

Point-of-use (that is, at the sink or faucet) water filtration systems are easy to install and help ensure clean and good-tasting water for drinking and cooking, while a simple gray water recycling system allows you to capture gallons of potable water daily that would otherwise go down the drain.

Minor changes at the kitchen sink can have a major effect on greening up the kitchen. Here, a simple filter on the faucet makes all of the cold water safer to drink, and a gray water system makes it easy to save clean water for reuse.

Water Filtration

Due to the glut of filtration products available and the relative dearth of definitive information about the health effects of water contaminants, the subject of water filtration can get a bit murky. Suffice it to say that all public water has some bad stuff in it. We know this because the EPA requires large water companies to submit an annual report showing tested levels of contamination of the water it supplies to its customers. Are the government's standards high enough to prevent you from harm? On this point many experts disagree.

Water can pick up contaminants from a number of sources, including erosion of natural deposits, water treatment chemicals and their byproducts, elements naturally present in the environment, and water supply piping. All municipal water contains trace pollutants, the variety and levels of which depend on where you live. Your home can add contaminants, too. For example, in old houses, lead supply piping or even lead-based solder on copper piping can leach lead into your drinking water.

If you're interested in filtering your drinking water, first find out what's in it.

Water utilities are required by law to submit a water quality report, officially called the Consumer Confidence Report, to their customers each year. The report shows the amounts of regulated contaminants in your water compared to the government's maximum allowable levels. It's important to note that not all potential pollutants are regulated and the water company can't test for pollutants that enter the water en route to your faucet. (Of course, if your water comes from a private well, testing and treating the water is your responsibility. It's a good idea to have well water tested regularly, particularly for bacteria and nitrates.)

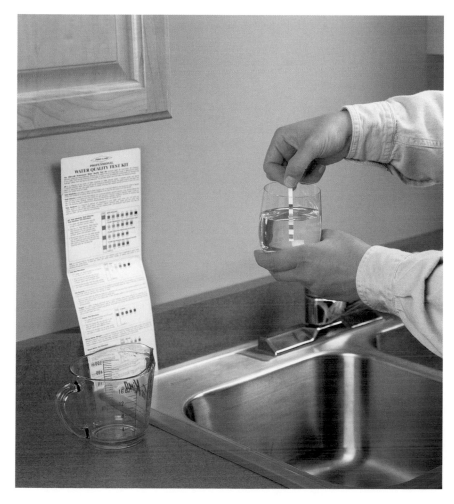

Do-it-yourself water testing kits offer a quick and easy way to test your water for many common contaminants. For true accuracy, however, professional testing is recommended.

For a more complete report of what's in your tap water, have a sample analyzed by a professional lab. Contact local water providers or visit www.epa.gov/safewater/labs for listings of state-certified water testing labs. Some local water suppliers also test water. In any case, use a certified lab that follows EPA protocols and one that doesn't sell filtration equipment on the side, so to speak, to avoid an obvious conflict of interest. You can also test water yourself using an at-home kit. While their accuracy may be questionable, these kits can indicate the types of contaminants in your water and help guide you toward the right kind of filter.

Once you find out what's in your water—and decide which pollutants concern you most—shop for the filtration system or systems that will reduce or eliminate the target pollutants. A combination of filters may be required. The chart on page 37 lists the main types of point-of-use filtration systems. Look for products bearing the NSF International (formerly the National Sanitation Foundation) seal, or visit www.nsf.org/certified/DWTU for a listing of certified water treatment products. Keep in mind that on all systems replacing filter cartridges and following other maintenance procedures are essential to proper performance.

The zero-installation option: Carafe water filters effectively improve taste and odor of drinking water while removing several common contaminants. Keep a full carafe in the fridge for instant cold water.

Note: Carbon filters are intended for cold water filtration only. Running hot water (greater than 100° F) through filters will render them ineffective.

Common Drinking Water Contaminants ▸

- Chlorine
- Pesticides
- Lead
- Nitrates, mostly from nitrogen fertilizers
- Cysts (giardia, cryptosporidium)
- Bacteria
- Mercury
- Perfluorochemicals (PFCs), a common man-made chemical used in many household items and food packaging
- Trihalomethanes, resulting from methane gas produced when water is chlorinated to kill bacteria
- Radon
- Asbestos
- Soft metals such as chromium, copper, and aluminum
- Volatile Organic Compounds (VOCs)
- Fluoride, a common water additive

Water test kits are available from online resources and home improvement stores (see Resources).

Filtration Systems ▸

Filter Type	Description*
Carbon (or Activated Carbon)	Uses absorption to remove chlorine byproducts, lead, some metals, and some organic chemicals. Most effective filter for improving taste and odor. Does not remove bacteria, heavy metals, dissolved minerals, nitrates, or microbes. Solid-block carbon filters typically are more effective than granular filters. May be combined with ceramic-type filter system to remove bacteria, cysts, asbestos, and sediment. Faucet-mounted and under-counter installation; also available in portable carafe designs.
Reverse Osmosis (RO)	A system involving pressure and a fine membrane reverses the osmotic process to remove heavy metals, nitrates, asbestos, industrial chemicals, arsenic, and some parasites. May reduce levels of pesticides, dioxin, petrochemicals, and chloroform. Improves taste and odor but does so more effectively when coupled with a carbon filter. Under-counter installation (see page 41). RO units waste 3 to 5 gallons of water for each gallon of filtered water.
Distiller	Purifies water by turning it to steam then back to water. Kills microbes and removes arsenic and other pollutants, but does not remove chlorine. Often combined with carbon system. Under-counter installation. Consumes a fair amount of electricity.
Ultraviolet	Disinfects water with ultraviolet light, eliminating bacteria and parasites. Most commonly used as a supplement to carbon filtration. Under-counter installation.

*Types of contaminants removed and overall effectiveness vary by product and application.

Reducing Waste at the Kitchen Faucet

Everyone does it: You go to the kitchen sink for a glass of water, but the water coming out of the tap isn't cold, so you let it run full blast. And you wait. And wait. In the meantime, all of that perfectly good drinking water is going right down the drain. Depending on the time of year and how much heated space the cold-water piping runs through, you might waste a gallon or more of water just to get eight ounces of cool water in your glass. The same thing happens when you wait for hot water before filling up the sink for dishes.

Factor in the number of people in the house and the number of occurrences each day and you end up with a fairly huge amount of wasted water each year. So what's the green solution? One easy remedy is to add a small sink for capturing the water while you wait for the tap to reach the desired temperature or while washing fruits and vegetables. The sink's drain, instead of leading to the sewer, is directed to a receptacle located under the kitchen sink or just outside. All of that captured gray water can be used for watering indoor and outdoor plants or the lawn.

Gray water in this type of system is considered "light gray," meaning it has very little or no pollutants, such as soap, cleaning chemicals, food waste, or other added organic and inorganic material. Allowing only clean water into the system means it's immediately ready for reuse. Gray water captured from sources like a bath or washing machine often must be treated before reuse or fed into a subsurface irrigation system for watering outdoor vegetation—a great way to recycle water but just a little more involved.

Tip: Insulate & Recirculate ▶

Reduce your waiting time at the tap (for the water to heat up or cool down) by insulating the water supply pipes to all faucets in the house. Hot-water pipes lose heat in transit from the water heater to the faucet, while cold-water pipes absorb heat, especially when they run near heating ducts or radiant tubing. Insulation slows the heat transfer to keep the water closer to the desired temperature. Another way to speed hot water delivery to the tap—and avoid the wasteful run-off—is to install a hot-water recirculation system (see page 110).

Bucket for gray water collection

A small gray water sink (see Resources, page 237) drains automatically to a reservoir (inset photo) for watering plants or gardens, making it easy to recycle thousands of gallons of tap water each year.

Additional Resources for Water Quality & Conservation ▸

- U.S. Environmental Protection Agency: www.epa.gov/safewater; or call the EPA's Safe Drinking Water Hotline: 800-426-4791
- NSF International: www.nsf.org
- National Resource Defense Council: www.nrdc.org
- National Testing Labs (mail-in water testing): www.watertest.com

Carbon Water Filtration Systems

Carbon-activated water filters are the most popular systems for home drinking water because they are inexpensive, easy to install, and they effectively improve the taste and odor of most municipal tap water. Most systems remove common contaminants, such as chlorine, lead, cysts, and particulates. Filters are readily available from home centers, hardware stores, and online through many manufacturers.

There are three main types of carbon filters: faucet-mounted, countertop, and under-counter. Faucet-mounted install directly to the kitchen faucet and have a simple diverter switch to provide filtered water directly from the tap. These are the easiest to use of the three systems, and they take up no counter or cabinet space. Countertop models also feed from the faucet spout but have a separate filter unit that sits on your countertop. Diverted water flows through the filter and out through a spout on the filter unit. Under-counter filters install under the sink and connect directly to the cold water supply piping. A separate, countertop-mounted spout delivers the filtered water.

When shopping for a filter system, compare ratings for contaminant reduction as well as flow rate and filter service life. Under-counter units typically offer the greatest service life per filter cartridge, followed by countertop models. Faucet-mounted filters typically offer considerably shorter service life before requiring a new cartridge. When comparing prices, be sure to calculate long-term costs for cartridge replacement.

Tools & Materials ▸

Adjustable wrench	Screwdrivers
Channel-type pliers	Teflon tape
Drill and bits	Plumbers putty
Tubing cutter	Filter system
or utility knife	

Faucet-mounted filters are easiest to install. Remove the faucet aerator, then thread the filter unit onto the spout and hand-tighten. Slowly turn on the cold water tap, then check for leaking. If necessary, carefully tighten the collar using pliers. Flush the filter before use as recommended.

Countertop water filters also are easy to install. First, remove the faucet aerator. Then, thread the filter's diverter valve onto the spout, using the appropriate adapter and gaskets. Place the filter unit and supply tubing in a convenient location. Test the system and check for leaks, carefully tightening the diverter with pliers if necessary. Flush filter as recommended.

How to Install an Under-Counter Filter System

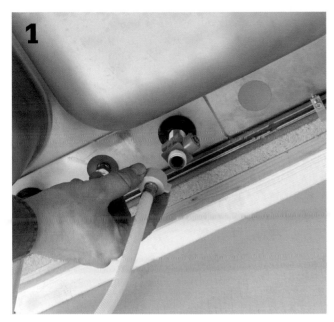

1

Shut off the cold water supply to the kitchen faucet at the fixture shutoff valve or main house valve; drain faucet. Remove the supply tubing from the faucet stud using a wrench. Wrap the stud with Teflon tape, then thread the filter's water supply fitting onto the stud and tighten carefully. Apply tape and connect the supply tubing to the fitting.

2

Secure the mounting bracket to the filter unit, then mount the unit at a convenient location under the sink, following the manufacturer's directions. Be sure to leave plenty of room for removing the filter housing for filter replacement.

3

If necessary, remove the sprayer from the sink, or cut a new hole through the countertop, following the countertop manufacturer's recommendations (some materials require a professional fabricator). Assemble the filter spout as directed, and then mount the spout into the sink hole, using plumbers putty as a sealant.

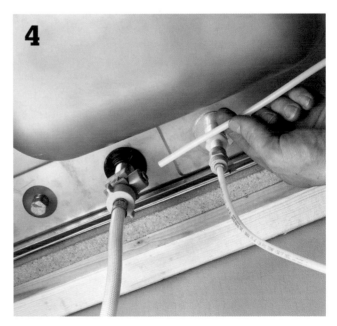

4

Cut lengths of tubing to run between the water supply, filter unit, and spout, making sure the cuts are square and the tubing ends are free of scratches, kinks, and rough spots. Connect the tubing at the push-in (or other) fittings. Test and flush the system as directed.

Reverse-osmosis Water Filtration Systems

Not all water is created equal. Some water tastes better than other water. Some water looks better than other water. And some has more impurities, too. Because no one wants to drink bad water, the bottled water business has exploded over the past twenty years. Home filtration systems have also grown by leaps and bounds, in part because there are so many different types of filters available.

For example, sediment filters will remove rust, sand, and suspended minerals, like iron. A carbon filter can remove residual chlorine odors, some pesticides, and even radon gas. Distillation filters can remove bacteria and organic compounds, while a traditional water softener can neutralize hard water. But many of the most toxic impurities, heavy metals like mercury, lead, cadmium, and arsenic, are best removed with a reverse-osmosis (RO) system like the one shown here.

These filters are designed to treat just cooking and drinking water. The system holds the treated water in a storage tank and delivers it to a sink-mounted faucet on demand. RO units feature multiple filter cartridges: in this case a pre-filter unit, followed by the RO membrane, followed by a carbon post-filter.

Tools & Materials ▸

Plastic gloves
Screwdrivers
Electric drill
Adjustable wrench

Teflon tape
Saddle valve
Rubber drain saddle

Reverse-osmosis filters can be highly effective for removing specific contaminants from drinking water. Because the filtration process wastes a lot of fresh water, it's a good idea to have your water professionally tested before investing in an RO system.

Point-of-use Filters ▸

Point-of-use water filtration systems typically are installed in the sink base cabinet, with a separate faucet from the main kitchen faucet. The setup shown here has an extra filter to supply a nearby refrigerator icemaker.

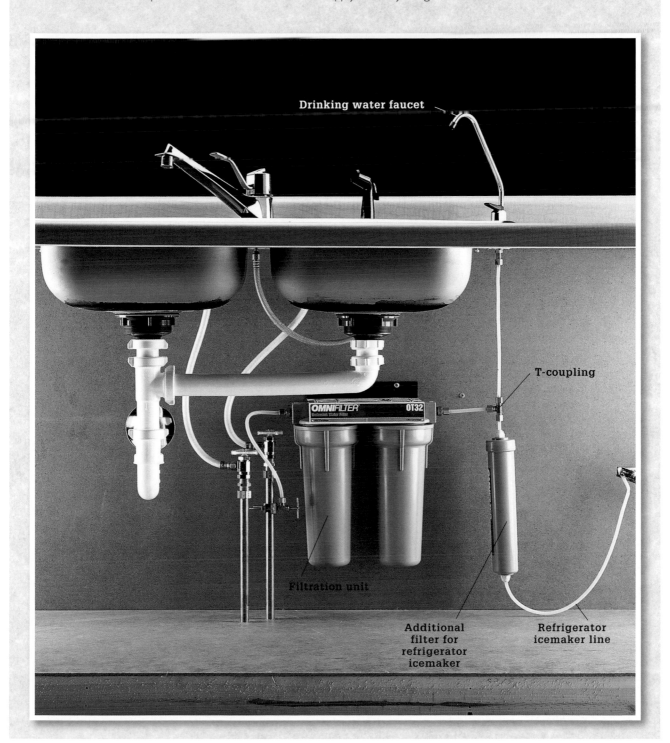

Drinking water faucet

T-coupling

Filtration unit

Additional filter for refrigerator icemaker

Refrigerator icemaker line

How to Install a Reverse-osmosis Water Filter

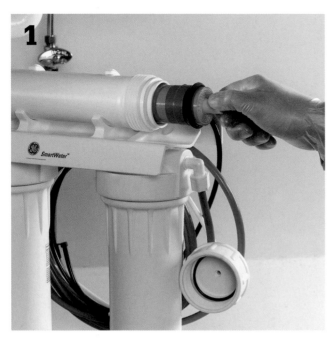

1

The RO membrane filter is shipped in a separate bag that is filled with antibacterial fluid. Wearing plastic gloves, remove the cartridge from the bag and install it in the filter unit. Make sure to touch only the ends of the cartridge when you handle it or you can damage the membrane.

2

Following the manufacturer's instructions, establish the best location for the filter inside your kitchen sink cabinet. Then drive some mounting screws in the cabinet wall to support the unit.

3

Assemble the entire filtration system and then hang it on the cabinet wall. The best system layout may be to locate the filter on one wall and the storage tank on the opposite wall.

4

The side of the storage tank has to be outfitted with a simple valve. To install it, just wrap its threads a couple of times with Teflon tape and screw the valve into the tank. Finger-tighten it, then turn it one more turn with an adjustable wrench.

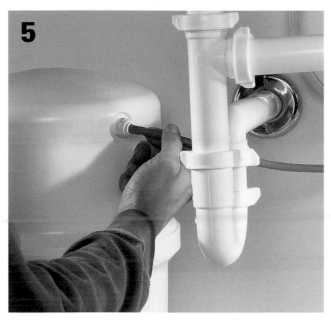

Connect the filter to the tank with plastic tubing.
In most units, the joint between the two is made with a compression fitting. On this filter, the fitting is a push-type collar. Simply insert the hose into the collar until it will not go any farther.

The water storage tank and faucet are connected with plastic tubing. Here, a push-type compression fitting on the end of the tubing was used. To install it, push the end of the fitting over the bottom of the faucet shank until the fitting bottoms out.

The filter faucet comes with a jamb nut and sometimes a plastic spacer (as with this unit) that goes on the shank of the faucet before the jamb nut. After the nut is finger tight, snug it securely with an adjustable wrench. This unit came with a C shaped collar and jamb nut, but a round collar would need to have hoses threaded through it prior to mounting the faucet.

Remove the cover from an unused sink hole, or remove the spray hose, or bore a mounting hole in the sink or into the countertop. Once you have prepared a suitable hole for the faucet stem, insert it from above.

(continued)

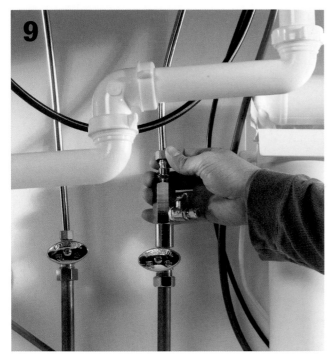

The water supply to the filter comes from the cold water supply line that services the kitchen sink faucet. The easiest way to tap into the supply line is to replace the shutoff valve at the supply riser with a new valve containing an additional outlet for tubing.

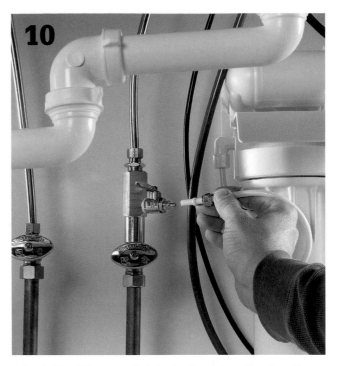

Attach the filter supply tube to the port on the shutoff valve with a compression fitting. Push the end of the tubing onto the valve, then push the ferrule against the valve and thread the compression nut into place. Finger-tighten it, then turn it one more full turn with a wrench.

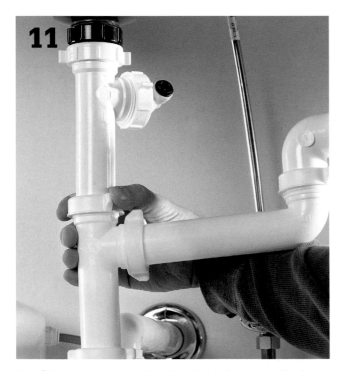

The filter must also be tied into the drain system. The best way to do this is to replace the drain tailpiece with a new fitting that contains an auxiliary port.

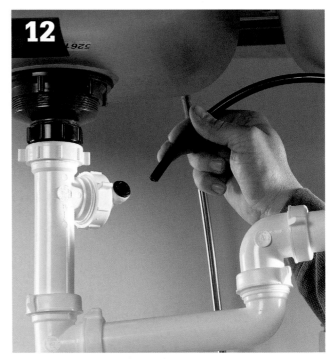

Attach the tubing from the drain to the auxiliary port on the tailpiece. Finish up by turning on the water and checking the system for leaks. Be sure to filter and drain at least two tanks of water to clean any contaminants from the system before drinking the water.

Installing a Whole-House Water Filtration System ▸

A whole-house water filtration system is installed along the supply pipe carrying water to the house, located after the water meter, but before any other appliances in the pipeline. A whole-house system reduces the same elements as an under-sink system and can also help reduce the iron flowing into the water softener, prolonging its life.

Always follow the manufacturer's directions for your particular unit. If your electrical system is grounded through the water pipes, make sure to install ground clamps on both sides of the filtration unit with a connecting jumper wire. Globe valves should be installed within 6" of the intake and the outtake sides of the filter.

Filters must be replaced every few months, depending on the manufacturer. The filtration unit cover unscrews for filter access.

Shut off the main water supply and turn on the faucets to the drain pipes. Position the unit after the water meter, but before any other appliances in the supply pipe. Measure and mark the pipe to accommodate the filtration unit. Cut the pipe at the marks with a pipe cutter. Join the water meter side of the pipe with the intake side of the unit, and house the supply side of the pipe with the outtake side of the unit. Tighten with a wrench.

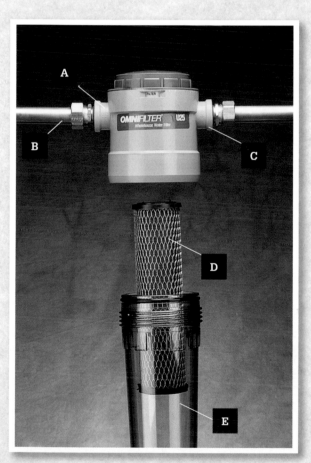

A whole-house water filtration system: (A) intake side, (B) supply pipe from the water meter pipe, (C) outtake side to the house supply pipe, (D) filter, and (E) filtration unit cover.

Install a filter and screw the filtration unit cover to the bottom of the filtration unit. Attach a jumper wire to the pipes on the other side of the unit, using pipe clamps. Open the main water supply lines to restore the water supply. Allow faucets to run for a few minutes, as you check to make sure that the system is working properly.

Kitchen Lighting

Kitchen lighting is a big deal—for homeowners everywhere and, of course, for the entire kitchen remodeling industry. And when confronted with the endless variety of fixture options, designers and their clients can be tempted to go a little nuts, often ending up with a complex array of interesting yet marginally effective lights. By contrast, lighting a kitchen with a green focus can be quite straightforward. The main objective should be comfortable and effective illumination without unnecessary and inefficient fixtures cluttering the plan.

Most people like bright kitchens, and with good reason: It's the home's primary gathering place and the stage for most of the household's everyday "work." A kitchen must be warm and inviting for all users at any hour. With that in mind, it's important to note that a green lighting plan is not about putting up with dim lighting or commercial-style ambience; it's about setting the right fixtures in the right places. It's also about maximizing natural daylight.

In a green kitchen, natural daylight, reflective surfaces, and judicious use of fixtures create a bright, dynamic environment with limited energy use.

Artificial Lighting

Kitchen lighting is often broken down into three main categories based on function: *Ambient* lighting provides the room with most of its general illumination. This is most often achieved with bright overhead fixtures that reflect light off of surrounding surfaces and set the overall light level in the room. The cumulative light from other fixtures also contributes to ambient lighting. *Task* lighting provides focused light in specific work areas, such as the cooktop, sink, and countertops. The third category, *accent* lighting, is used more sparingly and creatively to highlight special features or for decorative effect.

Ambient and task lighting together make up the core of a kitchen plan. With those types of lighting satisfied, accent fixtures can be added to provide layering and enhance the dynamics of light and shadow.

When it comes to overhead lighting, one or two well-placed fixtures will meet the demands of most kitchens. The most effective overhead fixtures are ceiling-mounted units that project light all around as well as onto the ceiling. Glass or acrylic globes offer the best illumination, while fixtures with opaque sides or shades limit brightness by focusing the light downward.

One of the most popular choices for overhead lighting is the recessed "can" fixture, which people like for its flush installation that doesn't break up the ceiling plane. However, because all of the light is directed downward, you need several fixtures to yield the same levels as one or two globe-type fixtures; thus, it is a less-green option. If you do opt for recessed cans, choose products rated "IC-AT," meaning the fixture housing can be covered with insulation and the cans are airtight to limit air infiltration.

The kitchen at left has several recessed fixtures just for overhead lighting, while the greener kitchen at right takes advantage of reflective surfaces and is brightly illuminated with only one overhead fixture.

When it comes to task lighting, nothing gets the job done more effectively or efficiently than under-cabinet fluorescent tube fixtures. These inexpensive units fit into the recess below most standard cabinets and can be plugged into a countertop receptacle or hard-wired with a wall-switch control (see pages 52 to 53). Their energy efficiency is unmatched by other fixture types, providing about 50 lumens per watt (or lpw—the true measure of lighting efficiency). A single bulb can burn for up to 20,000 hours before needing replacement.

Other popular types of under-cabinet lighting include halogen, xenon, and LED. Of the three, LED are the most energy-efficient but by far the most expensive. Halogen lights, which contain incandescent bulbs, are popular for their bright, even light, but they come with two significant drawbacks: They operate at only 20 lpw and they get very hot—hot enough to warm a stack of plates or even melt chocolate in the cabinet above the fixture. Xenon bulbs produce about 15 lpw and may require a separate transformer that you have to hide as part of the installation.

Ambient (and decorative) lighting may be less important from a practical view, but it can play a critical role in the overall quality of light in the kitchen. Eating areas, such as a bar or breakfast nook, often call for more atmospheric lighting. Dimmers let you set the light level to suit the mood of the specific meal or activity. Some compact fluorescent lamps (CFLs) and fixtures are available with dimming capability, so be sure to get the right products for the application.

Fluorescent under-cabinet lights run cool (unlike incandescents) and provide the most light with the least amount of electricity. The simplest way to add under-cabinet lighting is with plug-in fixtures (inset), while hard-wired installations don't use up outlet space.

Positioning Task Lights ▶

Here's a good rule of thumb for effective task lighting: Let nothing come between the light and the task. Lights placed under cabinets, inside range hoods, and directly over sinks follow the rule; overhead lights and soffit-mounted fixtures don't. Always place task lights where your body or head won't cast a shadow over your work.

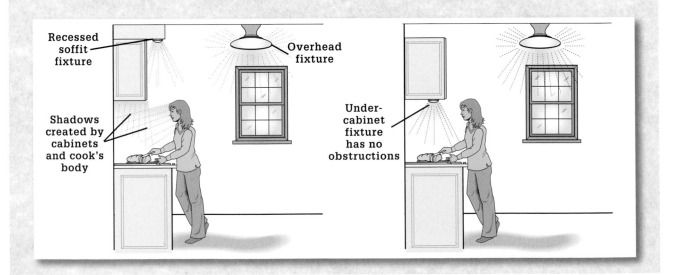

Natural Lighting

Nothing adds more life to a kitchen than a window. With a view to the outdoors, cooking and cleaning up feel less like work, and there's no sense of isolation that often plagues windowless kitchens. Operable windows on more than one wall can usher in generous cross-breezes to flush the kitchen with fresh air and remove excess heat from cooking. And all that natural light reduces the need for artificial lighting during the day.

When adding windows to a kitchen, orientation is a critical consideration. Glare and heat gain, primarily from south- and west-facing windows, can hinder visibility and make the room uncomfortably hot with the afternoon sun. North-facing windows offer more even light throughout the day, while east-facing windows can bring in pleasant morning sun without the heat gain from midday and afternoon sun exposure. On southern windows, you can use exterior awnings to block the hot summer sun but let in light and warmth in the winter when the sun is at a lower angle.

Of course, not every kitchen can accommodate windows or has the luxury of an exterior view. But good alternatives exist. Skylights are great for kitchens because they dramatically brighten the room even on cloudy days, and they psychologically expand the space. As with windows, skylights should face north or east whenever possible. If glare and heat gain are unavoidable, look into skylights with prismatic or translucent glazing, or provide means for shading the unit when needed. Where an attic above the kitchen makes a skylight impractical, a tubular skylight (see pages 214 to 215) may be a viable alternative.

Another way to bring natural light into a kitchen is to remove a wall or bank of cabinets to join the kitchen with an adjacent room that has windows. If the kitchen has a standard entry door, you can replace it with a glazed unit or add a transom or awning window above to increase daylighting.

Adding a well-placed window is always a good investment, particularly in smaller kitchens.

Under-Cabinet Fluorescent Task Lighting

Compact under-cabinet fluorescent fixtures mount directly to the underside of most standard cabinets and can be powered in a few different ways. Plug-in fixtures offer the simplest installation: Just screw the fixture in place and plug it into the nearest receptacle. Another option is to hard-wire the light to a convenient receptacle and use the fixture's ON/OFF switch to operate the light. The installation shown in the following steps involves hard-wiring a series of fixtures to an existing receptacle circuit and adding a new wall switch to control the lights.

Check with the local building department for code requirements surrounding the type of electrical wiring needed (some codes require armored cable) and the circuit you're tapping into. It's not always permissible to power kitchen lighting from small-appliance circuits. Also make sure the combined wattage of the new lights and appliances does not exceed the safe capacity of the circuit.

For best results, locate the light fixtures at the front edge of the cabinets, which provides the best light distribution over the counter area. If you think glare from the fixture will be a problem, you can add a thin strip of molding that extends about 1" below the front of the fixture. Slimmer fixtures (about 1⅛" thick) are the easiest to conceal, with or without molding.

Tools & Materials ▸

Circuit tester	Wire stripper
Utility knife	Under-cabinet
Wallboard saw	lighting kit
Hammer	14/2 NM cable
Screwdriver	Wire connectors
Drill and hole saw	Switch box
Jigsaw	Switch

How to Install Hard-Wired Under-Cabinet Lighting

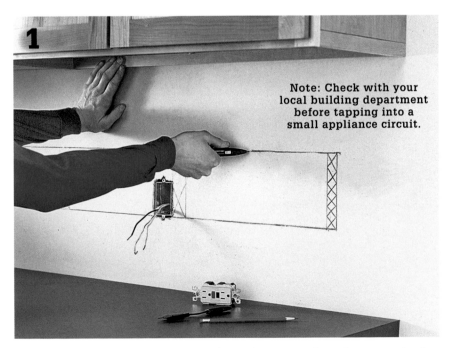

Note: Check with your local building department before tapping into a small appliance circuit.

Shut off the power to the device you plan to draw power from, then use a circuit tester to confirm the power is off. Disconnect the device from its wiring. Locate and mark the studs in the installation area. Mark and cut a channel to route the cable using a utility knife. In order to ease repair of the wallboard when finished, cut a wide channel bounded by studs in the center of the installation area.

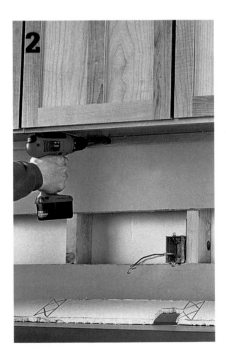

Drill holes through the cabinet edging and/or wall surface directly beneath the cabinets where the cable will enter each light fixture. Drill ⅝" holes through the studs to run the cable.

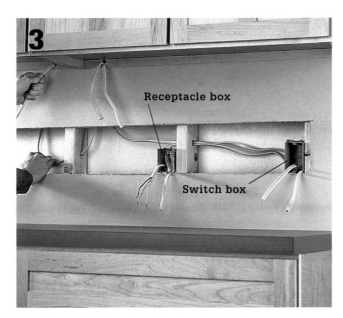

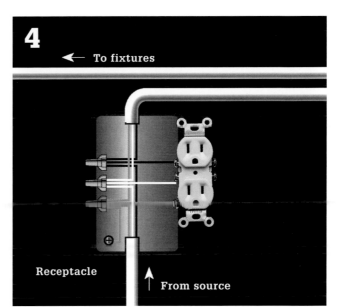

← To fixtures

Receptacle

From source →

Install a switch box by nailing it to the stud. Route a piece of 14/2 cable from the switch location to the power source. Route another cable from the switch to the first fixture hole. If you are installing more than one set of lights, route cables from the first fixture location to the second, and so on.

Hook up the new light power supply cable to the power source. The diagram above illustrates how to run cable from an existing receptacle to the under-cabinet light switch. Essentially, you join the like-colored wires from the cable feeding the receptacle and the new cable leading to the switch. Then, add a pigtail wire to each group, secure with a wire connectors, and attach the pigtails to the appropriate terminals on the receptacle.

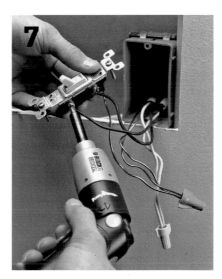

Remove the access cover, lens, and bulb from the light fixture. Open the knockouts for running cables into the fixture. Insert the cables into the knockouts and secure the clamps. Strip 8" of sheathing from the cables. Attach the light fixture to the bottom of the cabinet with screws.

Use wire connectors to join the black, white, and ground leads from the light fixture to each of the corresponding cable wires from the wall, including any cable leading to additional fixtures. Re-attach the bulb, lens, and access cover to the fixture. Repeat this process for any additional fixtures.

Strip 8" of sheathing from each cable at the switch and clamp the cables into the switch box. Join the white wires together with wire connectors. Connect each black wire to a screw terminal on the switch. Pigtail the ground wires to the grounding screw on the switch. Install the switch and coverplate; restore power. Patch removed wallboard.

Cabinets & Countertops

Now that you've looked at some of the simpler green improvements, like upgrading appliances and installing better lighting, you may be ready to consider some bigger changes. Of all the elements in a kitchen, cabinets and countertops have the greatest impact on the function of the space, and, along with flooring, they define its style and decorative character. These major features can play an equally important role in meeting your green objectives.

Repurposing a salvaged item, like this desk, for the kitchen makes for a one-of-a-kind piece and obviates the production of a manufactured good.

Cabinets for a Green Kitchen

Redoing your kitchen cabinets is complicated enough even with conventional design goals, so here's a simple way to look at incorporating green ideals; keep in mind that the best approach may be a combination of the following options:

Resurface or refinish—If you're happy with the layout of your existing cabinetry or it's not in your budget to buy new units, you can take the greenest route and simply renew your old cabinets. Options are numerous. You can freshen up painted cabinets with a new coat of paint or change the look entirely with a brand-new color. Natural wood cabinets can be refinished, and you may opt to send the doors out to a refinisher to have much of the work done offsite (see Cabinet Finishes, on page 60). Many cabinet styles are also suitable for refacing, which involves covering the visible surfaces with a new veneer of wood or even plastic laminate. Replacing the old hardware (drawer pulls and knobs) is an easy do-it-yourself upgrade with surprisingly dramatic results.

Of all the popular home improvements, replacing kitchen cabinets and countertops is one of the most rewarding. Choosing sustainable products, such as these beautiful bamboo cabinets, adds an even greater sense of renewal and sets a distinctly green tone for the entire room.

Refacing is a popular do-it-yourself technique for renewing old cabinets. If you use wood veneers that come from an FSC-certified supplier (see page 13), it's also a decidedly green alternative to buying new cabinets.

Reuse—A good green option when replacing cabinets is to buy salvaged items and customize them to fit your plan. For reclaimed cabinetry, shop around at architectural salvage dealers and retailers that carry recycled building materials. For modular items, such as tables and storage cabinets, check out restaurant supply houses and antique shops. On the salvage hunt, it pays to think creatively. How about an island made from an antique furniture piece topped with a new counter surface? Or maybe you'll be lucky enough to find a rolling stainless steel table secondhand. Always inspect the quality of reclaimed items carefully, and beware of old finishes, such as lead paint.

Buy new cabinets made from sustainable, non-toxic materials—Kitchen cabinets rank high on the not-so-green list for a couple of reasons. First, their boxes (or carcasses) are typically made with particleboard, MDF (medium-density fiberboard), or plywood, all of which commonly contain resins made with urea-formaldehyde (see Cabinet Materials, page 79). Second, cabinet faces (frames, doors, and drawer fronts) are often made with wood harvested in an unsustainable manner or with an endangered species of wood.

So how do you make sure your new cabinets are green? One way is to find a cabinet supplier who uses formaldehyde-free sheet goods and finish wood from certified forests (see page 13) or reclaimed lumber. Ideally, the supplier is close to your area so the cabinets don't have to be shipped a great distance. If you're in the market for truly custom cabinets, look for a local cabinet maker who is willing to use the green materials of your choice. You can also take a step away from the traditional path and go with cabinets made with a highly sustainable material, like bamboo, or with an eco-friendly sheet good, such as wheatboard.

Bamboo makes an exceptionally beautiful and durable cabinet material and is commonly available with blond (natural) and various darker colorings.

Stock cabinets that you buy off the floor or order in prefabricated sizes almost always are made with particleboard or MDF, which tends to offgas formaldehyde. Look for cabinets with panels that are lined with melamine, like those above, to trap most of this toxic gas.

Cabinet Materials

Most cabinet boxes are made with particleboard, MDF, or plywood. Particleboard and MDF are manufactured sheets containing small wood fibers and particles (usually recycled waste from milling) that are compressed and bound with glue. Of the two, MDF is generally a higher-grade material because it has smaller particles and greater density, and it mills more cleanly. Plywood is made with thin layers of wood glued together, often with an outer veneer of finish-grade wood. Generally speaking, all of these sheet goods are greener than solid wood, because they make much more efficient use of the source materials.

But here's the rub: Most manufacturers of these sheet goods use glues, or binders, containing formaldehyde. Formaldehyde (you might know it as a smelly preservative from biology class) is a pungent gas used in many adhesives, preservatives, and industrial applications. It has been identified by the EPA as a "known human carcinogen," and it can cause allergic reactions and respiratory problems, particularly in people with certain chemical sensitivities.

The binders used most commonly to make interior-grade sheet goods are urea-formaldehyde, which can offgas toxic levels of formaldehyde in decreasing amounts following production. Offgassing is most severe immediately following production and then tapers off over time but may continue for several years. Exterior-grade sheet goods, such as roof sheathing, siding, and marine plywood, are commonly made with phenol-formaldehyde binders, which offgas less than urea-formaldehyde products. For this reason, some cabinet manufacturers build their boxes with marine-grade plywood instead of particleboard or interior plywood.

Some brands of interior-grade MDF panels are made from 100% recycled wood fibers and are manufactured with a synthetic resin containing no formaldehyde (See Resources, page 237).

Given the formaldehyde risk, the healthiest options for cabinet boxes are formaldehyde-free MDF (See Resources, page 237) and biocomposite or agriboard products, such as wheatboard that is similar to MDF but is made from wheat stems recycled from agricultural harvesting.

If you end up choosing cabinets containing urea-formaldehyde binders, you can effectively seal the boards to prevent offgassing using an appropriate non-toxic sealer (see Sealing Particleboard Cabinets, on page 60). Many cabinets made with particleboard are lined on the inside with melamine, a plastic resin similar to laminate countertops, and on the outside with wood or plastic veneers. Many of these veneers significantly reduce levels of formaldehyde offgassing, but any exposed edges or cut surfaces must be coated with a sealant for effective protection.

When it comes to choosing a material for cabinet doors and other finish surfaces, don't worry—you can still use real wood. Just make it a green choice by specifying FSC-certified materials. Natural wood cabinet parts may be solid wood or an engineered material (plywood, MDF) covered with real-wood veneers. The latter, of course, requires much less virgin wood, but make sure that both the core material and the veneer come from certified suppliers. Painted cabinets may also be solid or engineered wood products and should come from sustainably managed sources. There are also vinyl-coated cabinets that have the look of painted cabinets and are made with MDF coated with a thin layer of heat-fused PVC (vinyl). Many green building experts recommend avoiding vinyl cabinets due to the potential health risks and environmental impacts of PVC (see The Great Vinyl Debate, on page 78).

If you like the appearance of natural materials but want something less traditional than hardwood, you should take a look at bamboo cabinets. Bamboo is a fast-growing grass that's harder than hardwood and can be sustainably harvested every three to five years. Given its durability and striking beauty, it's no surprise that bamboo is an increasingly popular choice for cabinets and other finish work (its most popular use in the U.S. is as an alternative to hardwood strip flooring). Most bamboo cabinets have doors, frames, and drawer fronts made of solid bamboo (or, rather, glued-together strips of solid bamboo) and boxes made of MDF or another engineered product.

Green cabinets may look like normal stock cabinets, but they are made differently. Many are built using FSC-certified plywood and formaldehyde-free bonding agents. The factory-applied finishes have low VOC content.

Tip: One Room's Trash is Another Room's Treasure ▶

Cabinets are indispensable for storage in the kitchen, but they can be just as useful in other rooms of the house. So instead of ditching your old boxes in the landfill, turn them into custom storage units in a laundry room, workshop, playroom, or home office. If you can't reuse them in your own home, donate the cabinets to a building materials recycler or charity organization.

Cabinet Finishes

Minimizing airborne toxins from finishes is an important goal in creating a healthy home environment. Unfortunately, most kitchen cabinets need plenty of finish to maintain a durable, washable surface and retain the beauty of natural materials. Most green-minded cabinet producers offer factory- or shop-applied non-toxic finishes. If your cabinets will be finished in situ, specify a low- or no-VOC finish material. These are available in a range of types, from water-based polyurethanes and varnishes to natural penetrating oils, such as linseed oil and tung oil.

Wax-based finish is another option, as well as soy and other vegetable-based coatings.

Be aware that natural finishes typically require reapplication on a regular basis (often once a year), and some carry an odor that can last for a while inside cabinet boxes. On the upside, natural coatings are easy to touch up when surfaces get scratched or worn, while varnish usually must be completely stripped prior to refinishing. See pages 134 to 135 for a discussion of low-toxicity paints.

Sealing Particleboard Cabinets ▶

Cabinet boxes made with conventional particleboard, MDF, and strandboard are likely to contain urea-formaldehyde binders that can offgas toxic formaldehyde gas for significant periods after installation in your kitchen. The best way to limit this potential health hazard is to seal all bare surfaces with a low-toxicity sealer designed to reduce offgassing on your specific material. Apply the sealer following the manufacturer's directions. Most sealers must be reapplied at recommended intervals to ensure protection.

Thoroughly coat all surfaces of the new cabinet with a sealer manufactured to prevent VOC offgassing.

Simplifying the Three Rs ▶

Reduce, reuse, recycle is a basic tenet to live by in any green home, and there's no better place than the kitchen to put this philosophy to work. Most of a household's trash comes from food—whether it's food containers, preparing food, or cleaning up after meals. By modifying shopping habits and setting up a convenient recycling system, most households can reduce their daily garbage output by 50% or more. The key to success is making the system convenient.

REDUCE

The simplest way to reduce everyday kitchen garbage is by choosing products with minimal packaging or that come in recyclable containers. Whenever possible, buy food and other household supplies in bulk. Wholesale clubs have made this easier than ever and with considerable savings for the consumer. At the opposite extreme, avoid food products sold in one-serving containers. Instead, choose larger-volume containers, then do your own portioning with washable containers at home. Even when small packages are recycled, they have a far greater environmental impact per use than large containers.

REUSE

The practice of reuse requires nothing more than a little old-fashioned thriftiness. Instead of throwing out or recycling old coffee cans, plastic containers, glass jars, etc., use them to store miscellaneous items around the house. Glass containers are great for storing leftovers, but be careful about reusing certain plastic containers for food storage. Studies have shown that certain plastics and other petroleum-based materials can degrade over time and leach chemicals into stored food. For more information on identifying plastic types and the potential health risks of plastic materials, visit The Green Guide at www.thegreenguide.com.

RECYCLE

Many homeowners are already in the habit of recycling glass, plastic, and waste paper, but if you're making upgrades to your kitchen cabinetry, now's the time to include a recycling center to simplify household recycling for years to come. A slide-out bin near the sink or where you normally keep a trash can stores all types of kitchen waste in one convenient location.

When planning a recycling center, first contact your garbage/recycling collection company to learn what types of materials it recycles. Collection companies and municipalities vary widely on what they do and do not recycle. If your service offers limited collection, look for a more eco-minded business, and contact your city office to learn about collection facilities for materials that your garbage company won't accept.

Keep in mind that the success of municipal recycling programs is largely the homeowners' responsibility. If your collection service accepts only 1 and 2 plastics (which is most common), but you're dumping all types of plastics into your recycling bin each week, you may be doing more harm than good. Improper materials have to be culled by staff at recycling facilities to prevent contamination of other materials. Always check the number on the bottom of each plastic container before throwing it into the recycling bin.

Bulk containers reduce a household's expenses and its environmental impact. The single container at right holds the same volume of soap as the nine containers at left.

Some plastics are safer than others. The familiar recycling emblem on the bottom of most plastic food containers shows an abbreviated code indicating the type of material used in the container.

Cabinet manufacturers offer a range of options for all-in-one, integrated recycling/garbage storage.

Countertops

As anyone in the building industry can tell you, there's no such thing as a perfect countertop material. Even the best surfaces have their drawbacks. Some stain, some burn, and some need regular upkeep and surface treatments to maintain sanitary and aesthetic standards. So, when you add green goals into the mix, the range of options becomes even more limited, right? Well, yes and no. It all depends on your priorities and the performance you require. In the end, you'll most likely choose from the list of familiar countertop materials or perhaps go with something funky like a recycled glass product.

From a green perspective, a counter surface should satisfy three demands: It must be durable (to prevent replacement in the near future), it must be sanitary and not require toxic treatments (for health reasons), and it should come with a reasonably low "price tag" of embodied energy (to minimize the ecological impact of production).

As an example, let's say you're considering three of today's most popular countertop materials: granite, stainless steel, and plastic laminate. Granite certainly is a nice material—it's natural, sanitary, durable, and beautiful. It's also an irreplaceable resource that must be mined from the ground, causing lasting damage to natural habitats. Then it gets shipped (most likely from very far away and at great expense because it's so heavy), cut, processed, finished, and shipped again (more pollution and use of natural resources).

On the surface, plastic laminate might not seem like a very green countertop option but, perhaps surprisingly, it offers quite a few advantages over other popular materials.

Okay, so maybe granite doesn't seem so green. What about stainless steel? Also sanitary, durable, beautiful, and even recyclable. Yet steel, too, comes from the ground (more mining), and the raw materials require energy-intensive processing before you have a sleek and shiny finished product. Then it has to be cut, shaped, and welded to your specifications. In the end, the material is a very good performer but maybe not so good for your wallet or the environment.

Finally, perhaps only half-seriously, you consider plastic laminate. It doesn't look or feel very "green." It's plastic. It's not exactly beautiful or showy and not all that durable compared to stainless steel. But it is quite sanitary and easy to clean, and it comes in a huge range of colors and styles. How is it made? Mostly with recycled paper and wood fibers and petroleum-based resins. No mining, less shipping and processing, and highly efficient use of a renewable resource (that is the wood, not the petroleum).

And the drawbacks? The particleboard substrate on most laminate countertops is made with a binder containing urea-formaldehyde (see Cabinet Materials, on pages 57 to 59). The paper in the laminate may also contain urea-formaldehyde, but it's pretty well locked in by the resins. As for the petroleum used to make the resin, it's hardly worth considering when compared to the fuel consumed by the mining equipment extracting a material like granite or by the cargo ship bringing it overseas.

Yet, you say, granite lasts for generations; it will never need to be replaced. True, in theory. But unless you live in Colonial Williamsburg, there's extremely little chance your kitchen will remain unchanged for generations. As popular as granite is today, it undoubtedly will be considered ugly or impractical by homeowners of the future, if only for a while. Nevertheless, you can always use reclaimed stone instead of virgin granite, and you can seal the particleboard of laminate countertops to prevent offgassing or build your own custom counters made with a formaldehyde-free substrate (see pages 58 to 59). As for the steel, its greatest green attribute is its durability and recyclability; the countertops can prove to be green if you keep them for a long time and then recycle the metal surfaces.

Stainless steel countertops score well on durability and sanitariness, but lose points on the embedded energy front since they require a lot of work to mine, forge finish and transport.

Granite and other natural stone materials make sense from a green perspective only if they are reclaimed for re-use by salvaging. Otherwise, the natural benefits of stone are offset by the environmental damage caused by mining and the high fuel consumption required for transport.

The universe of countertops doesn't end with the three we've discussed. There are some newer but very green countertop solutions. Although no countertop material is perfectly green, you still have many *greener* options to choose from (but let's face it, imported stone just doesn't make the cut). Topping the list of alternative products these days are surfaces made with recycled glass and a paper-resin compound that's sort of a cross between plastic laminate and solid-surface material.

Recycled glass countertops have a fun and funky look created by glass shards suspended in a cement-based or plastic resin binder. Their main green advantage is that most of the glass is recycled. Greener versions contain as much as 80% post-consumer recycled content. However, these surfaces must be custom-made to your specifications, which means the finished product has to be shipped from the factory; if you live far from the manufacturer, the green advantage of the material is offset by the environmental cost of shipping.

As their name implies, paper-resin countertops are made with layers of paper and petrochemical resins or water-based phenol resins. But unlike paper-resin laminates, they are manufactured into solid slabs that commonly range from ½" to 1¼" thick. The surface can be customized with drainboard cutouts and other integrated details. Paper-resin countertops are assembled on-site, where pieces are cut and fused with a special adhesive to create a seamless surface.

Countertops made with recycled glass and other composite materials (See Resources, page 237) offer a smooth, hard-wearing surface and can be produced with a high percentage of recycled content.

Certified paper-resin countertops are made with 100% FSC-certified recycled paper and water-based phenol resin and are formaldehyde-free. And perhaps equally important, you need not make any aesthetic sacrifices to use them.

Comparing Countertop Materials ▸

Material	Description	Making It Greener
Plastic Laminate	Paper and resin laminate glued to particleboard (or MDF) substrate Resistant to stains, scratches, and moisture; easy to clean; inexpensive Surface susceptible to chipping and burning; damage cannot be repaired	Use formaldehyde-free, recycled-wood substrate and low-VOC adhesive; laminate should be made with recycled paper and water-based resins, if possible
Paper-resin	Solid slab of paper and resin Highly workable for custom applications; solid color and same durability throughout slab; resistant to stains and heat May need Aeriodic cleaning and finishing treatments	Choose product with high recycled content; purchase from local or regional supplier/fabricator to minimize shipping
Tile	Ceramic, porcelain, or glass tiles glued to cementboard and wood substrate Durable and highly heat-resistant; tiles are highly washable; versatile material for custom applications Grout between tiles is prone to staining and must be sealed periodically	Use tiles with recycled content or locally produced tiles Use marine plywood and/or seal plywood to reduce formaldehyde offgassing; set tiles with low-VOC adhesive Seal grout and tiles (if necessary) with formaldehyde-free, low-VOC sealer
Glass Composite	Solid slab of glass and resin binder Durable; unique appearance; heat- and scratch-resistant May require periodic cleaning and/or sealing treatments	Choose product with high recycled content Purchase from local or regional fabricator to minimize shipping
Butcher block	Solid-wood strips laminated to form slab Natural, renewable material; good surface for cutting; can be refinished Must be oiled and sealed periodically to maintain appearance	Choose only FSC-certified wood Treat surface with food-safe finishes and sealers
Stainless Steel	Alloy of steel, nickel, and chromium; often glued to wood substrate Highly durable, rustproof, and easy to clean Can be scratched and dented	Recycle the metal if you replace the countertops Use formaldehyde-free substrate
Natural Stone	Solid quarried stone slabs or tiles glued to substrate Durable; heat-proof and waterproof Can chip and crack; some varieties will stain; dark colors make cleaning problematic	Look for salvaged slabs or buy stone from local quarry
Engineered Stone	Composite of quartz or other stone, pigments, and polyester resin Same color and durability throughout slab; doesn't require sealing	Purchase from a manufacturer in your region and use a local fabricator
Solid-surface	Composite of petrochemical-based resins (polyester, acrylic) and bauxite ore and/or other fillers Color and durability consistent throughout material; highly workable and customizable	Green options are limited; perhaps minimize quantity of countertop
Concrete	Available in various forms, including poured-in-place concrete, cast concrete, and fiber-cement composite materials Versatile material is highly customizable; durable and heat-resistant Can be very heavy; prone to cracking, chipping, and staining; must be sealed regularly	Look for products with high recycled content, such as fly ash (to replace high-embodied energy cement) and aggregates Color material with natural, non-toxic pigments added to concrete mix instead of stains applied to surface

Laminate Countertops

A custom laminate countertop offers some decidedly green advantages. First, you can select your own substrate—the wood structure underneath the laminate surface. Particleboard, or higher-grade MDF, made from recycled wood fibers and formaldehyde-free binders is an environmentally friendly material without the toxic formaldehyde offgassing you get with standard particleboard (see Cabinet Materials, on page 57). You can also use a low-VOC contact cement for adhering the laminate to the substrate. Be sure to choose a strong, high-quality adhesive designed for laminates.

Plastic laminate is readily available from local suppliers in a wide range of colors, styles, and finishes. Laminate sheets for countertops are typically $\frac{1}{20}$" thick and 30" wide and come in 8-ft. and 12-ft. lengths. 48"-wide sheets are also available for deeper surfaces, as are "color-through" laminates that don't have the dark exposed edge of standard laminates.

This project shows all of the steps for creating the main counter surface with a built-up, laminated front edge, as well as a laminated backsplash. Exposed edges of the laminate are filed to create a smooth, safe edge. Be careful when working with cut pieces: The edges are razor-sharp before they are filed at a slight angle.

Tools & Materials ▸

Tape measure	Screwdriver
Framing square	Belt sander
Straightedge	File
Scoring tool	Router
Paint roller	¾" particleboard
3-way clamps	Sheet laminate
Caulk gun	Contact cement
J-roller	and thinner
Miter saw	Wood glue
Scribing compass	Wallboard screws
Circular saw	

Compared with other popular materials, laminate countertops boast low embodied energy and minimal shipping and processing. Building your own countertop makes this inexpensive material even more economical.

Working with Laminate

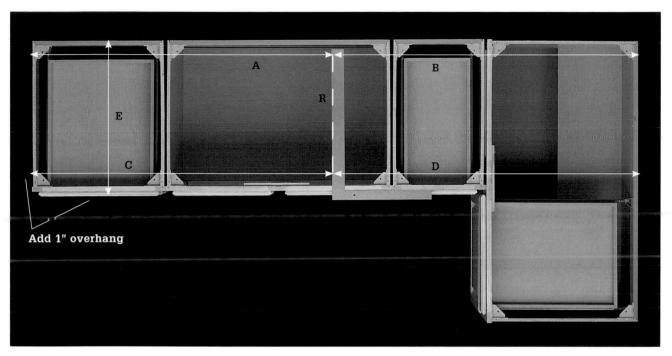

Add 1" overhang

Measure along tops of base cabinets to determine the size of the countertop. If wall corners are not square, use a framing square to establish a reference line (R) near the middle of the base cabinets, perpendicular to the front of the cabinets. Take four measurements (A, B, C, D) from the reference line to the cabinet ends. Allow for overhangs by adding 1" to the length for each exposed end and 1" to the width (E).

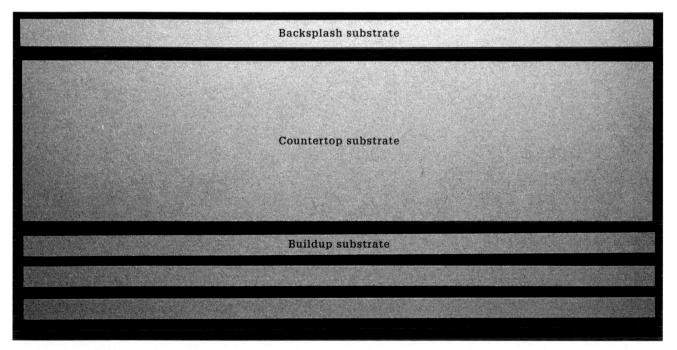

Backsplash substrate

Countertop substrate

Buildup substrate

Lay out cutting lines on the particleboard so you can rip-cut the substrate and buildup strips to size, using a framing square to establish a reference line. Cut the core to size using a circular saw with a clamped straightedge as a guide. Cut 4" strips of particleboard for backsplash and for joint support where sections of countertop core are butted together. Cut 3" strips for edge buildups. Seal all exposed particleboard or MDF surfaces.

How to Build a Low-Impact Laminate Countertop

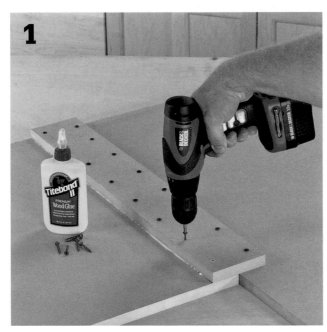

Join the countertop substrate pieces on the bottom side. Attach a 4" particleboard joint support across the seam using carpenter's glue and 1¼" wallboard screws.

Attach 3"-wide edge buildup strips to the bottom of the countertop using 1¼" wallboard screws. Fill any gaps on the outside edges with latex wood patch, and then sand the edges with a belt sander.

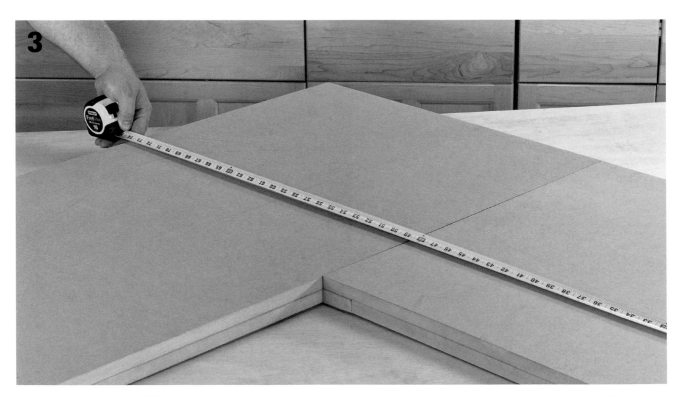

To determine the size of the laminate top, measure the countertop substrate. Laminate seams should not overlap the substrate. Add ½" trimming margin to both the length and width of each piece. Measure laminate needed for the face and edges of the backsplash and for the exposed edges of the countertop substrate. Add ½" to each measurement.

Cut the laminate by scoring and breaking it. Draw a cutting line, then etch along the line with a utility knife or other sharp cutting tool. Use a straightedge as a guide. Two passes of the scoring tool will help the laminate break cleanly.

Option: Some laminate installers prefer to cut the laminate with special snips that resemble aviator snips. Available from laminate suppliers, the snips are faster than scoring and snapping and less likely to cause cracks or tears in the material. You'll still need to square the cut edges with a trimmer or router.

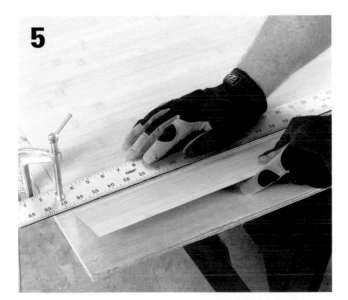

Bend the laminate toward the scored line until the sheet breaks cleanly. For better control on narrow pieces, clamp a straightedge along the scored line before bending the laminate. Wear gloves and safety glasses to avoid being cut by the sharp edges.

Create tight-piloted seams with the plastic laminate by using a router and a straight bit to trim the edges that will butt together. Measure from cutting edge of the bit to the edge of the router baseplate (A). Place the laminate on scrap wood and align the edges. To guide the router, clamp a straightedge on the laminate at distance A plus ¼", parallel to the laminate edge. Trim the laminate.

(continued)

Apply the laminate to the sides of the countertop first. Using a paint roller, apply two coats of contact cement to the edge of the countertop and one coat to the back of the laminate. Let the cement dry according to manufacturer's directions. Position the laminate carefully, then press against the edge of the countertop. Bond the laminate to the substrate firmly with J-roller.

Use a router and flush-cutting bit to trim the edge strip flush with the top and bottom surfaces of the countertop substrate. At the edges where the router cannot reach, trim the excess laminate with a file. Apply the laminate to the remaining edges, and trim with the router.

Test-fit the laminate top on the countertop substrate. Check that the laminate overhangs all edges. At the seam locations, draw a reference line on the core where the laminate edges will butt together. Remove the laminate. Make sure all surfaces are free of dust, then apply one coat of contact cement to the back of the laminate and two coats to the substrate. Place spacers made of ¼"-thick scrap wood at 6" intervals across the countertop core. Because contact cement bonds instantly, spacers allow laminate to be positioned accurately over the core without bonding. Align the laminate with the seam reference line. Beginning at one end, remove the spacers and press the laminate to the countertop core.

10

Apply contact cement to the remaining substrate and the next piece of laminate. Let the cement dry, then position the laminate on spacers and carefully align the butt seam. Beginning at the seam edge, remove the spacers and press the laminate to the countertop substrate.

11

Roll the entire surface with a J-roller to bond the laminate to the substrate. Clean off any excess contact cement with a soft cloth and mineral spirits.

12

Flush-cutting bit

Remove the excess laminate with a router and flush-cutting bit. At edges where the router cannot reach, trim the excess laminate with a file. Countertop is now ready for final trimming with a bevel-cutting bit.

(continued)

13

15° bevel-
cutting bit

Finish-trim the edges with a router and 15° bevel-cutting bit. Set the bit depth so that the bevel edge is cut only on the top laminate layer. Bit should not cut into vertical edge surface.

Tip ▸

File all edges and sharp corners smooth. Use downward file strokes to avoid chipping the laminate.

14

Cut 1¼"-wide strips of ¼" plywood to form an overhanging scribing strip for the backsplash. Attach to the top and sides of the backsplash substrate with glue and wallboard screws. Cut the laminate pieces and apply to the exposed sides, top, and front of the backsplash. Trim each piece as it is applied.

15

Test-fit the countertop and backsplash. Because your walls may be uneven, use a compass to trace the wall outline onto the backsplash scribing strip. Use a belt sander to grind the backsplash to the scribe line.

16

Apply a bead of silicone caulk to the bottom edge of the backsplash.

17

Position the backsplash on the countertop, and clamp it into place with bar clamps. Wipe away excess caulk, and let the caulk cure completely.

18

Screw 2" wallboard screws through the countertop and into the backsplash core. Make sure the screw heads are countersunk completely for a tight fit against the base cabinet. Install the countertops.

Flooring

Like the cabinets and countertops, flooring plays an important role in determining how well your kitchen functions and how good it looks. Green options for flooring cover a full range of readily available materials, many of which lend themselves to do-it-yourself installation. The following is a brief discussion of the front-runners—materials that meet the considerable demands of the kitchen environment and accomplish green-building objectives in a variety of ways.

Engineered wood floors offer a comparable look and feel to solid hardwood flooring but require much less material from old-growth trees.

Wood

Wood flooring has long been prized for its natural beauty, its comfortable feel underfoot, and its long-term durability. Day-to-day maintenance of wood flooring is generally more involved than with some other materials, particularly tile and concrete, but the fact that wood can be refinished means that the original flooring can serve you well for many decades.

Traditional solid hardwood flooring, although it uses considerable natural resources, can be a green option if you buy from a supplier who guarantees FSC-certified materials (see page 13). All of the standard species, like oak, maple, and cherry, are available from certified forests, as are tropical hardwoods such as teak and ipé. Solid-wood flooring made from salvaged or reclaimed lumber also is available from a number of suppliers. When it comes to floor finishes, healthier alternatives to oil-based polyurethane (the industry standard) include low-VOC water-based varnishes and natural penetrating oils, such as linseed oil and tung oil. And you can always select prefinished flooring for durable, factory-applied finish without the problem of fumes in the house.

Engineered wood flooring is a resource-efficient alternative to solid hardwood, but its appearance is virtually the same. Engineered flooring consists of a plywood core or substrate topped with a hardwood veneer (also called the wear layer). Flooring with a thick wear layer often can be sanded and refinished two or more times. Installation of engineered products is made easy with tongue-and-groove or snap-together joints that permit a floating floor application. For the greenest engineered flooring, look for products with FSC certification—for both the core and veneer—and low- or no-formaldehyde glues used in making the core.

Bamboo

As a popular wood alternative that's far too nice to be considered "the next best thing to wood," bamboo is steadily making its way into the mainstream flooring market. Because it can be harvested every three to five years (and without killing the plant, as an added bonus), bamboo is classified as a "rapidly renewable resource." Hardwood trees, by contrast, can take 25 years or more to reach maturity prior to harvesting.

Bamboo flooring is available in solid-strip and engineered versions. The latter has a similar construction to engineered wood flooring and can be installed with floating or glue-down methods. Solid bamboo products install much like traditional hardwood—they're typically nailed or glued to the subfloor—and are sold prefinished or can be sanded and finished on-site just like hardwood. The project on pages 146 to 151 shows you how to install solid-bamboo tongue-and-groove flooring using the nail-down technique.

When shopping for bamboo flooring, compare products and varieties for their suitability in kitchens. Vertical-grain (edge grain) bamboo typically stands up better to moisture than horizontal grain (flat grain), while carbonized bamboo (which has been steamed to produce darker coloring) may be somewhat softer than natural-color products. It's also important to buy from a reputable, experienced manufacturer to ensure high performance standards and (hopefully) ethical and sustainable practices in harvesting and producing the materials.

A kitchen floor made of grass. Bamboo (a woody grass) is a popular and widely available alternative to hardwood flooring.

Cork & Linoleum

These once-passé-but-now-cutting-edge flooring materials are grouped here because both are excellent green alternatives to resilient vinyl flooring (see The Great Vinyl Debate, on page 78).

Cork is a natural material that boasts a cook-friendly "give" underfoot and an uncommon advantage over other kitchen floors: it's quiet. Due to its porous structure, cork has remarkable sound-deadening properties, which can be a welcome feature in a room full of hard, sound-reflecting surfaces. As a raw material, cork is the dead bark stripped from cork oak trees (harvesting doesn't damage the tree), but most cork flooring is made with material recycled from cork stopper manufacturing.

Cork flooring materials come in glue-down tiles and glue-down or snap-together planks and may include a wood, layered cork, or PVC backing.

Cork lends a rich, natural character to kitchen floors and helps to keep noise levels down.

(continued)

If you're concerned about the health risks of PVC, avoid cork flooring with a vinyl backing or wear layer. Common finishes include acrylic, polyurethane, and wax. For a greener cork floor, look for products made with all-natural protein binders, or urea-melamine, phenol-formaldehyde, or polyurethane binders, as many cork manufacturers use urea-formaldehyde binders (see Cabinet Materials, on page 57). Also inquire about low-VOC sealants recommended by manufacturers.

Linoleum, which was used so widely in the early 1900s that its name remains the popular generic term for all resilient flooring, is making a huge comeback in the green-building industry. It's made with natural products including linseed oil, cork dust, wood flour, and pigments, plus jute, burlap, or wood composite as a backing—all renewable and resource-efficient materials. Linoleum is comfortable underfoot and comes in a range of appealing colors and patterns. It's also easy to install and is available in sheets, tiles, and snap-together planks.

Tile

It's hard to beat the durability and versatility of tile. With a scrubable, waterproof, and nearly indestructible surface, tile is ideal for hard working kitchens (and ones that don't always get swept every night). Tile can be produced with high percentages of recycled materials and may not need replacement for the lifetime of the home, so it can be a solidly green option for flooring. Because tile retains heat well, it's good for passive solar designs as well as radiant heat systems. Yet it must be said that tile comes with two significant drawbacks: Its grout is prone to staining, and its rock-hard surface is hard on your feet after a while.

But if tile is right for your needs, look for ceramic or porcelain tile containing recycled materials, such as glass, ground ceramic, and feldspar tailings (a mining byproduct). Because tile is made with clay, a plentiful resource, it usually comes with relatively low embodied energy, so if you choose virgin-material products (as opposed to recycled), you might look for regional suppliers who don't have to ship the product from afar. When it comes to adhesive, grout, and sealers, choose low-VOC products to minimize detrimental effects on your indoor air quality.

Tile flooring is always in style, and careful shopping for products made with some recycled content makes it a great green option.

Concrete

Decorative finishes and superb thermal qualities have made concrete a popular choice for green homes of any style.

Like tile, concrete as a floor surface is hard (too hard for some people), durable, versatile, and excellent for retaining and radiating heat. Concrete is a favorite of many green builders, particularly when the plan calls for a slab-on-grade floor and the homeowners don't intend to cover it with another type of flooring. This means the concrete can serve as both foundation and finished floor surface and makes it an ideal application for in-floor radiant heating systems.

From a green perspective, concrete's main drawback is that portland cement—the binder in concrete—requires a lot of energy to produce and emits a significant amount of carbon dioxide (a greenhouse gas) and other pollutants in the process. To reduce these environmental impacts, a portion of the cement can be substituted with fly ash, a byproduct of coal-fired power plants. Depending on

the application, fly ash can be used to replace 25% or more of the concrete's cement, but this must be done following strict engineering specifications, so it's important to work with an expert.

Concrete's recent popularity as a flooring material is largely due to a great expansion of its decorative possibilities. Poured concrete can be tinted for a range of coloring effects, and skilled finishers can give it the appearance of stone, tile, and even leather. Surface-applied stains are often used for various texture and color effects. These can contain highly toxic chemicals and may offgas noxious fumes into the area, so be sure to make educated decisions before using any applied treatments. Cured concrete should be sealed to reduce the risk of staining. Low-VOC water-based sealers and natural penetrating oils are recommended for the chemically sensitive.

The Great Vinyl Debate ▸

Polyvinyl chloride (or PVC), what most people call vinyl, is the most widely used plastic in the building industry today and is the primary ingredient in most resilient flooring products. But due to potential health concerns, vinyl is also one of the most hotly contested materials in the international building community.

PVC is found in a range of household products, including windows, gutters, siding, wallcoverings, shower curtains, roofing membranes, and, of course, kitchen flooring. It's also used in many behind-the-scenes applications, such as plumbing drain pipe and sheathing for electrical wire. From a builder's and consumer's perspective, PVC is hard to beat. It's inexpensive, durable, and can take virtually any form imaginable with a high degree of consistency. Vinyl siding, for example, is essentially maintenance-free and may be guaranteed for up to 50 years. Compare that to wood siding, which must be refinished every five to 10 years to maintain performance. For many homeowners and builders, it can be hard to justify the added expense of using alternative materials when vinyl does the job so well and often so affordably.

So what's wrong with vinyl? It depends on who you ask. Vinyl producers and manufacturers assert that PVC is safe to work with and to have in your home, and they often point to vinyl's durability when comparing it to other materials: The less frequently something has to be replaced, the better it is for the environment.

Opponents of PVC production are most concerned with the "life cycle" of vinyl, which takes into account the production, usable life, and destruction of a material. Although PVC manufacturing has cleaned up considerably in recent decades, sources including the U.S. EPA have reported that vinyl production emits significant levels of pollutants, particularly vinyl chloride. Others claim that certain processes in PVC production emit dioxin, a potent toxin linked to cancer in humans and a range of ecological effects.

Flexible PVC products, such as resilient flooring, shower curtains, and wallcoverings, are made flexible with the addition of plasticizers, including DEHP (di-2-ethylhexul phthalate), a suspected carcinogen and possible endocrine disruptor. Phthalate plasticizers can offgas over the life of a PVC product, creating a potential health hazard in the home. Another health risk raising concern occurs when PVC products are burned in house fires or in unregulated incineration (such as garbage-pile

Good or bad for consumers and the environment? Most residential green-building experts steer clear of vinyl flooring (and siding or wallcovering), but many have accepted the use of PVC for plumbing pipes and wire insulation, at least for now.

fires). Burning PVC produces hydrochloric acid and can emit dioxins.

If all of this seems a little vague to you, it's because the jury is still out on the overall effects of PVC. Even the U.S. Green Building Council, the group behind LEED certification for green buildings, has yet to make a definitive call of the use of PVC and whether avoiding it should constitute a point in LEED certification. An extensive study of PVC by the USGBC is underway. To learn more about both sides of the vinyl debate, you can contact the following sources:

- Healthy Building Network: www.healthybuilding.net
- Greenpeace USA: www.greenpeaceusa.org
- The Vinyl Siding Institute: www.vinylsiding.org
- The Vinyl Institute: www.vinylbydesign.com
- The U.S. Green Building Council: www.usgbc.org

Tip: Additional Resources for Cabinets, Countertops & Flooring Materials ▸

CABINETS & CABINET MATERIALS

Neil Kelly Cabinets—"Naturals Collection": www.neilkellycabinets.com (photo left, below)
Cabinet King—Green Leaf Series: www.cabinetking.com
CitiLog™: www.citilogs.com
Forefront Designs (Greenline): www.forefrontdesigns.com
Henrybuilt (bamboo cabinets): www.henrybuilt.com
Smith & Fong (bamboo products): www.plyboo.com
SierraPine Ltd. (Medite II MDF): www.sierrapine.com
Environ Biocomposites: www.environbiocomposites.com
Collins Products, LL (CollinsWood® FSC-certified particleboard): www.collinswood.com
Columbia Forest Products (hardwood plywood): www.columbiaforestproducts.com

COUNTERTOPS

Paneltech International LLC (PaperStone Certified paper-resin countertops): www.kliptech.com/paperstone certified/
Richlite® (paper fiber composite countertops): www.richlite.com
Counter Production (Vetrazzo recycled-glass countertops): www.counterproduction.com
IceStone, Inc. (recycled-glass countertops): www.icestone.biz (photo center, below)
Endura Wood Products, Ltd. (FSC-certified butcherblock countertops): www.endurawood.com
All Paper Recycling, Inc. (recycled-paper countertops): www.shetkastone.com

FLOORING

Bamboo Hardwoods, Inc.: www.bamboohardwoods.com
GreenFloors (bamboo): www.greenfloors.com
Teragren (bamboo): www.teragren.com
Natural Cork, Inc.: www.naturalcork.com
Nova Distinctive Floors (Nova Cork™ and Nova Linoleum™ flooring): www.novafloorings.com
Forbo Linoleum: www.forboflooringNA.com
Sandhill Industries (recycled-glass tile): www.sandhill.com
Eco-Friendly Flooring: www.ecofriendlyflooring.com (photo right, below)

Green Bathrooms

Like kitchens, bathrooms have received a lot of attention in recent years and have benefited from a number of practical changes. As a result, a new or remodeled bath today is trimmed and fitted with proven materials and relatively efficient fixtures. These days, most builders wouldn't even think of putting thick carpeting in the bathroom (or even hardwood in a full bath), and they're not even allowed to install an old water-hog toilet or ignore specifications for a ventilation fan.

So if you're considering some *really* up-to-date changes—that is, incorporating green design goals—much of the groundwork has already been laid for you. But that doesn't mean there's no room for improvement. Green bathrooms aren't just well-designed rooms full of water-saving fixtures; they're also built to protect against the ravages of excess moisture (think: mold), and they display a sense of environmental responsibility and a creative use of exciting materials, new and old.

In this chapter:

- Must Be Something in the Water
- Low-Flow Fixtures
- Low-Flush Toilets
- Water-Saving Urinals
- Hot Water Systems
- Preventing Mold
- Bathroom Vent Fans
- Bathroom Surfaces
- Preparing for New Tile in Wet Areas
- Converted Vanity Cabinet

Must Be Something in the Water

Not surprisingly, green bathroom design is keenly focused on the use and disposal of water. When you consider that the toilet and shower together account for about 45% to 55% of the average home's annual water consumption, it's easy to see how that "something" in the water is actually your money. As you'll learn in this section, a few simple fixture upgrades can dramatically reduce your everyday water use, even if you don't take a vow to change your showering habits (although you should try).

A typical full bath presents three primary opportunities for reducing water consumption (in order of significance): the toilet, the shower, and the sink faucets. Thanks to federal conservation laws, low-flow plumbing fixtures are now the industry standard, so finding what you want in a resource-efficient version is a no-brainer. But green bath design doesn't end with your personal use of water. There's also all that steamy vapor, puddling and splashing, and surface condensation to deal with. In the war against wetness, your main lines of defense are durable, water-resistant surfaces and a good ventilation system.

But enough about the water already. What about the decorative details, like vanity cabinets and countertops? You'll be glad to know that this is an area where the available green options can more than fill your palette. Bathroom vanities come in just as many eco-friendly materials as kitchen cabinets, and when it comes to countertops, the options are even greater because bath counters don't receive as much abuse as kitchen counters. Bath surfaces are also smaller, so it's easier to splurge on something special, like recycled-aluminum tiles or a recycled-glass countertop.

Reduced water flow doesn't mean reduced enjoyment. Today's new low-flow showerheads combine advanced technologies with popular usability features to provide a great showering experience.

Elements of a Green Bathroom

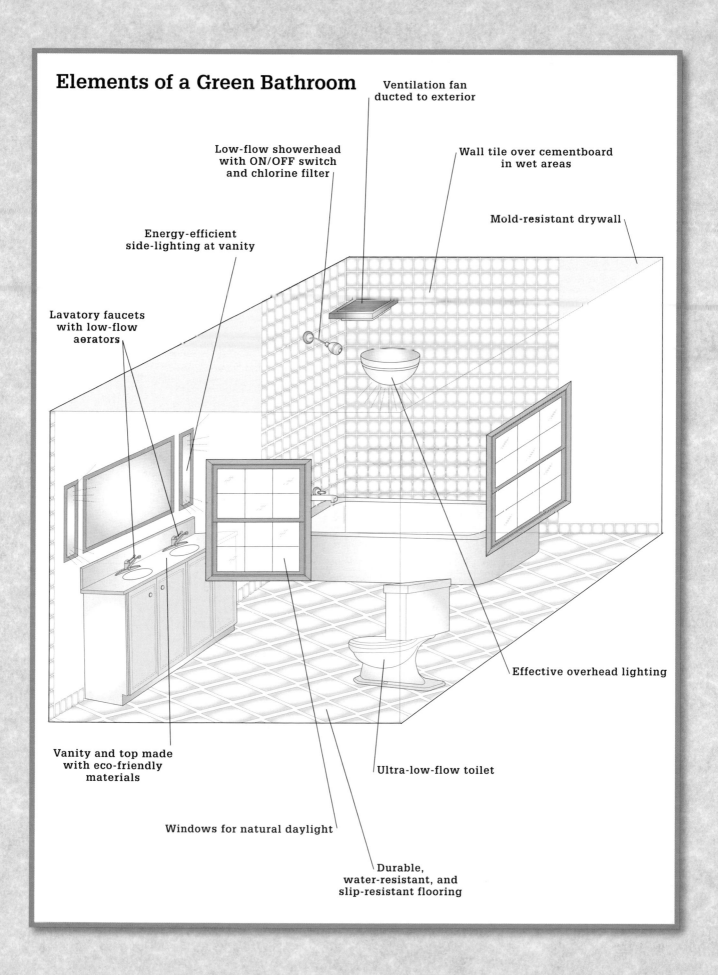

Ventilation fan ducted to exterior

Low-flow showerhead with ON/OFF switch and chlorine filter

Wall tile over cementboard in wet areas

Mold-resistant drywall

Energy-efficient side-lighting at vanity

Lavatory faucets with low-flow aerators

Effective overhead lighting

Vanity and top made with eco-friendly materials

Ultra-low-flow toilet

Windows for natural daylight

Durable, water-resistant, and slip-resistant flooring

Low-Flow Fixtures

Low-flow is a general description applied to water-saving bath fixtures, including showerheads, special aerators for lavatory (sink) faucets, and toilets (although "low-flush" are "ultra-low-flush" are more accurate descriptors for toilets). Flow rate is typically quantified in terms of gallons per minute, or gpm. In the cases of the bathroom's biggest water users, the toilet and showerhead, fixtures with "low-flow" ratings have been standard issue for over 10 years, but the description still has relevance because so many homeowners still have old fixtures made before the early-1990s changes in federal water conservation regulations.

When it comes to implementing water-saver upgrades, most do-it-yourselfers can tackle everything a typical full bath requires. See pages 90 to 93 for replacing a toilet, and page 100 for information on low-flow showerheads.

Toilets account for 30% to 40% of a home's indoor water use. Replacing an old fixture with a new 1.6 gpf model has instant payback. For even greater returns, you can buy a toilet that uses still less water, like the 1.28 gpf model seen here.

Water-Saving Toilets

When an appliance or other item in your home is working fine and meets your needs, replacing it with a new, more efficient model isn't always the greenest choice. This seldom is the case with old toilets. Due to their basic design and the durability of glazed porcelain, toilets can last seemingly forever. Unfortunately, older models simply waste too much water to warrant keeping them around.

On average, pre-1980s toilets use five to seven gallons of fresh water per flush, while those manufactured through 1992 use about 3.5 gallons per flush (gpf). Compared to today's standard 1.6 gpf models, even an early-90s toilet consumes 15,000 to 20,000 more gallons per year for a family of four. Multiply that number by your current per-gallon water charge (it should be on your water bill) and you'll clearly see how a new low-flow model can pay for itself in as little as three years' time. Yet, the environmental benefits are immediate. Reducing water consumption eases the strain on municipal water treatment facilities and saves wear and tear on home septic systems. And contrary to what many believe, fresh water (including water suitable for treatment) is not an inexhaustible resource.

In all fairness, it must be said that early versions of low-flow toilets, which first appeared in the U.S. in the 1980s, were rightly criticized for their poor flush performance among other problems. This was mostly due to the fact that many toilet manufacturers simply limited the amount of flushing water without redesigning the trap—the water channel inside the toilet that creates a siphoning effect to get rid of the waste. Older trap designs needed the greater water capacity to work properly. But that's all changed. Many new low-flow toilets outperform older versions with less than half the water per flush, so the naysayers no longer have a good excuse.

High-tech flushing systems like this flapperless tower system by Kohler have allowed for the development of toilets (like the one on the previous page) that use only a fraction of the amount of water older units consume per flush.

Tip: How Old is Your Toilet? ▸

Unless you're willing to measure the water in your toilet tank with a measuring cup, there's no easy way to accurately determine how much water an old toilet is using. But you can find out its age, which will give you a ballpark idea of its usage. Most toilets have the year of manufacture stamped underneath the tank lid. If your toilet was born before 1993, it may be time to consider putting it to rest.

Shopping for a New Toilet

Sounds like a great night out, right? Well, maybe not for everyone. But you might be surprised by how immersed you become in comparing technical data on features like trap-way diameter, flush-valve size, and kilograms of solid waste removal. In truth, the available options on toilets today can make your head swirl, so here's an abbreviated overview of the primary shopping decisions:

Aside from color, style, size, and other aesthetic criteria, there are two basic types of ultra-low-flush toilets. *Gravity* models work pretty much like your old toilet, except for the modernized trap-way and a few other improvements. *Pressure-assisted* toilets have a special reservoir inside the tank. As the reservoir fills with water, it becomes pressurized with air, resulting in a powerful, bowl-cleansing flush. If you've ever been scared by a flushing toilet, it was probably a pressure-assisted one. The noise can give you a start when you're not expecting it. But they do work well and are often recommended for applications when older plumbing hinders toilet performance.

A third type of toilet, called power-assisted, uses an electronic flush mechanism to create an effective and reasonably quiet flush, and, best of all, the toilet doesn't need a tank. However, these are priced well out of range for most consumers. They also present yet another unnecessary use of electricity. Unlike most household systems, toilets have never needed to be plugged in to work, so why start now?

Both gravity and pressure-assisted toilets are available with a clever feature that results in significant water savings over standard models. The *dual-flush* system has two flush buttons—one for a standard 1.6-gallon flush and one for a 0.8- or 0.9-gallon flush, for when you're flushing only liquids (which is what the majority of flushes are for). Dual-flush toilets are common in Europe and are gaining popularity in the U.S. due to the simple realization that you don't need over a gallon and a half of water to evacuate a small amount of liquid waste. If your household has a policy about not flushing liquids after every use, a dual-flush toilet offers an "out" from this sometimes unsavory (but admirable) water-saving technique.

Finally, there are toilets that use even less water than dual-flush, and some that use no water at all (see Composting Toilets, on page 87). Urinals are becoming popular features in residential bathrooms. In addition to obviating the age-old seat up/seat down debate, urinals help the primary throne-style toilet stay cleaner, and they use very little water. Flush versions may be rated at 0.5 gpf, while waterless designs use no water at all. For instructions on how to install a urinal, see pages 96 to 99.

When you're ready to plan your night on the town visiting plumbing showrooms, start with a little background research. Consumer Reports (www.consumerreports.org) has done their standard full write-up on today's water-saving toilets, including a performance test and model rating. One of the challenges that comes with choosing a toilet is that you can't take the products for a test-drive. Therefore, it's important to read performance reviews from third-party sources before making a decision.

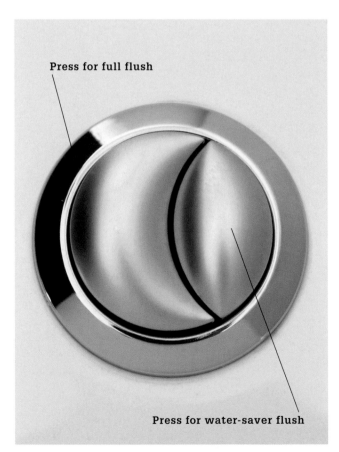

Press for full flush

Press for water-saver flush

Among new water-saving toilet technologies are dual flush buttons that allow you to select a low water volume flush for liquid waste or a full-strength flush.

Newer gravity-assisted toilets rely on taller tanks and steeper bowl walls to comply with the 1.6 gallon flush laws without any degradation of flush power, making them a perfectly fine (and readily available) green option.

This one-piece toilet uses only 1.0 gallons of water per flush. Its high-tech flushing system discharges compressed air to propel water forcefully out of the rim holes and effectively boost the flushing power. The manufacturer, Kohler, claims that for an average family the fixture will save 7,000 to 10,000 gallons of water per year compared to a 1.6 gallon toilet.

Composting Toilets ▸

If the reduced water usage of today's conventional toilets doesn't satisfy your green goals or if you have a rural home where a standard septic system is costly or inconvenient to install, a composting toilet is an excellent option. Composting toilets use little or no water and collect the waste in a repository underneath the toilet or in a crawlspace or basement below. Inside the enclosed collection bin, aerobic microorganisms quickly convert the waste into a dry, odorless, nutrient-rich material suitable for fertilizing trees, flower gardens, and other non-food plants.

But before you say "Eeewww!" and quickly turn the page, keep in mind that composting toilets have been used in homes for decades with proven standards of hygiene and performance in many different applications. (If you want something to exclaim about: The landscape-ready soil amendment created by composting toilets is sometimes called "hummus." Now you can say Eeewww!, so you don't have to do it in front of the salesperson.)

Low-Flush Toilets

Replacing an old (pre-1993) toilet with a new low-flush model will likely save your household more water than all other fixture and appliance upgrades combined. New toilets are commonly available in one-piece and two-piece designs. Most products in the low-to-mid price range are two-piece—the bowl and tank pieces are joined with bolts at the bottom of the tank. This project shows you how to drain and remove your old toilet before installing the new fixture. Be sure to purchase a new wax ring to use for the new installation.

Before you send your old toilet off to the landfill, see if you can find a local recycling center or manufacturer that recycles porcelain products. Porcelain can be recycled for use in concrete, road materials, and other applications.

Tools & Materials ▸

Pliers
Screwdriver
Putty knife
Utility knife
Adjustable wrench
Channel-type pliers
Hacksaw
Toilet seat & bolts

Wax ring
   without flange
Wax ring with flange
Supply tube
Penetrating oil
Teflon tape
Towels
Bucket and sponge

Replacing a toilet is simple, and the latest generation of 1.6-gallon water-saving toilets has overcome the performance problems of earlier models.

Buy a toilet that will fit the space. Measure the distance from the floor bolts back to the wall (if your old toilet has two pairs of bolts, go by the rear pair). This is your rough-in distance and will be either 10" or approximately 12". Make note of the bowl shape, round or oval (long). Oval bowls (also called elongated bowls) are a few inches longer for greater comfort, but may be too big for your space. The safest bet is to buy a replacement with the same bowl shape.

Round front

Rough-in distance 10", 12", or 14" (12" most common)

Floor bolt (cap on)

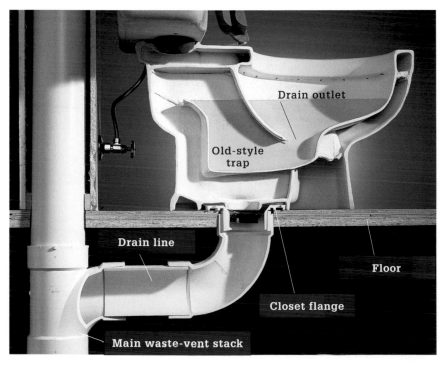

Knowing how a toilet works isn't essential to successful installation, but it helps. This cutaway photo features a pre-1.6-gallon law model, so your new toilet will have a much smaller trap. When the flush handle on the tank is depressed, the water in the tank rushes out through the hole in the underside of the bowl rim. The onrushing water forces the contents of the bowl and trap out through the closet flange and into the drain line, while the fresh tank water refills the bowl and trap.

Drain outlet

Old-style trap

Drain line

Closet flange

Floor

Main waste-vent stack

How to Replace a Water-hog Toilet

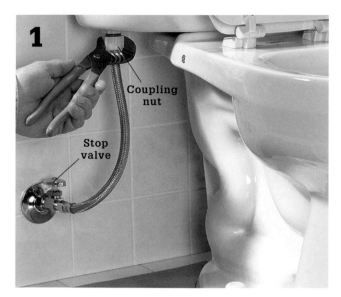

1

Remove the old supply tube. First, turn off the water at the stop valve. Flush the toilet, holding the handle down for a long flush, and sponge out the tank. Unthread the coupling nut for the water supply below the tank using channel-type pliers. Use a wet/dry vac to clear any remaining water out of the tank and bowl.

2

Grip each tank bolt nut with a box wrench or pliers and loosen it as you stabilize each tank bolt from inside the tank with a large slotted screwdriver. If the nuts are stuck, apply penetrating oil to the nut and let it sit before trying to remove them again. You may also cut the tank bolts between the tank and the bowl with an open-ended hacksaw. Remove and discard the tank.

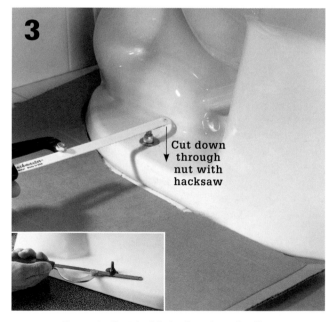

3

Cut down through nut with hacksaw

Remove the nuts that hold the bowl to the floor.
First, pry off the bolt covers with a screwdriver. Use a socket wrench, locking pliers, or your channel-type pliers to loosen the nuts on the tank bolts. Apply penetrating oil and let it sit if the nuts are stuck, then take them off. As a last resort, cut the bolts off with a hacksaw by first cutting down through one side of the nut. Tilt the toilet bowl over and remove it.

Tip ▶

Removing an old wax ring is one of the more disgusting jobs you'll encounter in the plumbing universe (the one you see here is actually in relatively good condition). Work a stiff putty knife underneath the plastic flange of the ring (if you can) and start scraping. In many cases the wax ring will come off in chunks. Discard each chunk right away—they stick to everything. If you're left with a lot of residue, scrub with mineral spirits. Once clean, stuff a rag in a bag in the drain opening to block sewer gas.

4

Clean and inspect the old closet flange. Look for breaks or wear. Also inspect the flooring around the flange. If either the flange or floor is worn or damaged, repair the damage. Use a rag and mineral spirits to completely remove residue from the old wax ring. Place a rag-in-a-bag into the opening to block odors.

Tip ▶

If you will be replacing your toilet flange or if your existing flange can be unscrewed and moved, orient the new flange so the slots are parallel to the wall. This allows you to insert bolts under the slotted areas, which are much stronger than the areas at the ends of the curved grooves.

5

Insert new tank bolts (don't reuse old ones) into the openings in the closet flange. Make sure the heads of the bolts are oriented to catch the maximum amount of flange material.

6

Remove the wax ring and apply it to the underside of the bowl, around the horn. Remove the protective covering. Do not touch the wax ring. It is very sticky. Remove the rag-in-a-bag.

(continued)

7

Lower the bowl onto the flange, taking care not to disturb the wax ring. The holes in the bowl base should align perfectly with the tank bolts. Add a washer and tighten a nut on each bolt. Hand tighten each nut and then use channel-type pliers to further tighten the nuts. Alternate back and forth between nuts until the bowl is secure. *Do not overtighten.*

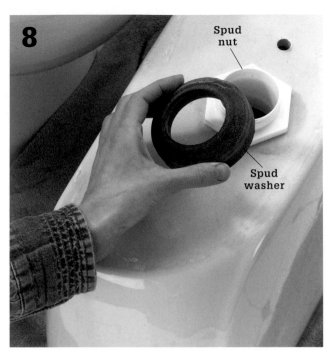

8

Spud nut

Spud washer

Attach the toilet tank. Some tanks come with a flush valve and a fill valve preinstalled. For models that do not have this, insert the flush valve through the tank opening and tighten a spud nut over the threaded end of the valve. Place a foam spud washer on top of the spud nut.

9

Threaded fill valve shank

Adjust the fill valve as directed by the manufacturer to set the correct tank water level height and install the valve inside the tank. Hand tighten the nylon lock nut that secures the valve to the tank (inset photo) and then tighten it further with channel-type pliers.

10

Intermediate nut goes between tank and bowl

With the tank lying on its back, thread a rubber washer onto each tank bolt and insert it into the bolt holes from inside the tank. Then, thread a brass washer and hex nut onto the tank bolts from below and tighten them to a quarter turn past hand tight. Do not overtighten.

11

Intermediate
nut

Position the tank on the bowl, spud washer on opening, bolts through bolt holes. Put a rubber washer, followed by a brass washer and a wing nut, on each bolt and tighten these up evenly.

12

You may stabilize the bolts with a large slotted screwdriver from inside the tank, but tighten the nuts, not the bolts. You may press down a little on a side, the front, or the rear of the tank to level it as you tighten the nuts by hand. Do not overtighten and crack the tank. The tank should be level and stable when you're done. Do not overtighten.

13

Hook up the water supply by connecting the supply tube to the threaded fill valve with the coupling nut provided. Turn on the water and test for leaks. Do not overtighten.

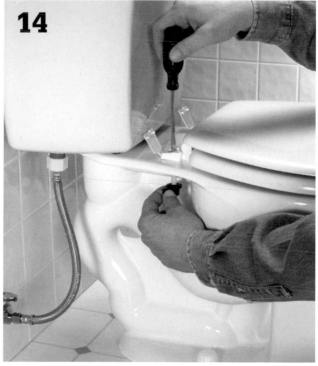

14

Attach the toilet seat by threading the plastic or brass bolts provided with the seat through the openings on the back of the rim and attaching nuts.

Water-Saving Urinals

Most people consider a urinal to be a commercial or industrial bathroom accessory, so why would you want one in your green home? The answer lies in the many advantages a urinal has to offer and the fact that most major bathroom fixture manufacturers are now producing urinals designed for residential installation.

A urinal doesn't take up much space and it uses much less water per flush than a standard toilet: 0.5 to 1.0 gallon of water per flush for the urinal, as opposed to the low-flow toilet's 1.6 gallons of water per full flush. You also have the option of a waterless urinal, a real boon in water-scarce areas. A urinal also has the emotional benefit of ending the great *up versus down* toilet seat debate. Finally, a urinal is generally easier to keep clean than a toilet because splashing is minimized.

Tools & Materials ▸

Tape measure	Urinal flushometer
Adjustable wrench	Emery cloth
Pencil	Wire brush
Level	Allen wrench
Sealant tape	Drywall
Utility knife	Drywall tape
Drywall saw	Drywall compound
Tubing cutter	2 × 6 lumber
Hacksaw	PVC 2" drainpipe
Miter box	PVC 2" male threaded
Hex wrenches	drain outlet
Smooth-jawed	½" copper pipe
spud wrench	Urinal
Slotted screwdriver	

Urinals are great water savers and are becoming increasingly popular among green homeowners.

Waterless Urinals ▸

For the ultimate in water conservation, you can now purchase a home urinal that uses zero water. A waterless urinal is never flushed, so you'll save about a gallon of water per usage. Naturally, waterless urinals are plumbed into your drain line system. But where typical plumbing fixtures rely on fresh water to carry the waste into the system, the waterless system relies simply on gravity for the liquid waste to find its way out of the fixture and into the drain. The secret is a layer of sealing liquid that is heavier than the water and forms a skim coat over the urine. When the urine enters the trap, it displaces the sealing liquid, which immediately reforms on the surface to create a layer that seals in odors. The Kohler fixture seen here (see Resources, page 237) is an example of the sealing liquid system. Other waterless urinals use replaceable cartridges.

A layer of sealing liquid forms a skim coat that floats on top of the liquid to trap odors.

Flushing Options for Urinals

A manual flush handle is still the most common and least expensive flushing mechanism for urinals. It is reliable but not as sanitary as touchless types, such as the Flushometer on page 99.

Motion sensors automatically flush touchless urinals, which is a great improvement in sanitation. These tend to be more expensive, however, and are more likely to develop problems. Also, because they flush automatically when users step away from the fixture, they don't allow you to conserve water by limiting flushing.

How to Install a Urinal

Remove the drywall or other surface coverings between the urinal location and the closest water supply and waste lines. Remove enough wall surface to reveal half of the stud face on each side of the opening to make patch work simpler.

2 × 6 mounting board

Following the manufacturer's directions for the urinal and flushometer, determine the mounting height of the urinal and mark the location of the supply and waste lines. For this installation, the 2" waste line is centered 17½" above the finished floor. Cut 5½" × 1½" notches in the wall studs centered at 32" above the finished floor surface, then attach a 2 × 6 mounting board.

Install the copper cold water supply line according to the manufacturer's specifications. Here, it is 4¾" to the side of the fixture centerline and 45" from the finished floor (11½" from the top of the fixture). Cap the stub-out 3" from the finished wall surface. Install the 2" drainpipe and vent pipe, making sure that the centerline of the drain outlet is positioned correctly (here, 17½" above the finished floor and 4¾" to the side of the supply line).

Attach the male threaded waste outlet to the drain pipe. It should extend beyond the finished wall surface. Replace the wall covering and finish as desired.

Attach the mounting brackets 32" above the floor, 3¼" to the sides of the centerline of the waste outlet.

Apply Teflon tape to the waste outlet. Thread the female collar onto the waste outlet until it is firmly seated and the flanges are horizontally level. Place the gasket onto the female collar. The beveled surface of the gasket faces toward the urinal.

Hang the urinal on the brackets, being careful not to bump the porcelain as it chips easily. Thread the screws through the washers, the holes in the urinal, and into the collar. Tighten the screws by hand, then one full turn with an adjustable wrench. Do not overtighten.

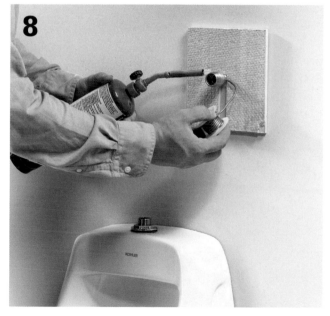

Determine the distance from the centerline of the water inlet on the top of the urinal, called the spud, to the finished wall. Subtract 1¼" from this distance and cut the water supply pipe to that length using a tubing cutter. Turn off the water before cutting. After cutting, deburr the inside and outside diameter of the supply pipe. Attach the threaded adapter to the cut pipe.

(continued)

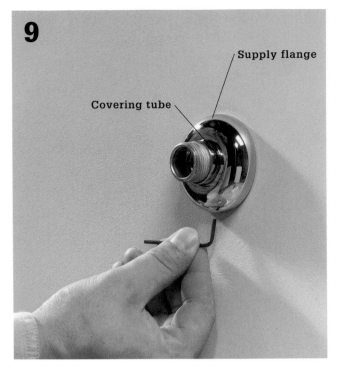

9

Covering tube

Supply flange

Measure from the wall surface to the first thread of the adapter. Using a hacksaw and a miter box or a tubing cutter, cut the covering tube to this length. Slide the covering tube over the water supply pipe. Slide the supply flange over the covering tube until it rests against the wall. Tighten the setscrew on the flange with an Allen wrench.

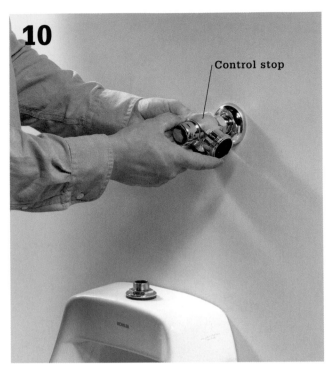

10

Control stop

Apply a small amount of pipe sealant to the adapter threads, then thread the control stop onto the adapter threads. Position the outlet toward the urinal so that it is horizontally level.

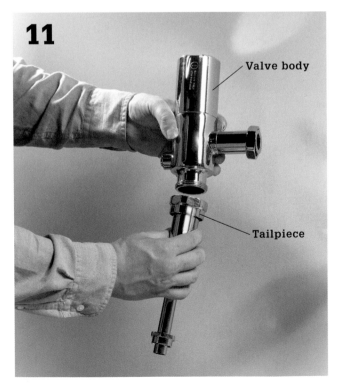

11

Valve body

Tailpiece

Hand-tighten the tailpiece into the flushometer valve body.

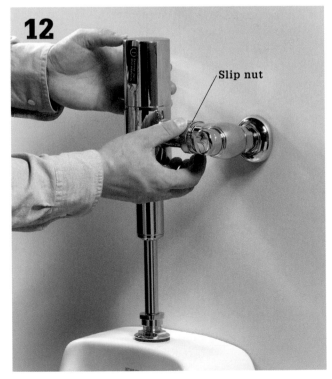

12

Slip nut

Hand-tighten the slip nut that connects the valve body to the control stop.

13

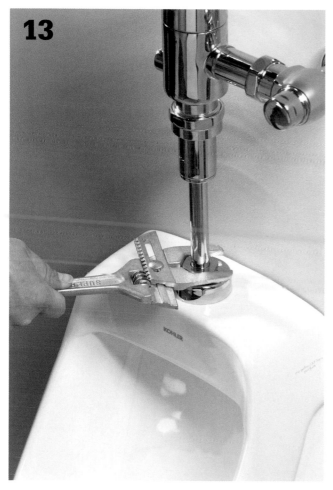

Use a smooth-jawed spud wrench to securely tighten the tailpiece, vacuum breaker, and spud couplings.

Tip ▸

For maximum sanitation, choose a urinal flush mechanism with an electronic sensor, like the Kohler Flush-o-meter being installed here. The electronic eye on this type of flush mechanism senses when a user approaches the fixture and then commands the fixture to flush when the user steps away. This eliminates the need to touch the handle before the user has the opportunity to wash his hands.

While testing the flush, adjust the supply stop screw counterclockwise until adequate flow is achieved.

14

Low-Flow Upgrades ▸

Replacing a toilet or adding a urinal are good ways to reduce your water consumption, but you needn't embark on ambitious plumbing projects to make a difference. Very simple projects like replacing a showerhead with a more efficient model or adding a flow restrictor to a faucet take only minutes to do.

SHOWERHEADS

The perfect showerhead is subject to personal taste. Some people like a strong, pulsating spray, while others prefer a gentle shower of water that falls vertically like rain. Some even claim to enjoy the piercing-needle sensation delivered by showerheads in budget hotels. But whatever your idea of a good spray may be, you can be sure of finding it in a new showerhead that uses no more than 2.5 gallons per minute.

The same federal act that limits water consumption in toilets (the Energy Policy Act of 1992) also requires that all showerheads made in the U.S. have a flow rate of 2.5 gpm or less. This has had several positive effects. It reduces household water consumption, of course, but it also leveled the playing field so that manufacturers must now compete by improving the spray of a showerhead without taking the easy route by adding more water. Unfortunately,

This showerhead (right) and this handshower (left) are engineered to operate with full performance at only 2.0 gallons per minute (gpm), saving 20% on water usage versus showerheads with a flow rate of 2.5 gpm. Made by Kohler (see Resources, page 237), they come with three spray options—soft coverage, rhythmic pulse, and aerated sprays.

Low-flow faucet aerators reduce water-flow rates from a typical 2.2 gpm to 1.5 gpm. You may be able to find a low-flow aerator that fits your current faucet—check with the manufacturer.

the law does not restrict the number of showerheads a shower can have.

Showering accounts for about 17% of household water use, and while 2.5 gpm is a decent benchmark for general conservation, there's plenty of room for improvement. Many showerheads offer lower flow rates, such as 1.0 gpm to 2.25 gpm. You can also choose a head with a built-in ON/OFF switch that allows you to conveniently shut off the water while you soap up. When the switch is turned back on for rinsing, the water is still mixed at the desired temperature. It's important to remember that most of what you're paying for when

showering is not the water itself but the gas or electricity used to heat the water. Shower water is typically about three-quarters hot water and one-quarter cold.

Replacing an old showerhead is an incredibly simple and usually inexpensive upgrade that can save water at the same time that it improves your showering experience and lowers your utility bill. There really aren't a lot of recommendations to follow when choosing a showerhead. Just take your time shopping around, ask your friends, maybe read some reviews, then take the plunge. You might find your ideal spray in a product that costs $15.

MEASURING SHOWERHEAD FLOW

Here's a simple method for testing the flow rate on an old showerhead: Turn on the shower full-blast with both hot and cold water and direct it into a 5-gallon bucket. Let the water run for exactly two minutes. If the bucket overflows before the time is up, it's not a low-flow showerhead.

A manual ON/OFF switch lets you stop the flow while you shampoo and soap up but keeps the water at the right temperature.

Today's showerhead designs use advances like air-inducing vacuum holes to provide a forceful spray that emits as little as 1.0 gpm.

Shower Filters

In addition to water conservation, another matter of consideration for a green home is the purity of the water. Most public water contains chlorine (and chlorine byproducts), which is added as a disinfectant. Chlorine is not listed as a carcinogen by the EPA, but some of its byproducts are, including trihalomethanes, chloramines, and chloroform. Chlorine is absorbed through the skin six times faster than through digestion, so showering exposes you to much more chlorine and some other contaminants than drinking the same water. People with sensitive skin and eczema are commonly affected by chlorine in shower and bath water.

Installing a water filter between the supply pipe (called the shower arm) and showerhead is an effective way to remove chlorine and other common water contaminants. Dechlorinating filters remove chlorine only, while some multistage carbon filters remove chlorine byproducts as well as some VOCs and pesticides. See page 35 for more information on analyzing your home's water. Many shower filters are rated at 2.5 gpm, so you don't have to worry about reduced flow.

How to Install a Shower Filter

Unscrew the old showerhead counterclockwise to remove it from the shower arm. Try turning it by hand first, then use pliers if necessary.

Apply one layer of Teflon tape wrapped clockwise around the threaded end of the shower arm. Install the filter unit and flush the filter as directed by the manufacturer.

Wrap the male filter end with Teflon tape, then install the showerhead and hand-tighten. If the showerhead or filter drips at the threaded joint, carefully tighten the appropriate connection until the leaking stops.

Faucet Aerators & Flow Reducers

Faucet aerators are the little disc-shaped fittings that screw onto the end of virtually all modern faucets. They mix the outgoing water with air to create a steady, even stream, increasing its pressure while deceptively reducing the faucet's flow rate. If you take the aerator off, the water comes out in a clumsy, usually off-center fashion that tends to cause a lot of splashing in the sink basin. Flow reducers perform a similar function to aerators but don't necessarily introduce air into the stream. Some flow reducers deliver a solid stream of water without the higher pressure that comes with aeration.

Because it's the last thing the water passes through on its way out, aerators and flow reducers determine a faucet's flow rate. On kitchen faucets, a higher flow rate is desirable to speed filling of pots and sinks for washing dishes. But on bathroom sink faucets, a high flow rate typically results in unnecessary water waste. This is because people tend to leave faucets running while brushing their teeth or shaving —a good habit to break, but not everyone in the house is likely to be very disciplined about it. For this reason, installing a low-flow aerator or flow reducer on all bathroom sink faucets can save significant amounts of water each year.

Green building experts generally recommend a maximum flow rate of 1.5 gpm on all lavatory faucets. With a good aerator or flow reducer, you'll find that this is plenty of water for everyday uses at the sink.

You can also find aerators and reducers with a 1.0 gpm flow rate for even greater savings. Replacing an old aerator (which is probably partially clogged with mineral deposits anyway) takes no more than a few minutes.

Replacing a Faucet Aerator ▶

To replace an aerator, unscrew the old aerator by hand or using channel-type pliers if necessary. Aerators typically screw into the faucet clockwise, but when you're standing above the fixture your hand motion is actually counterclockwise. Clean the faucet threads, then screw the new aerator or flow reducer into place and hand-tighten. Run the water to check for leaks. If necessary, carefully tighten the aerator using pliers (cover the aerator with a rag to prevent the plier's jaws from scratching the finish).

Low-flow aerators and flow reducers limit water consumption, often without making any perceptible change to the perceived water stream. Flow reducers (inset photo) have a perforated mesh that blocks water flow.

Hot Water Systems

Though you may not give it much thought, your water heater is arguably the second most important appliance in the house, behind only the heating and cooling system appliances. Not only is it the second-biggest energy user (next to heating and cooling), but its performance is reflected in so many other fixtures and appliances—from the clothes washer to the shower to the kitchen sink. As a result, the energy- and cost-efficiency of running those systems is directly linked to the efficiency of the water heater. For example, washing laundry in cold water may cost only pennies per load, while using warm or hot water can easily cost 10 times more.

Because we demand hot water almost the instant we turn on the tap, water heaters must keep the water hot at all times or, in the case of on-demand systems, blast cold water with an enormous amount of heat as it flows through the heater. That's why the water heater alone accounts for over 20% of a home's total energy use. So what's the solution for a green home? First, you can reduce hot water consumption, with water-saving appliances, low-flow bath fixtures, and simple habit modifications, such as taking shorter showers.

If it's time to replace your old water heater, you can make a significant green improvement by selecting a new high-efficiency unit that's sized to meet the specific demands of your household. If you're keeping your old tank-style heater but would like to improve its efficiency, you can insulate the tank to reduce standby heat losses (see pages 198 to 199). And any hot water system, old or new, can benefit from insulation on its water supply pipes (see page 38) and possibly a hot-water recirculating system (see sidebar on page 110).

Supplying the average home with hot water adds up to 21% of its annual energy usage.

Types of Water Heaters

Water can be heated with several different fuel sources, including natural gas, electricity, liquid propane (LP), oil, and solar energy. And there are two main types of water heating systems: tank-style and tankless. All of the abovementioned fuel sources can be used to serve a tank system, while tankless heaters are either gas, LP, or electric.

TANK (OR STORAGE) HEATERS

The most common type of water heater in use today is the direct-fired tank-style heater. Water is stored in a large tank that automatically refills itself with cold water as the heated water is used. Tank capacity in most home systems ranges between 40 and 80 gallons. As the water is heated—either from a gas (or oil) fire below the tank or from one or two electric elements submerged inside the tank—the hot water rises to the top where it is drawn off through a supply pipe to the home's fixtures. The main advantage of a tank system is that a large quantity of water remains heated and ready for use at all times. The downside is that the water loses heat sitting in the tank and must be reheated at regular intervals to maintain the set temperature. This is known as standby heat loss.

Indirect water heaters use the power of home-heating boilers to heat water with exceptional efficiency.

Conventional tank water heaters offer relatively low efficiency due to reheating of stored water.

Another type of tank heater, called indirect or indirect-fired, is used in conjunction with a boiler-driven home heating system. Indirect heaters have a large tank similar to standard water heaters, but the heat actually comes from the boiler. A closed loop of piping circulates hot water from the boiler into the tank, where a heat exchanger transfers the heat to the usable fresh water inside the tank. When properly designed, indirect water heaters can be the least expensive of all systems to operate, for two reasons: 1) boilers heat water more efficiently than standard

water heaters, and 2) when the boiler is already running to heat the home, some of that same energy is harnessed to heat the water in the tank. If your home uses hot water for its heat, have an HVAC or boiler specialist assess your system to determine the viability of an indirect water heater.

Solar water heaters are basically tank systems that use the sun as their primary energy source. Solar heat collected by panels on the roof or ground is transferred via fluid-filled tubes to a heat exchanger in or near a water storage tank in the house. Most systems also

Solar collectors for hot water are leaner and more versatile than ever. These flexible polymer collectors can be installed over roof shingles in a matter of hours.

Solar hot water systems typically preheat the water and rely on supplemental sources to add more heat.

include a secondary heat source, such as a gas burner or electric element, to bring the stored water up to temperature as needed. On an annual basis, solar systems typically rely on the sun for about 70% of the hot water heating, making it one of the greenest options if usually the most expensive in terms of setup cost. See page 228 for more information on solar hot water systems.

TANKLESS HEATERS

Tankless water heaters (also called on-demand or instantaneous) heat water only as it's used instead of stockpiling it in a tank. This technology offers several key advantages over tank systems. First, because there's no stored water to keep at temperature, there's no wasted energy due to standby losses. Second, the home never runs out of hot water—a tankless heater just keeps running as long as the hot-water taps are on. Third, tankless systems heat water more efficiently than tank heaters, reducing the home's everyday energy use. And finally, tankless heaters are small—about the size of a suitcase—so they can easily fit into a closet or even under a sink, and some units are designed for outdoor installation. There's also no risk of flooding caused by a ruptured water tank.

Given these clear advantages, are tankless heaters the best choice for every green home? Not necessarily. One common complaint from owners of tankless systems is that the supply of hot water is affected by the flow rate at the tap. If you want just a trickle of hot water, the heater's demand-sensitive burner switch might not turn on. Conversely, if you're using a lot of hot water (for example, when showering while the clothes washer is filling up) and exceed the heater's output capacity, the water temperature will drop. Also, the ability of the water heater to keep up with demand is affected by the ambient temperature of the water. In northern climates where the average water temperature is in the 40° F range, you'll need a bigger burner to satisfy the output rate. And if you choose to go with a tankless heater, plan on spending several thousand dollars with professional installation.

Of course, the high-demand problem isn't unique to tankless heaters. Most home water piping can't fully supply two hot-water fixtures at once, and even large storage tanks start running out of hot water after a couple of showers. For this reason, one of the main factors to consider when choosing a hot water heater is its "first hour" rating, discussed on page 108.

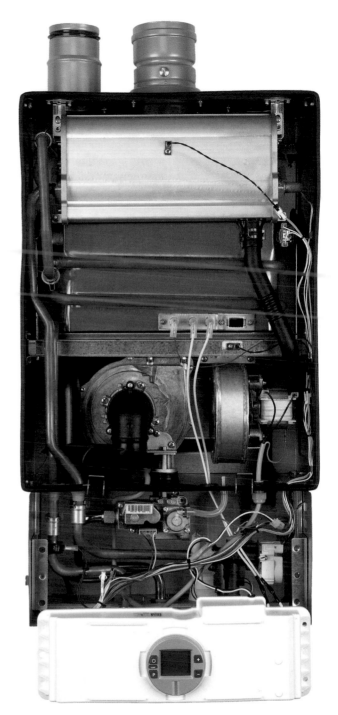

Tankless water heaters save energy because there's no stored water to keep hot.

Selecting a Water Heater

In theory, the best water heater for any green home is the one that meets the hot-water demands of the household while using the least amount of energy. In reality, your budget, space constraints, and other factors also will weigh in on the decision. But energy efficiency should be a top priority in any case.

The first thing to do is to estimate how much hot water your home uses during the busiest hour of the day. For example, let's say that between 6:30 and 7:30 am every weekday, three people take showers, one person shaves, and everyone uses a little hot water for washing their hands, etc. Depending on the flow rates of your various fixtures and your showering times, the house may go through 60 gallons of hot water in that hour. Therefore, if you're looking for a tank-style heater, you should narrow your search to units with *first hour* ratings of around 60 gallons. This is the amount of hot water the heater can deliver in one hour with a fully heated tank of water.

If you're looking at tankless heaters, compare units by their flow rate at the given temperature rise. For example, a residential heater may offer a temperature rise of 75° F at a continuous flow of three gallons per minute. Cold water starts at around 50° to 55°, so this heater can give you 125° to 130° water at three gpm. If your bathroom showerheads have a flow rate of 2.5 gpm and only one shower is going at a time, this size of heater could be what you're looking for.

To compare energy efficiency among heater models, look to the energy factor (EF), the measure of how efficiently a heater converts its energy source into hot water. The energy factor also takes into account standby loss in tank-style heaters. For an accurate comparison, it's important to consider EF ratings among models of the same type of heater. Here's why: A high-efficiency gas heater might have a rating around .62 (or 62% efficient), while an electric tank heater may score around .95 EF. This is because electric heaters don't lose heat through combustion exhaust, like gas heaters do. Yet, the EF doesn't account for the inefficiencies of generating electricity at the power plant and in transporting it to your home—inefficiencies that are reflected in the high cost of electrical power. Electricity is more expensive than gas; thus, the gas heater may cost significantly less to operate in the long run.

To determine the true cost of a water heater, you have to consider its purchase and installation price as well as its annual operating cost over the lifetime of the heater, or what you might call its *life-cycle* cost. Look to the Energy Guide label to find the estimated annual operating cost of each model. You should also take into account the life expectancy of different heaters. Tank heaters are generally expected to last 10 to 15 years, while many tankless heaters can last up to 20 years.

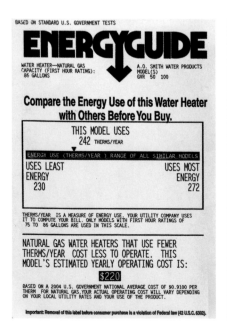

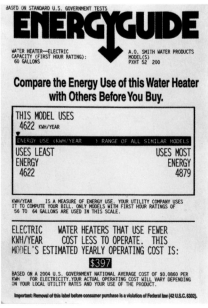

Rating appliances like water heaters for their energy efficiency is easy enough to do: just read the energy label. But if you're comparing costs, you'll need to do a little math, as is explained above.

Improving Efficiency on Older Tank Water Heaters ▸

In addition to regular maintenance steps to ensure optimal performance, there are a couple of add-ons that can make your old electric or gas water heater more energy efficient. The first, and easier, step is to wrap the tank with insulation. This can reduce standby heat loss by 25% to 45%, yielding a 4% to 9% savings in water heating costs.

Insulating jackets are available at hardware stores and home centers for around $10 to $20. Choose a jacket that fits your type and size of heater and offers an insulating value of R-8 or better. Your utility company also may sell insulating jackets and may install one for a small fee.

DOS & DON'TS FOR INSULATING A WATER HEATER

- Do check with the heater's manufacturer before adding insulation; some manufacturers consider this a warranty violation
- Do secure the jacket snugly around the tank
- Do check the jacket periodically to make sure nothing has come loose, is wet, or may be blocking air intakes

- Do make a cutout in the jacket for the pressure relief valve (TPRV), leaving an inch of clearance all around; also make cutouts for accessing thermostats and for heating coil elements on electric heaters
- Don't set the water temperature on electric heaters above 130° F, which can cause wiring to overheat
- Don't insulate the top of a gas heater, but you may do so on some electric heaters
- Don't cover or block the piping from the pressure relief valve (TPRV)
- Don't block the combustion-air intake on gas heaters or insulate within 2" of the floor

The other efficiency measure is to have heat traps installed on the hot and cold water pipes connected to your heater. Heat traps are valves or fittings that prevent heat from migrating out of the tank through the piping, an effect known as thermosyphoning and a contributor to standby heat loss. Heat traps should be installed by a qualified plumber, so this upgrade really makes sense only if you're replacing your heater and the new heater doesn't already have them.

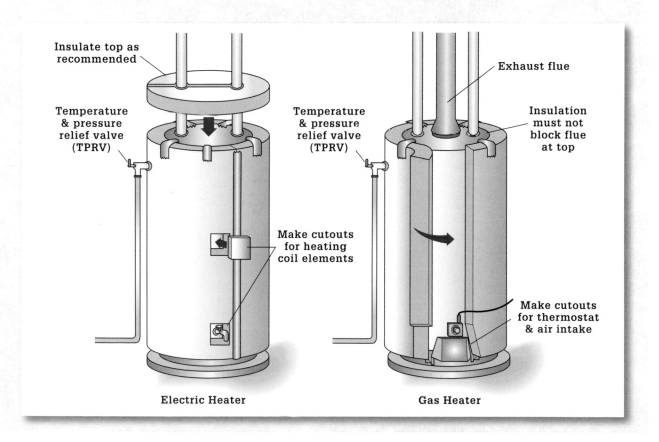

Insulate top as recommended

Temperature & pressure relief valve (TPRV)

Make cutouts for heating coil elements

Exhaust flue

Insulation must not block flue at top

Temperature & pressure relief valve (TPRV)

Make cutouts for thermostat & air intake

Electric Heater

Gas Heater

Hot-Water Recirculating Systems ▸

When you turn on the hot-water tap at the kitchen sink, how long do you have to wait before you actually get hot water? Depending on how far the tap is from the water heater, the wait can be an inconvenience as well as a big waste of water. All of that waste is the water that's been sitting—and cooling—in the hot-water supply lines, not to mention the energy required to heat it in the first place. Enter hot-water recirculation, a system that uses a pump to redirect all of that cooled water back to the water heater while it speeds the delivery of truly hot water to the tap.

Recirculation pumps may be activated in several different ways. Some work on a timer and can be set to circulate hot water during peak-demand times of the day. Others use temperature controls that trigger circulation whenever the water in supply pipes drops below a set temperature. And some versions combine timer and temperature controls. Still other systems circulate hot water continuously, although these tend to be the least energy-efficient.

A different type of pump control, called on-demand, starts working only when the tap is opened and shuts off when the hot-water supply is at temperature. There's still a wait for hot water, because the pump isn't running before you turn on the faucet, but on-demand systems tend to be the most energy-efficient types.

Adding a hot-water recirculation system during new construction involves putting in a dedicated return line that serves each fixture and takes the water back to the water heater. Typically there's one pump and it's located near the water heater. In existing homes, where adding a return line is problematic, recirculation systems use crossover valves that allow the cold-water supply piping to serve temporarily as the return line while the pump is on. The pump is located either at the water heater or under the sink farthest from the heater. On-demand systems in retrofit applications require a pump at the end of each hot-water supply loop.

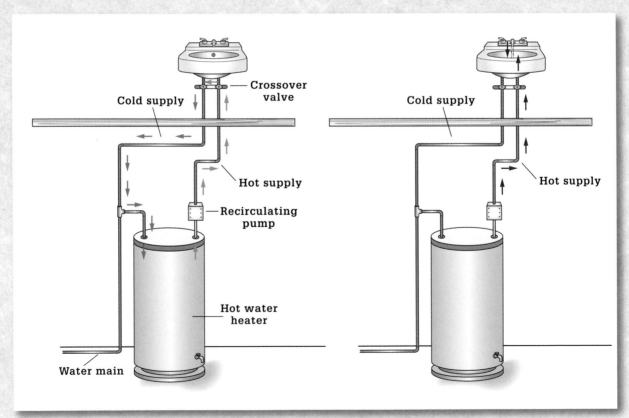

Hot-water recirculation as a retrofit: When the recirculating pump is on (left), water in the hot-water supply piping is diverted through a crossover valve and into the cold-water supply piping. When the crossover valve senses the hot water is at temperature (right) it closes, and hot water goes straight to the fixture.

Other Green Considerations

If you prefer not to have combustion appliances in the home, due to concerns about indoor air quality, you might consider a sealed combustion tank-style heater or a tankless heater suitable for outdoor installation. Standard gas water heaters draw air for combustion from the surrounding air in the house (that's why utility closet doors have vents in them), and they exhaust by natural draft through a chimney at the top of the unit. In super-airtight houses, there is a potential for backdrafting of combustion exhaust from the heater (see Kitchen Ventilation, on page 26). Also, when the burner of a gas heater turns on, often a small amount of unburned gas escapes—you can smell this if you're standing near the tank.

By contrast, sealed combustion water heaters draw in all of their combustion air and get rid of all exhaust gases through sealed outdoor vents. Because no part of the combustion system is open to the indoor air, there's no risk of backdrafting. There's also no loss of conditioned (heated or cooled) indoor air, yielding additional energy savings.

For the record, electric water heaters have no exhaust emissions and need no intake air. But again, the high operating cost for you and the significant emissions down at the power plant usually make electric heaters undesirable for a green home.

For more information on water heaters and the relative efficiency of currently available products, visit these websites:

- American Council for an Energy-Efficient Economy: www.aceee.org
- Gas Appliance Manufacturers Association: www.gamanet.org
- U.S. Department of Energy: www.eere.energy.gov

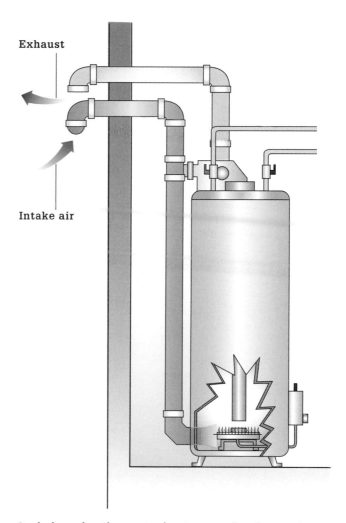

Exhaust

Intake air

Sealed combustion water heaters are directly vented to the outdoors, so there's no air exchange inside the house.

Tip: How Hot Is Your Water? ▸

For most households, setting the water heater at 120° F strikes the right balance between comfort and energy-efficiency. The normal temperature for shower water is between 104° and 110°, and the same level is good for washing hands or dishes at the sink. Some people keep their thermostats higher—at 140° or even 160°—with the thought that it's better for washing dishes in the dishwasher. But this practice is wasteful and even dangerous. At 140°, water causes a first-degree burn in only two seconds of exposure, while scalding is instantaneous at 154°. If your dishwasher doesn't have an internal water heater (many new models do), you can install a booster heater to raise the temperature of the 8 to 12 gallons required for a dish cycle, instead of heating the 30 to 80 gallons (depending on your heater's tank size) in your water heater at all times.

Preventing Mold

Mold is a naturally occurring fungus that can attack any home at any time. All it needs is a little moisture and some good stuff to eat. Mold's favorite foods in the home environment are paper and wood, especially engineered wood products like particleboard, OSB (oriented strandboard), and plywood. Given those conditions, bathrooms are prime breeding grounds for mold because they're frequently loaded with moist air—from showering and bathing—and they're most likely covered in paper—from the paper facing on drywall.

So, the first step in preventing mold in the bathroom is to install a ventilation system to rid the space of excess moisture. Modern building codes require vent fans in all bathrooms, although some may make an exception for rooms that have operable windows for passive ventilation. If you have an older bathroom with windows, you should still include a vent fan because windows are less effective at capturing and evacuating water vapor, and windows don't ventilate at all when they're shut tight during the winter. The project on pages 114 to 117 shows you how to install a new ventilation fan in a bathroom ceiling.

The next step for keeping mold out of your bathroom is to take away its sources of food. Most homes in the U.S. built since the 1950s use standard, paper-faced drywall for almost all wall and ceiling surfaces. Drywall is a great building material and can be very green if it's made with recycled content, but in high-moisture areas like bathrooms and kitchens, today's green builders are increasingly switching to mold-resistant versions of drywall as a preventive measure against mold.

Mold-resistant drywall has become widely available in different forms from several leading drywall manufacturers. Some products have treated facepaper to inhibit mold growth, while others eliminate the paper altogether and use a fiberglass skin for the surface layers; others are made with a gypsum-cellulose material that doesn't require paper to give the panel stability. Special fiber-faced drywall is also available for use as a backing for tile in showers and other wet areas. It's important to note that "mold-resistant" does not mean "mold-proof." Mold can grow almost anywhere given the right conditions. But by treating or eliminating paper, mold-resistant wallboards make your walls and ceilings much less inviting places for mold to reside.

Airborne moisture will almost certainly lead to mold problems if you do nothing to check it. Installing a vent fan in the bathroom and another in the kitchen is the best way to take the fight against mold right to the source.

If mold hasn't been a problem in your bathroom and you're not remodeling, it probably doesn't make sense to tear out all the old drywall and replace it with mold-resistant panels. Standard drywall won't promote mold growth unless there's too much moisture to begin with and the panels don't get a chance to dry out. But if you're planning a remodel that involves some surface changes, it's well worth the minor additional expense of using a mold-resistant product. Mold-resistant drywall typically installs and finishes just like standard drywall panels. Just be sure to check with the panel manufacturer for recommendations for taping and finishing materials.

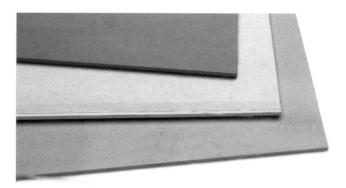

No more free lunch. Mold-resistant drywall products limit mold growth by chemically treating or eliminating mold's favorite food: wet paper.

Attack of the Mold Reports! ▸

Seems like mold is everywhere in the news these days. But mold won't invade your home of its own accord; you have to invite it in with the promise of excess moisture and a steady supply of food.

That said, mold can be a very serious problem. And cases of mold-related damage and health concerns do appear to be on the rise. Many building experts believe that the recent increase in mold-related problems is due in part to the materials used in modern homes, from man-made panel products like OSB and paper-faced drywall to (improperly applied) plastic vapor barriers that trap moisture inside walls. They also point to HVAC design that fails to isolate the interior space from the thermal envelope, introducing moisture and contaminants from exterior walls into the indoor air.

Mold can affect human health when its airborne spores are inhaled, ingested, or absorbed through the skin. Minor symptoms of mold exposure include headaches,

eye irritation, nausea, and several cold-like symptoms. More serious effects include breathing difficulty, severe headaches, immune system suppression, and possibly cancer and birth defects. People with mold allergies may suffer from chronic symptoms in moldy homes.

As a general rule, if you can see mold or smell a musty odor, you've got a mold problem. Common places where mold thrives include carpeting, drywall, wood paneling, ductwork, and porous materials like fabric and newspaper. Any sign of excess moisture or moisture damage is a good indication that mold is present or soon will be. If you find a plumbing leak or a breach in your home's exterior surface, deal with the moisture source immediately. Thoroughly dry the affected area as soon as possible. Most mold begins to grow within 48 hours.

For more information about mold and its potential effect on indoor air quality, visit the EPA's website at www.epa.gov.

Discoloration on interior surfaces and musty odors are sure signs that mold is growing in your home.

Bathroom Vent Fans

An electric vent fan is the most convenient and effective way to get rid of excess moisture and odors in the bathroom. A vent fan can be controlled by its own standard wall switch or can be wired to come on with the bathroom's overhead light. You can also add a timer switch to turn off the fan automatically or use a fan with a built-in humidistat, which turns the fan on and off based on the humidity level in the room.

This project shows the basic steps for wiring a new fan and timer to a single-pole wall switch. Standard fans usually can be tied into an existing bathroom circuit, while fans with heat lamps or blowers require separate circuits. Unless you have experience working with household circuits and making wiring connections, consult an electrician for the project. Refer to the manufacturer's wiring diagrams for the recommended configurations.

Most vent fans are installed in the center of the bathroom ceiling or over the toilet area. A fan installed over the tub or shower area must be GFCI protected and rated for use in wet areas. You can usually wire a fan that just has a light fixture into a main bathroom electrical circuit, but units with built-in heat lamps or blowers require separate circuits.

If the fan you choose doesn't come with a mounting kit, purchase one separately. A mounting kit should include a vent hose (duct), a vent tailpiece, and an exterior vent cover.

Venting instructions vary among manufacturers, but the most common options are attic venting and soffit venting. Attic venting (shown in this project) routes fan ductwork into the attic and out through the roof. Always insulate ducting in this application to keep condensation from forming and running down into the motor. And carefully install flashing around the outside vent cover to prevent roof leaks.

Soffit venting involves routing the duct to a soffit (roof overhang) instead of through the roof. Check with the vent manufacturer for instructions for soffit venting.

To prevent moisture damage, always terminate the vent outside your home—never into your attic or basement.

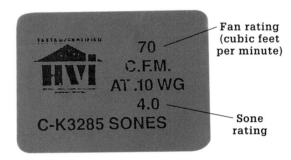

Check the information label attached to each vent fan unit. Choose a unit with a fan rating at least 5 CFM higher than the square footage of your bathroom. The sone rating refers to the relative quietness of the unit, rated on a scale of 1 to 7. (Quieter vent fans have lower sone ratings.)

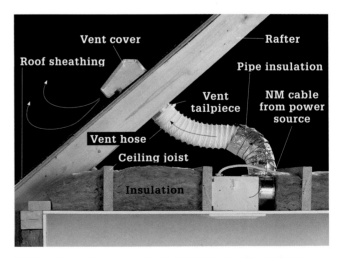

Bathroom vent fans must be exhausted to the outdoors, either through the roof or through a wall. Flexible ductwork is allowed for bath vent fans (but not for clothes dryers).

How to Install a Bathroom Vent Fan

Position the vent fan unit against a ceiling joist. Outline the vent fan onto the ceiling surface. Remove the unit, then drill pilot holes at the corners of the outline and cut out the area with a jigsaw or drywall saw.

Remove the grille from the fan unit, then position the unit against the joist with the edge recessed ¼" from the finished surface of the ceiling (so the grille can be flush mounted). Attach the unit to the joist using drywall screws.

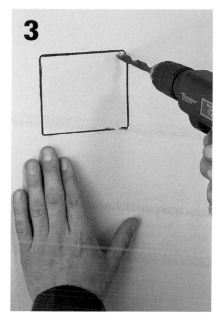

Mark and cut an opening for the switch box on the wall next to the latch side of the bathroom door, then run a 14/3 NM cable from the switch cutout to the fan unit. Run a 14/2 NM cable from the power source to the cutout.

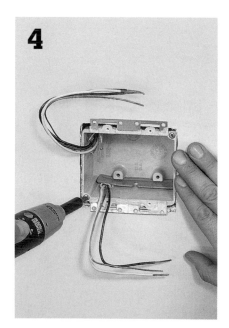

Strip 10" of sheathing from the ends of the cables, then feed the cables into a double-gang retrofit switch box so at least ½" of sheathing extends into the box. Clamp the cables in place. Tighten the mounting screws until the box is secure.

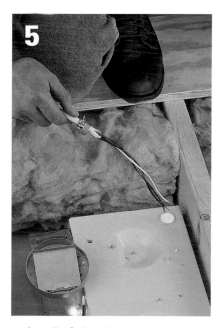

Strip 10" of sheathing from the end of the cable at the vent unit, then attach a cable clamp to the cable. Insert the cable into the fan unit. From the inside of the unit, screw a locknut onto the threaded end of the clamp.

Draw an outline of the duct onto the underside of the roof deck. Drill a pilot hole, then saw through the sheathing and roofing material with a reciprocating saw to make the cutout for the vent tailpiece.

(continued)

Remove a section of shingles from around the cutout, leaving the roofing paper intact. Remove enough shingles to create an exposed area that is at least the size of the vent cover flange.

Vent cover flange

If the hole for the vent does not abut a rafter, attach a 2 × 4 brace between the roof rafters. Attach a hose clamp to the brace or rafter about 1" below the roof sheathing (top). Insert the vent tailpiece into the cutout and through the hose clamp, then tighten the clamp screw (bottom).

Apply roofing cement to the bottom of the vent cover flange, then slide the vent cover over the tailpiece. Nail the vent cover flange in place with self-sealing roofing nails, then patch in shingles around the cover.

Connect the vent hose to the vent tailpiece and the outlet on the fan unit. Secure each end with clamps or straps. Wrap the hose with pipe insulation to prevent moist air inside the hose from condensing and dripping down into the fan motor.

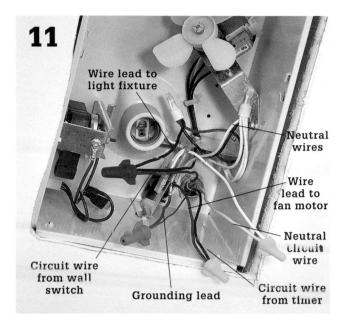

11

Wire lead to light fixture

Neutral wires

Wire lead to fan motor

Neutral circuit wire

Circuit wire from wall switch

Grounding lead

Circuit wire from timer

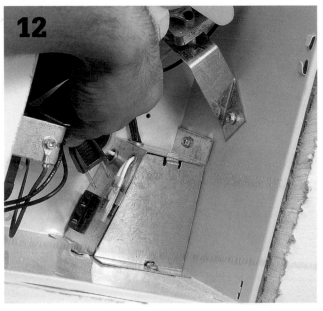

12

Make the following wire connections at the fan unit: the black circuit wire from the timer to the wire lead for the fan motor; the red circuit wire from the single-pole switch (see step 14) to the wire lead for the light fixture in the unit; the white neutral circuit wire to the neutral wire lead; the circuit grounding wire to the grounding lead on the fan unit. Make all connections with wire connectors. Attach the cover plate over the unit when the wiring is completed.

Connect the fan motor plug to the built-in receptacle on the wire connection box, and attach the fan grille to the frame using the mounting clips included with the fan kit. *Note: If you removed the wall and ceiling surfaces for the installation, install new surfaces before completing this step.*

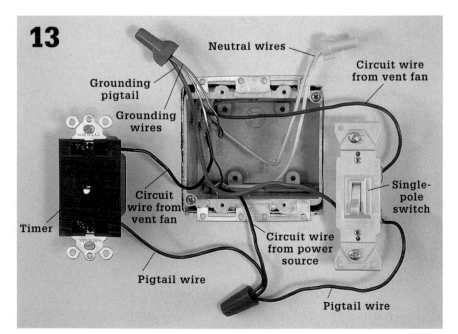

13

Neutral wires

Grounding pigtail

Grounding wires

Circuit wire from vent fan

Timer

Circuit wire from vent fan

Single-pole switch

Circuit wire from power source

Pigtail wire

Pigtail wire

14

At the switch box, add black pigtail wires to one screw terminal on the timer and to one screw terminal on the single-pole switch; add a green grounding pigtail to the grounding screw on the switch. Make the following wire connections: the black circuit wire from the power source to the black pigtail wires; the black circuit wire from the vent fan to the remaining screw on the timer; the red circuit wire from the vent fan to the remaining screw on the switch. Join the white wires with a wire connector. Join the grounding wires with a green wire connector.

Tuck the wires into the switch box, then attach the switch and timer to the box. Attach the cover plate and timer dial. Turn on the power.

Bathroom Surfaces

One of the primary goals in any green home is to use finish surfaces that are appropriate for the given space. In the bathroom, this means floors, walls, and ceilings should be covered with water-resistant materials that are easy to clean and highly durable. These requirements place tile and hard-wearing paints at the top of the list, while carpeting, unfinished wood, and fabrics rank at the bottom. The problem with soft, porous surfaces is that they trap moisture and airborne contaminants, which can quickly lead to mold and bacteria growth. Also, despite its continued popularity as a bathroom wallcovering, wallpaper is undesirable, too. For one, it's usually made with flexible vinyl that can offgas VOCs (see The Great Vinyl Debate, on page 78). And second, if the drywall behind the covering gets wet, the vinyl surface can seal in the moisture, at the same time concealing and promoting mold growth.

As a decorative and protective surface for bathroom floors, walls, and shower areas, tile offers many green advantages. It's durable and may never

Keeping it green means keeping it clean. If it can't be mopped, sponged, or sprayed down, it's not a good surface for a green bathroom.

need to be replaced. It's washable and virtually impervious to water when properly installed and maintained. And its manufacture involves relatively benign environmental impact and low embodied energy, especially when you consider its longevity. Locally made tiles or products made with recycled content offer additional green advantages. See page 74 for more information on choosing green tile materials.

For many years bathroom tile was installed directly over standard drywall on walls and over plywood on floors. In showers and other wet areas, modern builders commonly used "greenboard," a variety of drywall with a green-colored facepaper designed for tile applications. However, all three of these materials have a fatal flaw when used as a tile backer: If water gets past the tile, through a crack or a gap in the grout, the paper or wood surface beneath quickly becomes a haven for mold. Persistent water intrusion can lead to rotting in wall and floor structures, not to mention destruction of the tile surface. For new tile installation in wet areas and on all floors, start with a new substrate of cementboard or specialty drywall panel; see Tile Backer, below. Pages 120 to 123 show you the basic steps for installing cementboard on walls and floors.

When it comes to wall and ceiling areas that don't get a daily splashing of hot water, the best green option is a fairly glossy, low-VOC paint. Eggshell is a good level of sheen for most bathrooms, but some people prefer the greater washability and higher surface sheen of a semigloss. Zero- and low-VOC paints are readily available from most major paint manufacturers, so you can get the color you want without the noxious fumes of standard paints. See page 134 for more help with choosing paint.

Tile Backer ▸

If you're planning to tile new walls in wet areas, such as tub and shower enclosures, use tile backer board as a substrate rather than drywall. Unlike drywall, tile backer won't break down—and ruin the tile job—if water gets behind the tile. There are three basic types of tile backer (see photo, right):

Cementboard is made from portland cement and sand reinforced by a continuous outer layer of fiberglass mesh. It's available in ½" and ⅝" thicknesses. See pages 120 to 123 for installation instructions.

Fiber-cement board is similar to cementboard but is somewhat lighter, with fiber reinforcement integrated throughout the panel material. It comes in ¼" and ½" thicknesses. Cementboard and fiber-cement board cannot be damaged by water, but water can pass through them. To prevent damage to the framing, install a water barrier of 4-mil plastic or 15# building paper behind the backer.

Dens-Shield®, commonly called glass mat, is a water-resistant gypsum board with a waterproof fiberglass facing. Dens-Shield cuts and installs much like standard drywall but requires galvanized screws to prevent corrosion. Because the front surface provides the water barrier, all untaped joints and penetrations must be sealed with caulk before the tile is installed. Do not use a water barrier behind Dens-Shield.

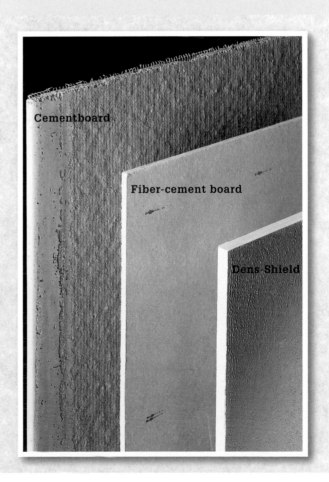

Cementboard

Fiber-cement board

Dens-Shield

Preparing for New Tile in Wet Areas

The following procedures show you the basic steps for installing a substrate of cementboard or fiber-cement board (see Tile Backer, on page 119) before laying tile in a shower/tub enclosure or onto a bathroom floor. Unlike drywall or plywood substrates, cementboard panels won't be damaged by water, and they're made without paper or wood for effective mold-resistance.

Cementboard, which comes in ½" and ⅝" thicknesses, is most commonly used on walls and ceilings but is equally suitable as a floor substrate. However, when the total thickness of a new tile floor is a concern, thinner fiber-cement panels (starting at just ¼"-thick) are a better choice. Both panel types are installed with similar methods, using thinset mortar as an adhesive and to finish the joints between panels.

Tools & Materials ▸

4-mil plastic sheeting and staple gun (walls and ceilings only)
Utility knife
Straightedge
Jigsaw with bimetal blade
Drill
¼" notched trowel (floors only)

Cementboard screws or galvanized deck screws (length based on panel thickness)
Bucket
6" drywall knife
Alkali-resistant fiberglass mesh joint tape
Thinset mortar.

Mix thinset mortar following the manufacturer's directions. Add liquid a little at a time to the dry powder and stir to a creamy consistency. Mortars commonly are supplemented with a latex additive for strength and crack resistance.

How to Install Cementboard on Walls

Staple a water barrier of 4-mil plastic sheeting or 15# building paper over the framing. Overlap seams by several inches, and leave the sheets long at the perimeter. *Note: Framing for cementboard must be 16" on-center; steel studs must be 20-gauge.*

Cut cementboard by scoring through the mesh just below the surface using a utility knife or a special carbide-tipped cementboard knife like the one shown here. Use a drywall T-square as a cutting guide.

Snap the cementboard along the scored cutting line and then finish the cut by slicing through the backing with your utility knife or cementboard knife.

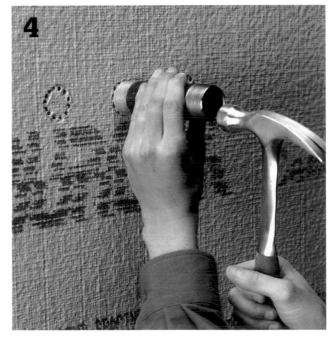

Make cutouts for pipes and other penetrations by drilling a series of holes through the board using a small masonry bit. Tap the hole out with a hammer or a scrap of pipe. Cut holes along edges with a jigsaw and bimetal blade.

(continued)

5

Install the sheets horizontally. Where possible, use full pieces to avoid cut-and-butted seams, which are difficult to fasten. If there are vertical seams, stagger them between rows. Leave a ⅛" gap between sheets at vertical seams and corners. Use spacers to set the bottom row of panels ¼" above the tub or shower base. Fasten the sheets with 1¼" cementboard screws, driven every 8" for walls and every 6" for ceilings. Drive the screws ½" from the edges to prevent crumbling. If the studs are steel, don't fasten within 1" of the top track.

6

Cover the joints and corners with cementboard joint tape (alkali-resistant fiberglass mesh) and latex portland cement mortar (thinset). Apply a layer of mortar with a wallboard knife, embed the tape into the mortar, then smooth and level the mortar.

Variation: Finishing Cementboard ▶

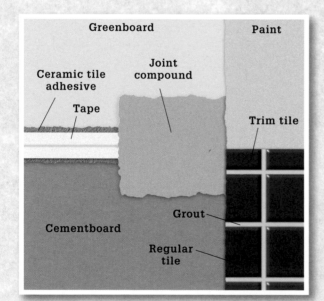

To finish a joint between cementboard and greenboard, seal the joint and exposed cementboard with ceramic tile adhesive, a mixture of four parts adhesive to one part water. Embed the paper joint tape into the adhesive, smoothing the tape with a drywall knife. Allow the adhesive to dry, then finish the joint with at least two coats of all-purpose wallboard joint compound.

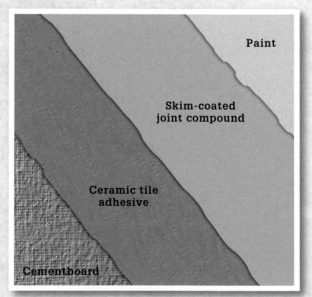

To finish small areas of cementboard that will not be tiled, seal the cementboard with ceramic tile adhesive, a mixture of four parts adhesive to one part water, then apply a skim-coat of all-purpose wallboard joint compound using a 12" drywall knife. Paint the wall.

How to Install Cementboard on a Floor

Mix thinset mortar (see page 120) according to the manufacturer's directions. Starting at the longest wall, spread the mortar on the subfloor in a figure-eight pattern using a ¼" notched trowel. Spread only enough mortar for one sheet at a time. Set the cementboard on the mortar with the rough side up, making sure the edges are offset from the subfloor seams.

Fasten the cementboard to the subfloor using 1½" galvanized deck screws driven every 6" along edges and 8" throughout the sheet. Drive the screw heads flush with the surface. Continue spreading mortar and installing sheets along the wall.

Cut cementboard pieces as necessary, leaving a ⅛" gap at all joints and a ¼" gap along the room perimeter. For straight cuts, use a utility knife to score a line through the fiber-mesh layer just beneath the surface, then snap the board along the scored line.

To cut holes, notches, or irregular shapes, use a jigsaw with a carbide blade. Continue installing cementboard sheets to cover the entire floor. Inset: A flange extender or additional wax ring may be needed to ensure a proper toilet installation after additional layers of underlayment have been installed in a bathroom.

Place fiberglass-mesh wallboard tape over the seams. Use a wallboard knife to apply thinset mortar to the seams, filling the gaps between sheets and spreading a thin layer of mortar over the tape. Allow the mortar to cure for two days before starting the tile installation.

Converted Vanity Cabinets

Inspired by high-end custom bath vanities made to look like furniture, here's a fun project with an especially green twist: by using a salvaged furniture piece for the vanity, you're recycling in the greenest possible way—that is, reusing materials with only minor modifications in the finished product.

If you already have an old wood bureau, desk, or dressing table, read through the steps here to see if the old piece is suitable for the project. Otherwise, you can shop around at architectural salvage dealers and antique shops for just the right unit to fit your bathroom and fixtures. The easiest type of sink to use with a custom vanity is a self-rimming (or

Tools & Materials ▸

Adjustable wrench	Wood screws
Channel-type pliers	Metal brackets
Circular saw	and angles
Jigsaw with	(as needed)
down-cutting blade	Cardboard
Drill	Wood finishes
Level	(as desired)
Hole saw	Plumber's putty
¾" plywood	Silicone caulk
Construction adhesive	

An antique dresser with a built-in mirror makes a perfect bathroom vanity. The dresser used in this project was mostly open underneath, so we included a new chrome drainpipe and silver braided-metal water supply tubes to dress up the exposed plumbing connections. A more enclosed piece, such as a chest of drawers, would work equally well, although it may require more modifications to the drawers and other parts to accommodate the plumbing.

drop-in) style, which gives you a good, watertight seal around the vanity top and won't expose the sink cutout like an undermount sink would. Some countertop-style sinks can work, too, but keep in mind where the faucet spout and handles will go. If you have reasonably good woodworking skills, however, you may prefer to undermount a sink and profile the sink cutout edges with your favorite router bit. Make sure to seal the exposed edges very thoroughly, though.

For a durable, water-resistant finish, you will most likely have to strip and refinish the vanity top, as well as any parts likely to get wet behind the sink. Refinishing the rest of the piece is also recommended for a good color match and additional water resistance and washability. Refinishing the vanity as a last step before installation allows you to keep dust and fumes out of the house. Also, consider using low- or no-VOC finishes to minimize the health risks from offgassing. A high quality, low-VOC, water-based polyurethane is a good choice for a transparent topcoat finish.

Tip ▸

Internal reinforcements make for a sturdy conversion. Add metal brackets and angles to reinforce construction joints inside the vanity. New plywood panels help strengthen and stiffen the original top and back of the piece.

Option: Replace the original furniture top with a green countertop material. A salvaged stone slab or custom surface made from recycled glass can add durability and plenty of "wow" factor to the finished project.

New or Old?

Converting a piece of furniture into a vanity isn't the only way to get that repurposed look. Several cabinetry manufacturers now offer bathroom vanities and other furnishings that are designed to look like freestanding pieces of furniture. These, naturally, do not have the same green benefit as a used piece of furniture that is given new life.

How to Convert a Dresser to a Vanity

Remove the old vanity. Close the water shutoff valves and disconnect the supply tubes from the sink. Disassemble the drain trap, leaving only the wall stubout, then block the drainpipe with a rag to trap sewer gases. Pull out the sink. Remove the screws securing the vanity cabinet to the wall, then pull the cabinet out of the way.

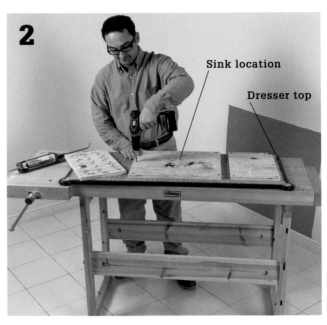

Reinforce the top of the dresser with ¾" plywood. One continuous piece of plywood will be strongest; otherwise, try to keep seams away from the sink area. Secure the plywood to the underside of the cabinet top using construction adhesive and wood screws. Make sure the screws don't go through the finished top.

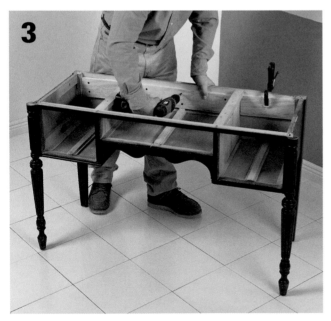

Add more reinforcement as needed to the back of the cabinet and to the internal construction joints. Install plywood or lumber crosspieces along the back to create secure points for mounting the vanity to the bathroom wall. Make sure reinforcements will not hinder the movement of usable drawers and doors.

Shorten or extend the legs of the vanity if necessary to set the desired height. Standard height for bathroom sinks is 32" to 36" from the floor to the sink's rim.

5

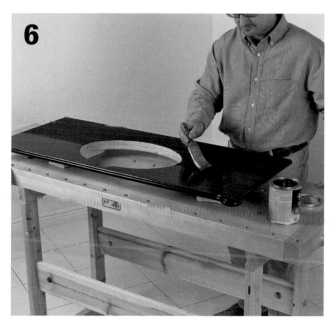

6

Make the sink cutout. If you're reusing the old sink, use a cardboard template traced from the cutout in the old vanity. A new sink should come with a cutting template. Drill a starter hole inside the cut line, then complete the cutout with a jigsaw.

Refinish the wood surfaces as desired. The entire top should have a continuous water-resistant finish, such as two or more coats of polyurethane or other varnish.

Tip: Converting Cabinets with Back Panels ▸

Cabinet back

Measure the plumbing locations and mark them on the cabinet back. First, draw a plumb line along the wall, centered on the drain stubout. Then draw a plumb line down the center of the cabinet back (assuming the sink is in the center). Measure over from the wall line to the center of each supply pipe, then transfer those measurements to the cabinet. Measure up from the floor to the centers of the pipes and drain, then transfer the measurements to the cabinet.

Cut the holes for the plumbing connections using a drill and hole saw, and a jigsaw if necessary. Make the holes slightly larger than needed to allow for adjustments. *Tip: Remove the handles on the water shutoff valves for sizing the holes and installing the cabinet.*

(continued)

Modify the drawers by making cutouts and rebuilding drawer boxes as needed. If the vanity has drawers that you'd like to use for storage, make cardboard templates that match the drawer boxes. Slide the templates in and out of the drawer cavities, trimming away the cardboard until it fits around the sink and plumbing pieces, as applicable.

Install the cabinet. First, mark the locations of the wall studs used to secure the old vanity. Set the new vanity cabinet into place, centering the back cutouts over the plumbing penetrations. Drive screws through the cabinet back (or crosspieces) to secure the cabinet to the wall. If necessary, shim between the vanity and wall to make sure the vanity legs remain squarely on the floor.

Option: Reconfigure the drawer boxes as needed using the templates to determine the final shapes. Where box sides are cut away, install plywood or lumber partitions to enclose the boxes and keep stored items at hand. Install the drawers and/or doors to complete the vanity.

Install the sink using a new bead of plumber's putty or as directed by the manufacturer. Reconnect the supply tubes and drain assembly. When everything is in place, carefully seal around the sink rim with a fine bead of clear silicone caulk and let dry.

Tiled Sink Base ▶

There was a time not so long ago when sewing machines almost always included a base. Some were wood cabinets from which the machine popped up on top, and this type frequently is a great candidate for conversion to a vanity. Even older sewing machines that predated the cabinet style were foot-powered treadle machines that were mounted to a cast iron base. Many of these machines were removed and electrified, leaving a mostly useless base behind. The bathroom vanity seen here is a good example of how some creativity and some basic tiling skills can be used to reclaim a discarded object (and keep an all-new cabinet out of the production stream).

A new subbase made of plywood and cementboard was screwed to the sewing base, then tiled.

An old-fashioned cast iron sewing machine base is a unique option to using a reclaimed dresser cabinet when constructing your own reuse vanity.

A vessel-style sink is a perfect complement to the freeform tile countertop.

Green Living Spaces

It's often estimated that we spend, on average, 90% of our daily hours indoors. And rooms where you and your family spend the most time probably include the family room, bedroom, nursery, dining areas, and home office. These spaces are, in essence, your "indoor environment."

From the floors and walls to the furniture and decorations, living spaces are filled with materials and finishes that affect your comfort, quality of life, and quite possibly your health. Selecting new products for these rooms requires careful consideration. When produced with conventional methods and materials, elements like carpeting, paint, and furniture can introduce an array of chemicals into your home. Some of these come with known risks to our health. And experts are quick to point out that even less is known about the cumulative effects of household toxins or the risks of exposure to combinations of chemicals.

An important part of creating a green home is minimizing unnecessary toxins while supporting the production of sustainable and natural goods. Your living spaces offer many opportunities to do both.

In this chapter:

Comfy, Cozy & Green

There's a definite line between the living spaces of a home and all of its other rooms: While the kitchen, bath, laundry room, mudroom, and garage are designed around tasks, the primary living spaces are set up for everything *but* work. Perhaps that's why we save the good stuff—the plush furnishings, the softer rugs, the finer decorations—for our rooms of leisure. And in a green home it's no different.

But green improvements in living spaces can foster some big changes, most notably in the quality of the indoor air. As an example, imagine walking into a new model home that's completely furnished and loaded with all of the upgrades available from the builder. The floors gleam, the walls are pristine, and the whole place exudes an aura of freshness and a sort of homier version of a "new car smell." As nice as this

picture may seem, that familiar smell is precisely what you want to avoid in a green home. This is because the "aura" most likely includes a brew of toxins being released into the air from the home's interior finishes. We've grown to like the new house smell, no doubt, but chances are its sources are not so good for our health.

Getting back to your own house: If you're hoping to make some positive changes to your living spaces, you'll be glad to know that meeting green standards shouldn't slow you down much. Virtually every conventionally made home furnishing and finish has a greener substitute, from flooring, paint, and wallcoverings to furniture and even fireplaces. Here's a look at some upgrades you might consider:

Green décor isn't always obvious to the eye. This elegant setting uses building materials and furnishings featuring natural sustainable elements with low embedded energy costs and no offgassing potential.

Elements of a Green Living Space

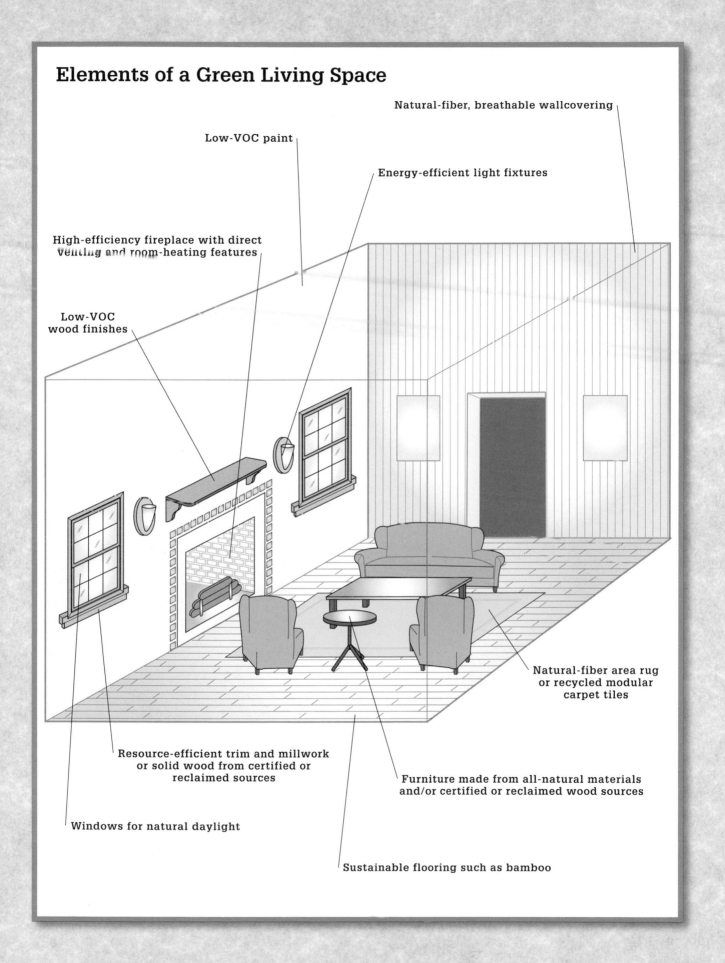

Natural-fiber, breathable wallcovering

Low-VOC paint

Energy-efficient light fixtures

High-efficiency fireplace with direct venting and room-heating features

Low-VOC wood finishes

Natural-fiber area rug or recycled modular carpet tiles

Resource-efficient trim and millwork or solid wood from certified or reclaimed sources

Furniture made from all-natural materials and/or certified or reclaimed wood sources

Windows for natural daylight

Sustainable flooring such as bamboo

Choosing Paints & Other Finishes

In recent years, most paint and finish manufacturers have moved away from toxic solvent-based finishes to develop more and more water-based and plant-based products that perform just (or nearly) as well as their oily forebears. The triumph of water-based paints was an early big step, but more recent trends aim to minimize the toxicity of paints, particularly the levels of VOCs released into the air as the material dries. As a result, green builders and homeowners now have a wide range of products to choose from. They can also enjoy greater availability of green options for decorating materials like trimwork and wall and ceiling treatments.

Choosing low-VOC and low-toxicity paints for your living spaces can be one of the most important steps to reducing indoor air contaminants.

Paints & Wood Finishes

There's nothing like the feeling of renewal that you get with a fresh coat of paint. Surfaces marred by unsightly scuffs and years of grime are quickly transformed into pure planes of vibrant color. Even the smell of new paint adds something to our response; it has come to represent positive change, a fresh start. Unfortunately, much of that "fresh" smell comes from chemicals offgassing from the paint as it dries.

All liquid coatings, like paints and wood finishes, contain a carrier (traditionally petroleum-based solvent but now commonly water) that evaporates when exposed to the air. What's left behind are the active agents that make up the permanent coating. Evaporating solvents can be highly toxic in heavy concentrations, and they contribute to ground-level ozone, among other environmental problems. Water, of course, comes without these negatives, but that doesn't mean all water-based coatings are completely safe. Conventional paints may contain mildewcides, pesticides, formaldehyde, and toxic metals in pigments.

As paint ages, it releases microscopic flakes into the air and onto surrounding surfaces, which are easily picked up or ingested by the home's occupants. Exposure to this ongoing breakdown of paint is typically minute and has little noticeable effect on most people. However, people with chemical sensitivities may suffer irritations from certain chemicals released from dried paint. For these folks, natural paints may be the best option.

LOW-VOC PAINTS

Due to public support for healthier products, many major paint manufacturers now offer low-VOC paints in a full range of colors and sheens. You can also find many zero-VOC products, although color options are more limited. In general, custom coloring often introduces higher levels of VOCs, as can greater sheen levels; it all depends on the manufacturer and the product.

"Low" is a relative term when used with paints and other finishes. Generally, a low-VOC rating means the product contains up to 200 grams of VOCs per liter, although many products go much lower. The GreenSpec directory sets its threshold at 50 grams per liter and has a fairly extensive listing of products. Check the paint container or the product's MSDS (Material Safety Data Sheet) for the rated VOC levels. Most standard low-VOC paints are made with petrochemicals. With any type of paint, the majority of VOC offgassing occurs during drying, so always ventilate the work area well to minimize exposure.

NATURAL PAINTS

"Natural paint," when used accurately, generally describes a category of paints made primarily from plants and/or minerals rather than petrochemicals. Many natural paints are also biodegradable, and some have a high percentage of food-grade ingredients. Natural paint products typically offer very low toxicity, but be aware that some plant-based formulations may come with relatively high VOCs (some people are more comfortable with plant-based VOCs than with petroleum-based VOCs). In general, the production of natural paints involves reduced environmental impact over synthetic paints.

MILK PAINT

Milk paint is a traditional natural paint made from milk protein (casein), lime, and mineral pigments. These paints have a soft, chalky finish that's especially suited to historic interiors and period decorating schemes. Milk-based products are often recommended for porous surfaces, such as unfinished wood, but generally do not perform well in damp areas like bathrooms. Once mixed, milk paint has a short shelf life, so it usually comes in powdered form that you mix with water when you're ready to paint.

Most of the big names in commercial paint offer high-performance synthetic paints in low-VOC formulations.

Natural paints are often made from plant sources, such as citrus fruits, tree resins, and seed oils.

Traditional milk paints are available in a range of historical colors (although soft blue is by far the most common) and can be mixed or tinted for custom coloring.

(continued)

WOOD STAINS, OILS & TRANSPARENT SEALERS

Many stains and topcoats for wood are still made with solvent-based carriers and come with high levels of VOC offgassing. While you have to shop carefully to find healthier alternatives with proven performance, options do exist. Natural stains made from plant and mineral sources may be biodegradable and free of petroleum products. Clear primers, or stain sealers, are also available in all-natural formulations.

Penetrating oils, such as linseed and tung oil, have always been based on natural ingredients, but many products are diluted with petroleum solvents. Look for oils made without chemical additives, petroleum products, or heavy metals (commonly used as drying agents). Pure tung oil is non-toxic and can be used as a protective topcoat on furniture and food-preparation surfaces. Natural waxes include beeswax and plant-based products such as carnuba wax. Hand-rubbed or applied with a brush or spray gun, liquid and paste waxes are buffed to a velvety finish that brings out the natural beauty of many types of wood. Waxes and penetrating oils often require periodic reapplication but are much more forgiving than varnish when it comes to spot repairs.

Varnishes and other topcoats like polyurethane are commonly available in water-based formulations, but you should always check the product data for VOC levels and chemical additives. Many clear sealers are petrochemical-based, while others are derived from natural materials. Water-based polyurethane offers comparable finish quality and durability to conventional solvent-based products but with significantly less VOC offgassing.

Natural stains, oils, and waxes and low-VOC water-based topcoats cover a range of options for finishing wood with reduced health risks.

Tip: What to Do with Leftover Paint? ▶

Always save some paint for future touchups: Seal the lid tightly, label the can, and store it someplace where it won't freeze. If you have more leftover paint than you're willing to store, you can donate it to a low-income building organization or community theater. Or, contact your local hazardous waste authority to find out about recycling the paint. Some communities hold "paint swaps," where residents can unload their unwanted paint or pick up donated paint for free (for more information about paint exchanges, visit the website of the National Paint & Coatings Association, at www.paint.org). While most municipalities allow you to clean water-based (latex) paints from brushes in your kitchen sink, they don't want you pouring gallons of paint down the drain. And why send it off for disposal as a hazmat when someone else can make good use of it?

Empty paint cans are allowed by most trash disposal services, but normally they require that you leave the can open so the wet paint left inside dries fully before disposal.

Wallcoverings

Wallcoverings made with natural fibers offer beautiful, breathable alternatives to vinyl-based products.

In general, wallpaper and other rolled wallcoverings have declined in popularity in recent years. Vinyl and paper wallcoverings have been the industry standard for several decades now, but that's starting to change. Due to widely reported health concerns related to PVC (and especially flexible PVD products like vinyl-coated wallpaper), green builders and homeowners are turning to natural wallcoverings and are finding a wealth of eco-friendly options to meet the residual demand. Many of these natural materials are not just washable but also permeable, so there's less risk of trapping moisture and possibly promoting mold growth behind the covering—a common problem with conventional vinyl coverings. The renewed interest in natural interior décor has encouraged fashionable new designs as well.

It seems that wallcoverings can be made with almost any material. Here's just a partial list of what's available:

- sisal
- paper and cellulose
- cork
- bamboo
- linen and other natural fabrics
- silk
- wood pulp
- honeysuckle vine
- polyester, nylon, and other synthetic materials

Many natural and other non-PVC wallcoverings come with a Class A fire rating and are more durable than you might expect.

Paneling

Conventional forms of wood paneling can consume a great deal of resource material (in the case of solid-wood paneling) or introduce formaldehyde and other indoor air contaminants, usually from particleboard or other composite panel materials. Green alternatives include bamboo paneling, milled products made from wheatboard or formaldehyde-free MDF, and veneered panel systems that mimic the look of solid hardwood. Ideally, all wood used in any type of paneling should come from FSC-certified forests.

Bamboo paneling is available in a range of colors, finishes, and thicknesses. The tambour paneling shown here has a fabric backing, allowing for easy installation over curves, columns, and flat surfaces (See Resources, page 237).

Real hardwood veneers over MDF cores make this modular paneling an affordable and highly resource-efficient alternative to custom solid-wood paneling.

Trimwork

The importance of trim materials can't be overstated. Elements like baseboards, window and door trim, wall and ceiling moldings, and decorative stair parts play a critical role in making a house a home. In the past, most wood trimwork was milled from high-quality, "clear" (knot-free) materials, regardless of whether the final product was to be stained or painted. The reason being that knots create surface flaws and don't accept paint well. But producing clear lumber is wasteful and places enormous strain on mature forests. Today, you can choose from several resource-efficient alternatives to solid-wood trimwork or find sources for sustainably produced new products as well as reclaimed or salvaged materials.

For trimwork that will be painted, you still want to use knot-free material, and this is commonly available in finger-jointed lumber made from small pieces of clear wood joined with strong interlocking joints. Finger-jointed trim is less expensive and usually straighter than trim milled from a single piece of lumber, and you can't tell the difference once it's painted. MDF (medium-density fiberboard), which is made from compressed wood fibers and can contain a high percentage of recycled content, is another green option. MDF mills very cleanly and is great for detailed moldings with fine edges and contours. Because MDF is commonly made with urea-formaldehyde glues, you may want to find a supplier of formaldehyde-free products.

For stain-grade trimwork, look for products with MDF or finger-jointed cores covered with a finish-grade wood veneer. Once installed, this looks just like solid lumber but uses far less virgin material. If your application requires solid lumber, specify FSC-certified products (see page 13), especially for tropical hardwoods. Another green option for using solid-wood trim and millwork is to buy from a supplier that uses reclaimed lumber.

Salvaging materials is a great way to save resources and also to bring one-of-a-kind and/or historical pieces into your home. It's also a good way to acquire authentic period details and old-growth wood that may no longer be available in new products. Stair parts can be great salvage pieces, along with architectural details like ceiling medallions, fireplace mantels, columns, and built-in features.

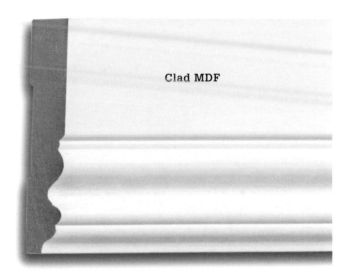

Beautiful wood details don't have to be wasteful. Finger-jointed (top), clad MDF (middle), and hardwood-veneer (bottom) moldings offer the look of solid lumber with greatly reduced environmental impact (and cost).

Flooring

Due to the wide selection of flooring materials that fit into a green plan, choosing floors for your living spaces is more about what you like than about what's green. Many of the popular options are discussed in the Green Kitchens section, including wood, tile, bamboo, and finished concrete, as well as some you may not have considered, like cork and linoleum. What's missing from that discussion is carpet, which is a lousy material for the kitchen but is by far the most popular choice for many living spaces. Here, you'll learn some greener ways to use this traditionally not-so-green floor covering. You'll also see how to install solid bamboo flooring (pages 146 to 151).

As a flooring material for a green home, carpet is definitely a mixed bag. On one hand, carpet and carpet padding are often made from petroleum products and typically contain an assortment of toxic chemicals—from dyes, binders, anti-stain treatments, fire retardants, and backing adhesives—that can offgas into your home for years. Carpet doesn't last as long as many other flooring materials. This means it gets replaced more often, and, unfortunately, old carpet is hard to recycle. The EPA reports that 4.7 billion pounds of carpet were discarded in 2002 in the U.S., while only 3.8% of carpet discards were recycled that year. Unlike tile, wood, and other floor coverings that are made up of smaller pieces, wall-to-wall carpet can't easily be repaired, so even localized damage usually results in the entire carpet getting replaced. Finally, carpet is often criticized for holding onto, and thereby increasing, dust and allergens in the home, and it can quickly encourage microbial growth if allowed to stay wet.

On the other hand, carpet can be made with recycled material, like plastic beverage bottles, which can't be said of wood, bamboo, and many types of tile flooring. If you shop carefully, you can also find carpet padding made with all-natural materials such as jute, natural rubber, and wool, and from recycled carpet materials. For the record, conventional synthetic carpet padding is widely recycled for use in producing new padding, but it's the chemical makeup of all synthetic padding that raises concerns among health experts. Carpet recycling programs do exist in several states, although that's still a far cry from curbside pickup. To find out if there's a program in your area, visit the Carpet America Recover Effort, at www.carpetrecovery.org.

Rugs and carpet made from natural fibers come with many green advantages, including use of sustainable materials, minimal environmental impact, and little or no chemical offgassing in the home.

As for the dust and allergens that can be difficult to extract from carpeting, you may be able to minimize the problem with a high-quality vacuum that uses a HEPA (high-efficiency particulate air) filter. Another option is to use area rugs, which you can clean by hanging them over a clothesline outside and whacking them with a broom, as in days of old. Instead of conventional carpet and area rugs made with synthetic materials like nylon and polyester, consider natural fibers such as sisal, jute, sea grass, coir, organically grown cotton, and wool. Be sure to inquire about chemical treatments applied to any natural-fiber product, as pesticides, flame-retardants, and other chemicals are common, especially in imported goods.

If you're thinking about new carpeting, here's another green option: carpet tiles that install with low-tack adhesive tabs, making it easy to replace individual tiles that are worn or damaged. Carpet tiles also are ideal for do-it-yourself installation. They come with their own pad and don't need to be stretched and held with tackless strips like conventional wall-to-wall carpeting. Tiles are available in a range of colors and styles, making them great for custom designs, and their small unit size means you can fit them to any space with little or no waste. Some carpet tiles contain recycled materials, and some manufacturers accept used tiles for recycling. The projects on pages 142-145 show you how to install carpet tiles in both "area-rug" and wall-to-wall applications.

Carpeting & VOCs ▸

Carpet systems, including pad, backing, stain-resistance treatments, and adhesives used for installation, have been the target of much debate over the health risks of chemical offgassing and its effect on indoor air quality. Carpet is also a likely candidate for "greenwashing," evident in deceptive marketing that implies greenness without definitive backing to prove it.

In response to widespread health concerns surrounding carpeting in the home, the Carpet and Rug Institute (CRI) has established a testing and monitoring program through which it awards *Green Label* and *Green Label Plus* certification for products that meet specific standards for lowered levels of VOC offgassing. While certification alone doesn't mean the product is right for every homeowner, it's a good place to start. For more information about the CRI's labeling program and testing criteria, visit the organization's website at www.carpet-rug.org. Also visit the EPA's website, at www.epa.gov, and search "carpet."

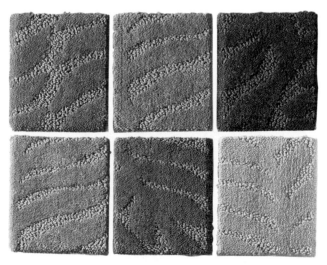

Carpet made from recycled materials can offer the same look, feel, and durability you get with standard virgin-nylon products.

Carpet Tiles

Carpet tiles offer an easy-to-install, and often economical, alternative to conventional wall-to-wall carpeting. They can also offer several green advantages. Because tiles are individual units, you can order the exact number that you need, so there's very little or no waste. By contrast, standard carpeting comes in 12-ft.-long rolls, and the amount of wasted material can be substantial. If carpet tiles become damaged, they can be replaced a la carte, while damage to standard carpeting means an entire room's worth of material must be replaced. And to make the greenest carpet choice, select tiles made with recycled materials. The makers of the tiles used in this project sponsor a recycling program through which they will take back and recycle your old tiles if you ever decide to replace them.

The installation shown here involves laying tiles onto the floor following simple grid lines. Individual tiles are held together with one-sided adhesive tabs. The tiles stay together, but they don't stick to the floor, so you can lay them over hardwood or tile without damaging the underlying finish. You can also move the entire carpet installation to clean the floor surface or to redesign the tile configuration. Spills and stains are no problem because you can simply pull up the affected tiles and wash them off. When the tiles have dried completely, fit them back into place using new adhesive tabs if necessary.

Carpet tiles can be laid over most smooth, flat surfaces, including wood, tile, vinyl, plywood or particleboard subflooring, and wood underlayment. Over concrete floors, the surface must be fully cured to minimize surface moisture and sealed with a water-based concrete sealer. Waxed flooring and some wood finishes may not be suitable for carpet tile. Check with the tile manufacturer for recommended surface preparation prior to installation.

Tools & Materials ▸

Chalk line	Framing square
Tape measure	Carpet tile
Carpet knife	
or utility knife	

Carpet tiles combine all the warmth and comfort of carpeting with do-it-yourself installation, custom designs, and easy replacement. They can be laid wall-to-wall or in an area rug fashion, as shown above.

Working with Carpet Tiles

Move the cartons of carpet tile into the room at least 12 hours prior to laying them so they have a chance to acclimate to the temperature and humidity in the room.

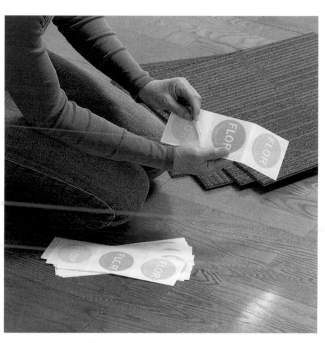

Study the installation methods for the specific brand of tile you purchase. Some tiles have a very heavy construction and are held in place simply by bonding the individual tiles to one another, as above.

Directional arrows are printed on the reverse face of the tiles to indicate which direction the grain runs. The arrows are a handy reference for ensuring that the layout has either a homogenous look or a regularly repeating pattern, depending on your design preference.

Save cut pieces of tile to fill in leftover sections, around obstacles, and underneath permanent elements like radiators.

How to Install Carpet Tiles Wall-to-Wall

Clean the floor thoroughly and make sure it is completely dry. Snap a chalk line between opposing corners of the room to create an X marking the room's center.

Measure and mark the exact center of each wall, then snap chalk lines between the marks to create two additional perpendicular grid lines.

Lay perpendicular starter rows of carpet tiles along the second set of chalk lines. Make sure the tiles are butted squarely together. If necessary, adjust the layout to minimize cut tiles or to make cut border tiles of equal size at opposite sides of the room. Re-snap chalk lines as needed after adjustments.

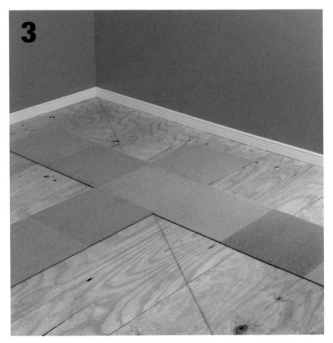

Connect the tiles in the starter rows together using the provided adhesive tabs. Place one tab at each seam, sticky side up, so the tab is centered on the seam. Press the tile edges down onto the tab to adhere them.

5

To mark border tiles for cutting, place a new tile face down on the floor, and slip it underneath the last full tile in the starter row. Make sure the new tile is oriented properly based on the back markings. Mark the new tile for cutting along the edge where the tiles overlap.

6

Cut the border tile with a carpet knife or utility knife using a framing square to ensure a straight cut. Start with a few light passes before cutting completely through the tile. Stick each cut border tile into place using adhesive tabs, so the cut edge is against the wall.

7

Complete the installation by filling in each of the four quadrants, working outward from the center of the room. *Tip: You'll use fewer adhesive tabs by placing them only at the corners where four tiles meet. Check the alignment of the tiles as you work to make sure the seams are straight. To reposition a tile, simply pull it off of the tabs; the adhesive bond becomes stronger after a couple of hours.*

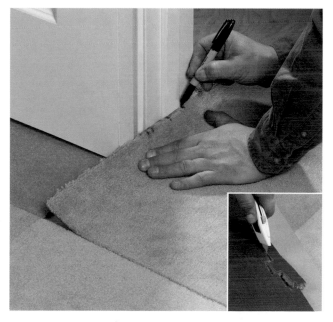

Tip: To fit tiles around doorways and wall openings, position a full tile against the wall and mark the edges of the tile where they meet the opening and the wall or baseboard. Use a framing square to make the two perpendicular cuts. For doorways, you may need to cut a notch for the door stop (inset).

Bamboo Flooring

It looks like hardwood and is available in traditional tongue-and-groove form and in laminate planks. But bamboo is not wood. It's really a grass—and one of the most popular flooring materials today.

Bamboo flooring is made by shredding stalks of the raw material, then pressing them together with a resin that holds the shreds in their finished shape. Not only is bamboo a fast-growing and renewable crop, the companies that make bamboo flooring use binders with low emissions of volatile organic compounds (VOCs). The result is tough, economical, and ecologically friendly. In other words, it's just about perfect for flooring.

If you choose tongue-and-groove bamboo, the installation techniques are the same as for hardwoods. Bamboo is also available as a snap-fit laminate for use in floating floors. In this project we show Teragren Synergy Strand in Java (see Resources): thin, durable planks that are glued to the underlayment.

Tools & Materials ▸

Adhesive	Moisture level meter
Carpenter's level	Notched trowel
Carpenter's square	Rubber mallet
Chalk line	Scrap lumber
Cleaning supplies	Shims
Flat-edged trowel	Straightedge
Marking pen or pencil	Weighted roller
Measuring tape	

Tips for a Successful Installation ▸

60° 70°
RECOMMENDED TEMPERATURE RANGE

40% 60%
RECOMMENDED HUMIDITY RANGE

Bamboo plank flooring should be one of the last items installed on any new construction or remodeling project. All work involving water or moisture should be completed before floor installation. Room temperature and humidity of installation area should be consistent with normal, year-round living conditions for at least a week before installation. Room temperature of 60 to 70° F and humidity range of 40 to 60% is recommended.

About radiant heat: The subfloor should never exceed 85° F. Check the manufacturer's suggested guidelines for correct water temperature inside heating pipes. Switch on the heating unit three days before flooring installation. Room temperature should not vary more than 15° F year-round. For glue-down installations, leave the heating unit on for three days following installation.

How to Install Bamboo Planks

Give the bamboo time to adjust to installation conditions. Store it for at least 72 hours in or near the room where it will be installed. Open the packages for inspection, but do not store the planks on concrete or near outside walls.

Even though thin-plank bamboo is an engineered material, it can vary in appearance. Buy all planks from the same lot and batch number. Then visually inspect the planks to make sure they match. Use the same lighting as you will have in the finished room.

Inspect wood surfaces. The planks and underlayment should have no more than 12% moisture. Bamboo planks can be installed on plywood or oriented strandboard at least ¾" thick. The underlayment must be structurally sound.

Make sure the underlayment is level. It should not change by more than ⅛" over 10 feet. If necessary, apply a floor leveler to fill any low places, and sand down any high spots. Prevent squeaks by driving screws every 6" into the subfloor below.

5

Sweep and vacuum the floor surface, then measure all room dimensions.

6

3'
4'
5'

Check corners for squareness using the 3-4-5 triangle method.

7

The planks should be perpendicular to the floor joists below. Adjust your starting point if necessary. Snap a chalk line next to the longest wall. The distance from the wall should be the same at both ends, leaving ½" for expansion.

8

Lay the first course of planks with the tongue edge toward the wall. Align the planks with the chalk line. Hold the edge course in place with wedges or by nailing through the tongue edge. This row will anchor the others, so make sure it stays securely in place.

(continued)

Once the starter row is in place, install the planks using a premium wood-flooring adhesive. Be sure to follow the manufacturer's instructions. Begin at the chalk line and apply enough adhesive to lay down one or two rows of planks. Spread the adhesive with a V-notched trowel at a 45° angle. Let the adhesive sit for the specified time.

When the adhesive is tacky and ready to use, lay the first section of bamboo planks. Set each plank in the adhesive by placing a clean piece of scrap lumber on top and tapping it down with a rubber mallet. Check the edge of each section to make sure it keeps a straight line.

After you finish the first section, cover the next area with adhesive and give it time to become tacky. This slows down the project, but it prevents you from using more adhesive than you can use—and it allows the section you just finished to set up.

When the adhesive is ready, lay down the next section of planks. Fit the new planks tightly against the previous section, taking care not to knock the finished section out of alignment. If the planks have tongue-and-groove edges, fit them carefully into place.

Continue applying adhesive and installing planks, one section at a time, to cover the entire floor. When adhesive gets on the flooring surface, wipe it off quickly.

At the edges and around any fixed objects, such as doorways or plumbing pipes, leave a ½" gap for expansion. Use shims to maintain the gaps if needed. These spaces can be covered with baseboards, base shoes, and escutcheons.

As you finish each section, walk across it a few times to maximize contact between the planks and the adhesive. When all the planks are in place, clean the surface and use a clean weighted roller. Push the roller in several directions, covering the entire surface many times.

In places that are difficult to reach with a roller, lay down a sheet of protective material, such as butcher paper, and stack weights on the paper. Let the finished floor sit for at least 24 hours, then clean the surface and remove any spacers from the expansion gaps. Finally, install the finishing trim.

Can a Green Home Have a Hearth?

Interestingly, the subject of fireplaces has been given the cold shoulder by many green sources. One likely reason for this is the belief that fireplaces are unnecessary decorations that waste a lot of energy and pollute the air—a fair indictment if you're talking about conventional wood-burning fireplaces. But today's high-efficiency fireplaces and other "hearth products," as they're called in the industry, can provide energy-efficient zone heating with very little outdoor air pollution and virtually no effect on indoor air quality. And they still make a nice decoration.

Thanks primarily to the innovation of direct venting, modern fireplaces are not only more environmentally friendly than their traditional counterparts, they're much easier to install in an existing home. So easy that many homeowners do most of the work themselves. The project on pages 154 to 159 shows you what's involved. Fireplaces with direct venting pull in combustion air from outdoors, instead of from the home's interior, and they get rid of exhaust gases through the same run of ducting. Because there's no mixing of interior air and combustion air, the indoor air stays clean and none of the heated air in the room is lost up the chimney.

In terms of fuel type, gas fireplaces far outsell all other types, but they're not the only option. Wood pellet stoves and some cord wood appliances can offer high efficiency along with some of the same space-heating features found on gas systems. If you're interested in a solid-fuel hearth product (as opposed to gas), look for EPA-certified models with high efficiency ratings. Also consider pollution controls. Some units have catalytic converters and other features to reduce air pollutants, but many control systems must be maintained and/or replaced regularly to ensure proper performance. Also be aware that solid-fuel stoves and fireplaces may be subject to wood-burning restrictions in your community.

Given that standard open-hearth wood-burning fireplaces are only about 10% to 15% efficient and emit a significant amount of particulate air pollution, it's safe to say the beloved decorative fireplace really has no place in a green home. However, if you already have a traditional fireplace and want to use it as more than a backdrop for candles, you can quickly bring it up to date with a high-efficiency insert. Inserts are available in a range of fuel types and offer similar heating performance to freestanding gas fireplaces.

Old-fashioned allure in a high-tech system. Efficient gas fireplaces mean you don't have to take a pass on this timeless feature for your green home.

Choosing a Gas Fireplace

For most homes, including green homes, a natural gas or liquid propane fireplace is the best all-around option. Gas burns cleaner than wood and requires less start-up time, and the fuel is plumbed directly to the appliance so it's always available (as long as you pay your utility bill). Gas hearth products come in a wide range of styles and are good for replicating the look of traditional fireplaces. They're also the most versatile in terms of locating and ducting the units. All of these advantages make a gas fireplace a great option for zone or supplemental heating. For example, you can use the fireplace to quickly heat a bedroom or basement space as needed while keeping your home's primary heating system set at a lower temperature.

Gas fireplaces and other heating appliances are rated for efficiency in a couple of different ways. AFUE (Annual Fuel Utilization Efficiency) is the same rating system used for comparing furnaces and other heating equipment. This tends to be the more accurate rating because it takes into account start-up time and standby heat loss (heat lost up the chimney when the appliance is off). Steady state ratings tell you the fuel-to-heat transfer efficiency at a constant temperature. These are typically a few points higher than AFUE ratings due to the narrower criteria. Both ratings are meaningful, but not all manufacturers use both systems. In any case, be aware of which rating system is used when comparing models. High-efficiency products score upward of 70% on the AFUE scale and mid-70% to 80% and up in steady state ratings.

Fireplace inserts fit into the firebox of conventional masonry fireplaces. Be sure to choose a style that complements the existing fireplace surround.

Depending on its output and other performance factors, a direct-vent gas fireplace can be used to heat a large room or a significant portion of the house.

Here are some other features to look for in a gas fireplace used for heating:

- direct-vent, sealed combustion—means the combustion system is totally independent from indoor air
- ceramic-glass front—seals heat in, preventing the transmit of heat through the front glass; ceramic-glass is better than tempered glass and it is shatter-resistant
- circulating fan—sends heat farther into the room; squirrel-cage fans are the most effective and tend to be quieter than other types
- automatic starter—uses less energy than a standing pilot light
- variable control settings—allow you to adjust the unit's temperature and, consequently, energy use; look for units with a wide range of control
- secondary heat exchanger—helps the unit capture more heat and send it into the room

In addition to direct-vent models, there are also unvented fireplaces and heaters that offer very high efficiency ratings. However, some industry and health experts recommend against unvented appliances due to concerns about indoor air quality and high levels of moisture (a natural byproduct of combustion) being released into the home. Some states and municipalities prohibit them entirely.

Direct-Vent Gas Fireplace

A high-efficiency gas fireplace can be the perfect addition to any green home. Direct venting is a ventilation system that uses a special 2-in-1 vent pipe: The inner pipe carries exhaust fumes outside, while the outer pipe draws in fresh air for combustion. The vent pipe can be routed in many different ways, which means you can install a fireplace in almost any room.

Installing a gas fireplace is a great do-it-yourself project because you can design and build the fireplace frame to suit your needs and add your own finish treatments. It all starts with some careful planning. Once you decide on the fireplace model and determine where to place it, order all of the vent pipes and fittings needed to complete the vent run.

Note: Consult the manufacturer's instructions for the specifications regarding placement, clearances, and venting methods for your fireplace.

Start your planning by determining the best location for the fireplace. Placing the unit next to an exterior wall simplifies the venting required. One important specification for a basement fireplace is that the termination cap (on the outside end of the vent) must be 12" above the ground. In the project shown, the vent runs up 3 ft. before it turns at an elbow and passes through a masonry wall. Because the wall is non-combustible, no heat shield is needed around the vent penetration.

For help with any of these planning issues, talk with knowledgeable dealers in your area. They can help you choose the best fireplace model for your situation and help you with venting and other considerations. And remember, all installation specifications are governed by local building codes: Check with the building department in your area to make sure your plans conform to regulations.

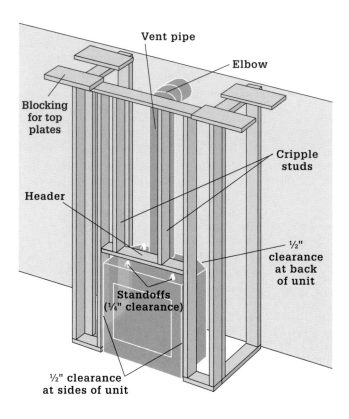

Vent pipe

Elbow

Blocking for top plates

Cripple studs

Header

½" clearance at back of unit

Standoffs (¼" clearance)

½" clearance at sides of unit

Tools & Materials ▸

Framing square	Nail set	Masonry fasteners	Mantle
Chalk line	V-notched trowel	3" wallboard screws	Wood-finishing materials
Plumb bob	Screwdriver	Sheet metal plates	6d and 4d finish nails
Circular saw	Grout float	Plastic sheet	Wood putty
Drill	Sponge	Scrap plywood	Ceramic tile
2-ft. level	Fireplace unit	Sheet metal screws	Tile spacers
Hammer drill	Vent sections	Caulk	Latex tile adhesive
Masonry bit	Termination cap	⅝" wallboard	Masking tape
Masonry chisel	½" copper tubing	Wallboard finishing materials	Grout
Hand maul	2× blocking lumber	High-temperature sealant	Cap rail trim
Adjustable wrenches	2 × 4 lumber	Primer	Buildup strips
Brush	Construction adhesive	Paint	

How to Install a Direct-Vent Gas Fireplace

BUILD THE FRAME

Mark the outer edges of the frame onto the floor. Use a framing square to draw a perpendicular line through each mark to indicate the locations of the side walls. Measure out along these lines and mark the front of the frame, then snap a chalk line through the marks. Measure diagonally from corner to corner to make sure the layout lines are square; adjust the lines, if necessary.

Use a plumb bob to transfer the lines from the floor to the joists above. If any top plates of the frame will fall between parallel joists, install 2× blocking between the joists. Snap a line through the marks to complete the top-plate layout.

Cut the bottom plates to size from pressure-treated 2 × 4s. Position the plates just inside the layout lines, and fasten them to the floor using construction adhesive and masonry screws or a powder-actuated nailer. Cut the top plates from standard 2 × 4s, and attach them to the joists or blocking with 3" screws

or 16d nails (drill pilot holes for screws) (photo 1). If the plates are attached directly to parallel joists, add backing for attaching the ceiling wallboard.

Mark the stud layout on the bottom plates, then transfer the layout to the top plates using a plumb bob. Measure to determine the length of each stud, then cut the studs to length. Attach the two studs along the back wall using construction adhesive and masonry screws or a powder-actuated nailer. Attach the remaining studs to the top and bottom plates with 3" screws or 8d nails.

Measure up from the floor and mark the height of the header onto each stud at the side of the front opening. Cut and install the header (photo 2). Cut the cripple studs to fit between the header and top plate. To allow easy access for running the vent pipe, do not install the cripple studs until after the vent is in place. Add any blocking needed to provide nailing surfaces for the tile trim.

Draw layouts for the plates. Attach the bottom plates to the floor and the top plates to the joists.

Cut and install the studs, then install the header piece to complete the front opening.

(continued)

SET THE FIREPLACE & CUT THE VENT HOLE

Bend out the nailing tabs at the sides of the fireplace unit. Slide the unit into the frame until the tabs meet the framing around the opening, then center the unit within the opening. Make sure the unit is level from side to side and front to back, and make any adjustments by shimming underneath with thin sheet metal plates (photo 3). Apply a small amount of construction adhesive to the shims to hold them in place. Measure at the sides and back of the unit to be sure the clearance requirements are met.

Dry-fit the vent pieces. Fit the flared end of the first vent section over the vent collars on top of the unit, aligning the inner and outer pipes of the vent with the matching collars (photo 4). Push straight down on the vent until it snaps into place over the lugs on the outside of the collar. Pull up on the vent slightly to make sure it's locked into place.

Attach the 90° elbow so that the free end points toward the exterior wall. *Note: Horizontal vent runs must slope upward ¼" per foot. If your vent includes additional horizontal sections leading from the elbow, adjust the vent pieces and elbow to follow the required slope. Trace the circumference of the elbow end onto the wall (photo 5).*

Remove the vent from the unit, and set it aside. Cover the fireplace with plastic and scrap plywood to protect it from debris. Using a long masonry bit and hammer drill, drill a series of holes just outside the marked circle, spacing them as close together as possible. Drill the holes all the way through the block. Be patient; the block cavities may be filled with concrete (photo 6).

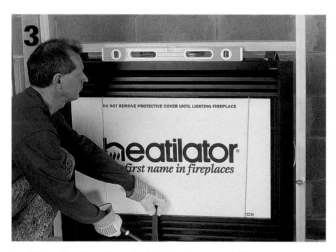

Position the fireplace inside the frame and, if necessary, install shims to bring it level.

Mark the position of the vent hole by tracing around the circumference of the elbow.

Dry-fit the first section of vent over the vent collars and snap it into place.

Drill a series of holes through the block wall using a hammer drill and long masonry bit.

Carefully knock out the hole, using a masonry chisel and a hand maul. Work inward from both sides of the wall to ensure a clean cutout on the wall surfaces (photo 7). Smooth the hole edges, test-fit the horizontal vent piece, and make any necessary adjustments. Uncover the fireplace, and clean up around the unit.

INSTALL THE VENT & TEST THE FIREPLACE

Reinstall the vertical vent section and elbow, locking the pieces together, as before. To install the adjustable horizontal vent section, measure the distance from the elbow to the termination cap. Adjust the section to length, and secure the sliding pieces together with two sheet metal screws. Install the horizontal vent section and termination cap, following the manufacturer's instructions. Seal around the perimeter of the cap with an approved caulk (illustration).

When the vent run is complete, fasten the fireplace unit to the framing by driving screws through the nailing tabs. Install the cripple studs between the header and top plate.

To make the gas connection, remove the lower grill from the front of the unit. Feed the gas supply pipe into the access hole on the side of the unit, and connect it to the manual shutoff valve (photo 8). Tighten the connection with adjustable wrenches.

Turn on the gas supply, and check the connection for leaking by brushing on a solution of soapy water (photo 9). Bubbles indicate leaking. If you see bubbles, turn off the gas, tighten the connection, then retest it before proceeding.

Break out the vent hole with a masonry chisel and hand maul, then carefully smooth the rough edges.

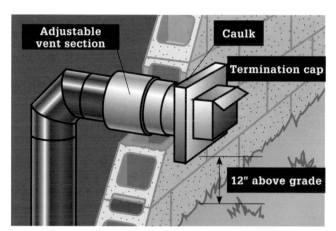

Complete the vent run by installing the adjustable vent section and termination cap. Fasten the cap to the exterior wall and seal around it with caulk.

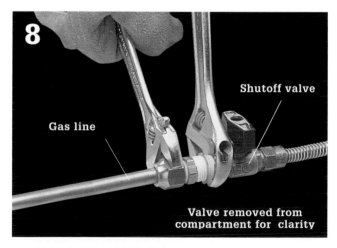

Connect the gas supply line to the manual shutoff valve, and carefully tighten the connection.

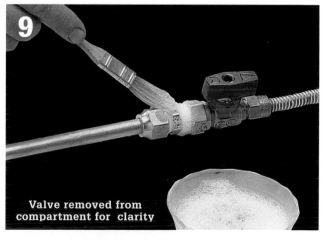

Test the gas connection for leaks by brushing on soapy water and checking for bubbles.

(continued)

Prepare the firebox, and light the fire, following the manufacturer's instructions. Let the fire run for about 15 to 20 minutes while you inspect the flame and make sure there are no problems with the vent. Report any problems to the manufacturer or dealer. After the test is complete, turn off the fireplace and let it cool down completely.

APPLY THE FINISHES

Install ⅝" wallboard over the framing, running the panels horizontally and attaching them with screws. To provide space for sealant, leave a ⅛" gap between the wallboard and the top and sides of the front face of the unit (photo 10).

Fill the gap around the front face with a high-temperature sealant supplied (or recommended) by the manufacturer (photo 11). Tape and finish the wallboard seams and inside corner joints, and install and finish corner bead at the outside corners. Prime and paint the areas of wallboard that won't be covered with tile.

To install the mantle, measure up from the floor and mark the height of the support cleat. Use a level to draw a level line through the mark. Mark the stud locations just above the level line. Position the cleat on the line, centered between the frame sides, and drill a pilot hole at each stud location. Fasten the cleat to the studs with screws provided by the manufacturer (photo 12).

Finish the mantle as desired, then fit it over the support cleat, and center it between the frame sides. Holding the mantle tight to the wallboard, drill pilot holes for 6d finish nails through the top of the mantle, about ¾" from the back edge. Secure the mantle to the cleat with four nails (photo 13). Set the nails with a nail set, fill the holes with wood putty, then touch up the finish.

Cover the frame with wallboard, leaving a gap around the black front face of the unit.

Seal around the unit's front face with high-temperature sealant.

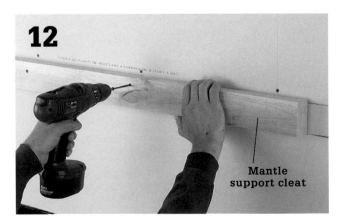

Draw a level line for the mantle support cleat, then attach the cleat to the studs with screws.

Fit the mantle over the cleat, and secure it with finish nails driven through pilot holes.

INSTALL THE TILE & TRIM

Dry-fit the tile around the front of the fireplace. You can lay tile over the black front face, but do not cover the glass or any portion of the grills. If you're using floor tile without spacer lugs on the side edges, use plastic tile spacers to set the grout gaps between tiles (at least ⅛" for floor tile). Mark the perimeter of the tile area and make any other layout marks that will help with the installation (photo 14). If possible, precut any tiles.

Using a V-notched trowel, apply latex mastic tile adhesive to the wall, spreading it evenly just inside the perimeter lines. Set the tiles into the adhesive, aligning them with the layout marks, and press firmly to create a good bond (photo 15). Install spacers between tiles as you work, and scrape out excess adhesive from the grout joints using a small screwdriver. Install all of the tile, then let the adhesive dry completely.

Mask off around the tile, then mix a batch of grout, following the manufacturer's instructions. Spread the grout over the tiles using a rubber grout float, forcing the grout into the joints (photo 16). Then, drag the float across the joints diagonally, tilting the float at a 45° angle. Make another diagonal pass to remove excess grout. Wait 10 to 15 minutes, then wipe smeared grout from the tile with a damp sponge, rinsing frequently. Let the grout dry for one hour, then polish the tiles with a dry cloth. Let the grout dry completely.

Cut pieces of cap rail trim to fit around the tile, mitering the ends where the pieces fit together. If the tile is thicker than the trim recesses, install buildup strips behind the trim using finish nails. Finish the trim to match the mantle. Drill pilot holes and nail the trim in place with 4d finish nails. Set the nails with a nail set (photo 17). Fill the holes with wood putty and touch up the finish.

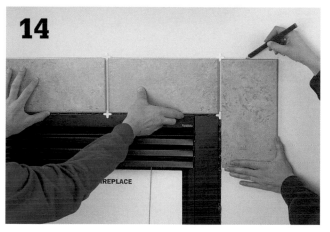

Dry-fit the tile around the fireplace front, and mark the wall to indicate tile positions.

Apply adhesive inside the layout lines, then press the tile firmly into the adhesive.

Force grout into the joints with a grout float, then make two passes to remove excess.

Attach the trim pieces around the tile with finish nails, and set the nails with a nail set.

Green Yards

Our room-by-room tour of a green home concludes with a stroll through the grounds (whatever your "grounds" may include). And as we make the move to the outdoors, we also adjust our focus to take a broad view of the home in its natural surroundings. We consider not only the plantings and hardscape surfaces, but also the local climate and the property's impact on municipal systems and nearby wildlife. For as much as a home and its yard should feel like a private oasis, it cannot be an island unto itself.

Above all, a green outdoor home is designed for its immediate environment: It celebrates local flora with both practical and ecological benefits; it uses rainwater for nourishing plants and returns excess storm water to the ground instead of the sewer system; and it enriches the local ecosystem with plants that appeal to wildlife. A well-planned landscape also improves the environment inside the home with trees and shrubs that provide shade in the summer and help buffer cold winter winds, adding comfort indoors and easing the demand for mechanical heating and cooling. In light of these important roles, it's easy to see how the landscape is an integral part of a green home and, ultimately, a green community.

In this chapter:

- As Green as It's Meant to Be
- Greening Up Your Outdoor Home
- Efficient Watering Techniques
- Drip Irrigation Systems
- Rainwater Collection Systems
- Patios, Decks & Paving
- Composite Decking
- Permeable Patio Surfaces

As Green as It's Meant to Be

As any backyard gardener knows, getting things to grow involves a great deal of trial and error . . . and also time, money, patience, and even wonder: How can it be that your next-door neighbor has more perfect tomatoes than she knows what to do with when all you can produce is a handful of mealy specimens each year? It could be her soil or her technique, but most likely the difference is that her backyard's microclimate is a better environment for growing tomatoes.

In the bigger picture, this imbalance occurs not just across the globe but also from county to county. Yet, you can visit any garden center in, say, Colorado, and find a huge selection of plants that evolved not on the Western plains but in coastal climates or even the dampest regions of Scotland. These plants may survive in the dry Colorado air with enormous amounts of irrigation and probably lots of chemicals, but it begs the question: Why fight nature?

Choosing plants that are well-adapted to the local climate (and your yard's microclimate) is the first step in creating a green landscape, both literally and figuratively. In many regions, this also means limiting the amount of conventional grass because of its insatiable thirst for water. The next step is to look for ways to use water more efficiently and for collecting free water when Mother Nature provides it (good luck to those of you in Colorado and the Southwest).

When it comes to the manmade elements of the landscape, the basic precepts of green building apply: Choose renewable, recyclable, and healthful materials such as recycled-plastic decking and locally produced mulch. Also consider permeable paving in place of concrete and asphalt to keep storm runoff in the ground instead of loading up the sewer system with water and all the yard and driveway chemicals it brings with it. In this illustration you'll find some of the features you'll find in a well-planned, low-maintenance landscape.

A green yard tends to look very natural and very at-home in its surroundings. It should be populated with native plants that don't require heroic efforts to thrive and it should require little or no watering or chemical fertilization. Ideally, a green yard also has a positive impact on your home and property by providing valuable shade or preventing soil erosion.

Elements of a Green Yard

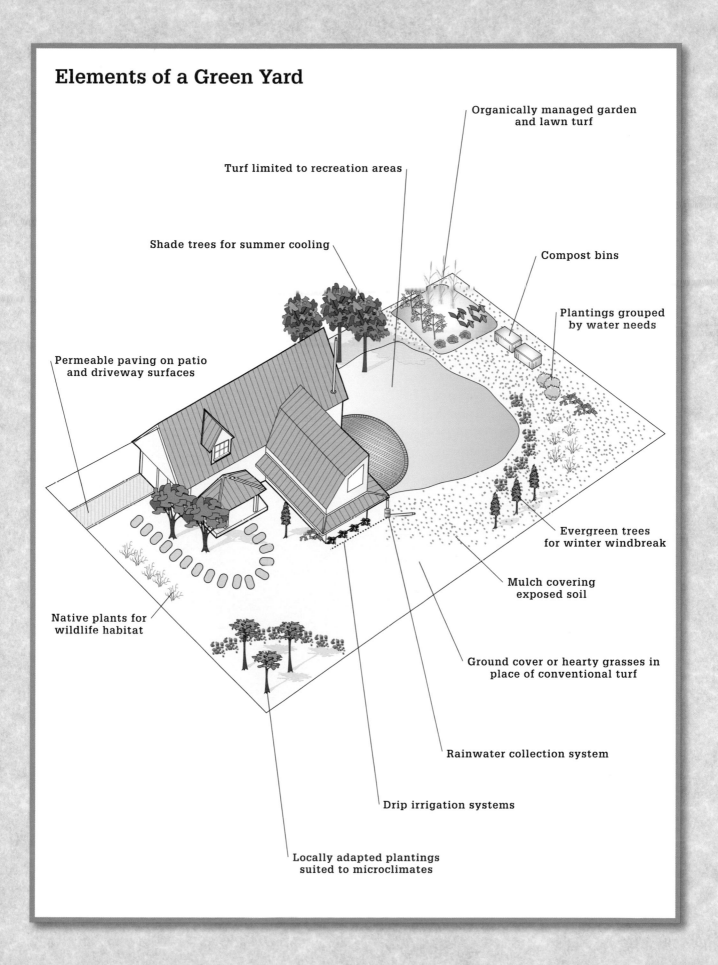

Organically managed garden and lawn turf

Turf limited to recreation areas

Shade trees for summer cooling

Compost bins

Plantings grouped by water needs

Permeable paving on patio and driveway surfaces

Evergreen trees for winter windbreak

Native plants for wildlife habitat

Mulch covering exposed soil

Ground cover or hearty grasses in place of conventional turf

Rainwater collection system

Drip irrigation systems

Locally adapted plantings suited to microclimates

Greening Up Your Outdoor Home

The following is a list of suggestions and considerations for making your outdoor home as green as your indoor one. Not all of these ideas will apply to your landscape or your climate, which, of course, is a critical factor. For help with choosing the right plants, treatments, and techniques for local conditions, seek the advice of local gardening and horticultural experts—your state or local extension office is a good place to start (see Extending a Helping Hand, on page 167).

LIMIT THE TURF AREAS

Conventional turf grass is pretty undesirable from a green perspective. It simply requires too much water and, when traditionally maintained, too many chemicals to stay healthy. Lawns are great for play areas and outdoor entertaining, but for strictly decorative areas, consider alternatives like drought-resistant ground covers, native grasses, and low-maintenance landscaping.

FEED AND FERTILIZE ORGANICALLY

This is a biggie. One of the primary sources of pollution in ground water and in homes comes from chemicals in synthetic fertilizers, insecticides, and weed killers. Organic lawn care is a holistic system that focuses on soil enrichment to improve water retention and promote natural organisms, making the lawn healthier and less dependent on applied treatments. Organic management techniques have proven to be effective in all climates. For more information, visit www.safelawns.org.

PLANT TREES

Mature trees offer many environmental benefits. They improve air quality by absorbing carbon dioxide and releasing oxygen, and they cool your yard's microclimate by releasing moisture into the air. Trees provide shade for nearby plantings and ground covers and can significantly reduce the need for watering. They also protect your home from hot summer sunlight and cold winter winds.

Generally speaking, deciduous shade trees are best near east- and west-facing walls and windows, where they block low-angle sun in the summer. Be careful about placing trees near south-facing walls: They help cool the house in summer, but in winter, even bare trees can block desirable solar heat. Evergreen trees and shrubs are best on the north, northeast, and northwest sides of the house or wherever the prevailing winds strike the house in winter.

Grass isn't always greener. In fact, it's one of the most resource-intensive plants you can have. Limiting turf to areas that really get used is a big first step to greening up your landscape.

Trees cool your home by shading it in the summer, and they cool the outdoor air through transpiration.

Xeriscaping is not only resource-efficient and water-wise, it also displays the beauty of locally adapted plants—an attractive alternative to generic, non-native turf grass.

Planting for wildlife adds a magical element to your outdoor home and a safe place for animals and insects to thrive in.

SELECT PLANTS ACCORDING TO YOUR MICROCLIMATES

Within the confines of a single yard there can be many different climatic zones. Factors, such as shade, ground contours, orientation to the sun, outdoor structures, and nearby plantings, can affect the growing conditions in each area. Choosing plants suited to its immediate environment will promote healthy growth and limit measures like extra watering to compensate for poor placement.

XERISCAPE

Xeriscaping is the practice of landscaping with regionally appropriate plants. In dry climates, this means using highly drought-resistant species that can survive primarily on natural precipitation. People unfamiliar with xeriscaping are often surprised at the range of naturally adapted plants available in a given area. A well-designed landscape can be quite diverse, colorful, and beautiful and doesn't have to look like a desert setting, unless you want it to. A properly xeriscaped yard also groups plants by their water needs so that higher-maintenance plants can be managed more efficiently.

COMPOST YARD DEBRIS

Instead of sending trimmings, weeds, and other organic yard waste to the landfill, set up a compost bin to turn the material into free fertilizer. Not everything is suitable for composting, so check with local experts about what to compost and what to throw away.

MULCH EXPOSED SOIL

A layer of organic mulch, such as wood chips, bark, and even grass clippings, helps soil in gardens and planters retain water by reducing evaporation.

PLANT FOR WILDLIFE

Providing a home for birds, butterflies, and other species is an important part of many green landscapes, as it helps replace natural habitat lost or endangered through land development. Planting for wildlife can be as simple as selecting a few plant varieties that appeal to local animal species. For more ambitious projects, the Wildlife Federation sponsors a certification program for homeowners interested in turning all or part of their landscape into a wildlife habitat site; visit www.nwf.org/gardenforwildlife for more information.

Lawn Equipment for the Green Homeowner

Ah, the sounds of summer...Full trees rustling in the breeze, kids running through sprinklers, and the deafening, percussive whine of gas-powered motors. If you live in the suburbs, you're no stranger to the sounds of motors at all hours of the day, from lawnmowers, weed trimmers, edgers, and leaf blowers. And you've certainly grown to accept the sudden onslaught of landscaping crews—the mow-and-blow S.W.A.T. teams—descending upon your neighbors' lawns (or your lawn) and filling the air with noise and noxious exhaust.

But there is indeed a better way: The first step is taking your foot (or your finger) off the gas. Studies have shown that mowing a lawn for one hour with a gas-powered mower pollutes the air as much as a 100-mile car trip. Older mowers and weed trimmers with two-stroke engines (the kind where you add the oil directly to the fuel) are the worst polluters, but even newer mowers with four-stroke, overhead-valve engines contribute disproportionately to the nation's air pollution. However, if your yard is so big (say, larger than ½ acre) that an electric or reel mower is too impractical, replace your old mower with the most efficient gas model you can find.

Electric mowers and trimmers are greener alternatives to gas-powered equipment. Electric mowers produce only a tiny fraction of the carbon monoxide and hydrocarbons that gas mowers do (but only about six fewer pounds of carbon dioxide). Electric motors are also considerably quieter than their gassy counterparts. Electric mowers and weed trimmers are commonly available in corded and cordless (battery-powered) versions; choose the type that best suits the size and configuration of your lawn.

Of course, the truly green option for lawn mowing is an old-fashioned, human-powered reel mower. Reel mowers are pollution-free, exceptionally quiet, and far more reliable than all types of power mowers. They're also much better for your health: Your body enjoys some mild exercise without a constant flow of exhaust going into your lungs. If you're wary of reel mowers because you've heard they're too much work, take a quality new mower out for a test drive; you'll

If a gas-powered mower is the only realistic option, choose a new model with an efficient overhead-valve engine.

While they still rely on conventional power sources, electric lawn mowers and rechargeable cordless mowers pollute far less than gas-powered equipment.

be surprised at how easy it is to push. The need for sharpening reel mowers also tends to be exaggerated. Many manufacturers recommend sharpening every one to two years (just like with power mowers), while some models can go five to eight years without needing to be sharpened.

However, there is one important rule to follow when using a reel mower: Mow regularly. If the grass gets too long, the mower simply won't cut it. Reel mowers lack the suction effect that power mowers have, so long grass just lies down and lets the mower go right over it. If you mow once a week like you would with a power mower, you shouldn't have any problems. But if you let the lawn go for a couple of weeks, you'll have to borrow a power mower or hire a neighborhood kid to give your lawn a once-over and shorten it to a workable length.

Finally, regular mowing with a reel mower means you don't have to catch and bag the grass clippings. Contrary to popular belief, lawn experts say that short grass clippings left on the lawn help to retain moisture and don't contribute to thatch buildup. Besides, sending dozens of garbage bags full of lawn clippings to the landfill each summer is downright silly.

Today's reel lawn mowers are lightweight, low-maintenance, and come with cutting widths up to 20".

Tip: Extending a Helping Hand ▸

For free advice on all things garden- or yard-related, contact your state or local Cooperative Extension office. Every state has an office at its land-grant university, as well as local and regional branch offices. As part of an educational program that awards Master Gardener certification, participants operate a help line for residents with gardening questions. To find the state or local extension office in your area, visit the U.S. Department of Agriculture's extension service website, at www.csrees.usda.gov. Other sources for information on planting and watering include your local water department and experts at local landscaping companies and garden centers.

Efficient Watering Techniques

Watering yards and gardens can account for a significant portion of a household's annual water use—up to 50% or more in most western states. Xeriscaping with dry-adapted plants can reduce water use considerably, but careful, systematic watering techniques can be just as important. Here are a few ways you can easily cut down on water use and make sure your plants are getting just what they need without unnecessary waste.

A MEASURED APPROACH

When watering a lawn manually or with an automatic sprinkler system, it's difficult to gauge how much water is getting to the grass. Measuring a sprinkler's output takes the guesswork out of watering and gives you a baseline for making adjustments to your watering as needed. Another thing to measure is the rainfall your lawn receives, so you'll know how much additional water is required.

First, determine how much water your lawn needs during its active season. This varies by climate, so consult local experts for recommendations for your type of grass. For example, in many areas Kentucky Bluegrass lawns (what most people have) need about 1" of water per week. If it rains ¼" in a given week, you'll need to add ¾" of water to keep the lawn in good shape.

Invest in a good gauge. A rain gauge gives you an accurate reading of how much rainfall is getting to your lawn.

Keep it low and localized. When watering, avoid sprinklers that spray high into the air—a lot of water is lost simply to needless evaporation. It's also a good idea to set a few empty cans around the lawn while you water so you can measure the time it takes your sprinklers to deliver 1" of water. This tells you how long to run sprinklers to water the desired amount.

Use hose bib timers for manual watering. These shut off the water automatically, so you don't have to keep track of watering times. They also help prevent wasteful over-watering.

To measure the output of your sprinkler(s), set out several cans or containers of the same size (tuna cans work well for this), then run the sprinkler at its normal setting, and watch the clock. Time how long it takes to collect 1" in each can. This test will also tell you if a sprinkler isn't working properly and where watering is unusually high due to overlap in the sprinkler arrangement.

The best way to measure rainfall is with a rain gauge. Set up one or more gauges in open areas around the yard. The combined precipitation from rainfall and watering should meet the recommended weekly allowance.

USING DRIP IRRIGATION

Drip irrigation systems reduce water use dramatically by delivering a steady drip of water directly to plantings. The water goes right where it's needed, minimizing waste through evaporation, and there's no risk of "leaf burn" caused by the magnification of sunlight on freshly watered foliage. The project on pages 170 to 171 shows you how to install a basic drip irrigation system.

COLLECTING RAINWATER FOR REUSE

Setting up a simple rainwater collection system is incredibly easy because most of the system is already in place. Your home's roof and gutters collect and channel the water for you. All you have to do is redirect the runoff from one or more downspouts into a rain barrel, then hook a hose up to the rain barrel to water your landscape. See pages 172 to 173 for step-by-step installation instructions.

MINIMIZING EVAPORATION

Watering plants and especially lawns during the hot hours of the day results in a great deal of waste through evaporation. Therefore, the best times to water are in the early morning and late evening, when water has time to settle into the ground instead of being vaporized by the sun and hot air. Mulching around gardens, trees, and decorative plantings also helps reduce evaporation and helps to enrich the soil and protect it from direct sunlight.

Healthy soil is critical for retaining water and nutrients that plants and grass need. Rich topsoil holds onto water like a sponge, while hard, nutrient-poor soil sheds water, and sandy soil lets water pass through to a depth where roots can't be fed properly. Talk to local experts about having your soil tested and amending the soil as needed.

Mulches made of wood chips, compost, and other materials are especially important in dry climates, where exposure to harsh sunlight leads to rapid evaporation during the day.

Drip Irrigation Systems

Installing a water-efficient drip irrigation system is very easy. A typical system consists of ½" plastic pipe that routes water from a hose spigot to trees, shrubs, and garden beds. The plastic tubing is fitted with small plastic nozzles, called emitters, at plant locations. Emitters are essentially mini-sprinklers, and they come in a variety of forms depending on the type of plant you need to water. If you're watering plant beds, assume you'll need 1 ft. of tubing with emitters for every square foot of plant bed space.

Tools & Materials ▸

Tubing punch
Drip irrigation kit
Extra fittings, as needed

Drip irrigation systems offer many different types of fittings, including the spray head shown here. Because they precisely direct water exactly where it's needed, drip systems waste very little water. A thick layer of mulch around plants will help keep soil moist.

Irrigation Equipment

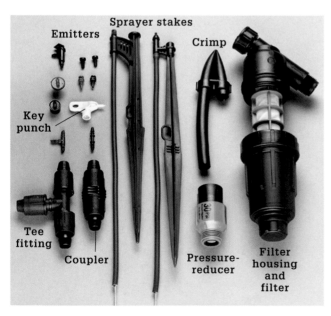

Basic kits come with only a few components, but can be augmented with pieces purchased "ala carte." You'll also need a punch for piercing the tubing and "goof plugs" for repairing errant punches.

Tubing for drip irrigation is thin-wall flexible polyethylene or polyvinyl, typically ¼" or ½" in diameter. Internal diameters can vary from manufacturer to manufacturer, so it's a good idea to purchase pipe and fittings from a single source.

How to Install a Drip Irrigation System

Connect the system's supply tube to a water source, such as a hose spigot or a rainwater system. If you tap into your household water supply, use a pressure gauge to check water pressure. If pressure exceeds 50 pounds per square inch (psi), install a pressure-reducing fitting before attaching the feeder tube. A filter should also be attached to the faucet before the feeder tube.

At garden bed locations, begin installing drip emitters every 18". You can also purchase ½" PE tubing with emitters preinstalled. If you use this tubing, cut the feeder tube once it reaches the first bed, and attach the emitter tubing with a barbed coupling. Route the tubing among the plants so that emitters are over the roots.

For trees and shrubs, make a branch loop around the tree. Pierce the feed tube near the tree and insert a T-fitting. Loop the branch around the tree and connect it to both outlets on the T-fitting. Use ¼" tubing for small trees, ½" for larger specimens. Insert emitters in the loop every 18".

Use micro sprayers for hard-to-reach plants. Sprayers can be connected directly to the main feeder line or positioned on short branch lines. Sprayers come in a variety of spray patterns and flow rates; choose one most appropriate for the plants to be watered.

Potted plants and raised beds can also be watered with sprayers. Place stake-mounted sprayers in the pots or beds. Connect a length of ¼" tubing to the feeder line with a coupler, and connect the ¼" line to the sprayer.

Once all branch lines and emitters are installed, flush the system by turning on the water and let it flow for a full minute. Then, close the ends of the feeder line and the branch lines with figure-8 end crimps. Tubing can be left exposed or buried under mulch.

Rainwater Collection Systems

One of the simplest, least expensive ways to irrigate a landscape is with a system that collects and stores rainwater for controlled distribution either through a garden hose or a drip irrigation system.

The most common system includes one or more rain barrels (typically 40 to 80 gallons in capacity) connected to downspouts. Valve fittings at the bottoms of the barrels let you connect them to a hose or to a drip irrigation line. The system can be configured as a primary irrigation system or a secondary system to augment a standard irrigation system.

Some communities now offer subsidies for rain barrel use, offering free or reduced-price barrels and downspout connection kits. Check with your local water authorities.

Tools & Materials ▸

Drill
Hacksaw
Rain barrel kit
Downspout diverter (optional)
Pavers or blocks (optional)

How to Install a Rain Barrel System

Select a location for the barrel under a downspout. Locate your barrel as close to the area you want to irrigate as possible. Make sure the barrel has a stable, level base. Connect the overflow tube, and make sure it is pointed away from the foundation.

Connect the spigot near the bottom of the barrel. Some kits may include a second spigot for filling watering cans. Use Teflon tape at all threaded fittings to ensure a tight seal. Remove the downspout, and set the barrel on its base.

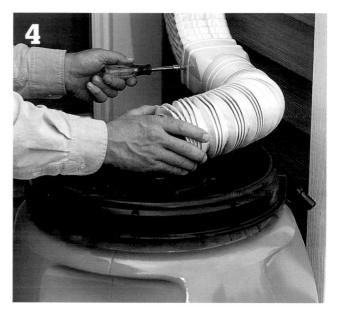

Cut the downspout to length with a hacksaw. Reconnect the elbow fitting to the downspout using sheet metal screws. Attach the cover to the top of the rain barrel. Some systems include a cover with porous wire mesh, to which the downspout delivers water. Others include a cover with a sealed connection (next step).

Link the downspout elbow to the rain barrel with a length of flexible downspout extension attached to the elbow and the barrel cover.

Variation: If your barrel comes with a downspout adapter, cut away a segment of downspout and insert the adapter so it diverts water into the barrel.

Connect a drip irrigation tube or garden hose to the spigot. A Y-fitting, like the one shown here, will let you feed the drip irrigation system through a garden hose when the rain barrel is empty.

If you want, increase water storage by connecting two or more rain barrels together with a linking kit, available from many kit suppliers.

Patios, Decks & Paving

When it comes to choosing materials for outdoor surfaces, the greenest choices meet three criteria: durability, sustainability, and permeability. Durable materials last a long time, of course, but they also are made to withstand outdoor exposure without the protection of toxic treatments, sealants, stains, or cleaning solutions. For example, brick, stone, or concrete pavers are more durable and need less maintenance than wood decking. Sustainable materials are resource-efficient and are produced with minimal impact on the environment: Think recycled plastic or wood composite decking in place of solid redwood or cedar.

Permeability is a factor that relates to runoff water. When driveways, walkways, and patios are laid with poured concrete or asphalt, rainwater is shed from the surface, down into the gutter along the street, and into the municipal storm sewer and/or nearby rivers and lakes. During heavy rains, this runoff unnecessarily burdens sewer systems and contributes to flooding problems. It also pollutes natural bodies of water with fertilizers, oil, and other contaminants carried off of the paved surfaces. An effective solution to this common problem is to use permeable paving that allows rainwater to percolate into the ground, purifying the water in the process and replenishing subsurface groundwater.

Made with locally produced pavers, this circular patio has the added benefit of permeability to reduce water runoff so it can remain in the yard.

Choosing a Decking Material

The beauty of natural wood decking is undeniable, but so is the fact that that beauty comes with some drawbacks. In most climates, cedar and redwood decking must be refinished every two years or so to retain the desirable coloring and delay the natural decay of the material. This typically involves cleaning the wood with bleach and/or applying a chemical brightener, followed by a heavy coating of exterior stain. Most conventional stains are solvent-based and contain mildewcide and other chemicals that can pollute the air, your landscape, and your home.

Cedar and redwood are naturally rot-resistant species. Higher grades of decking are cut from the heartwood at the center of the tree and are more resistant to rot than lower grades cut from the outer sapwood. This means that the better stuff comes from more mature trees and places greater stress on old-growth forests. The other type of decking is pressure-treated lumber, which comes from pine, fir, and other species of trees and must be chemically treated to withstand outdoor exposure; see Pressure-treated Lumber, on page 177.

If you're using cedar or redwood decking (or even imported hardwoods like Ipé), the only green options are materials from FSC-certified sources (see page 13) or reclaimed lumber. You can also choose a low-toxicity, low-VOC stain/protectant for the decking. However, durability is still an issue, as wood decking often lasts only eight to ten years in many climates. That's why many green builders and homeowners are switching from solid wood decking to products made with recycled plastics. Many of these materials require no stain or sealer and can last 25 years or longer. But once again proving that there is no perfect solution, once composite decking is no longer usable it cannot be further recycled and degrades very slowly.

Wood composite decking is the most popular alternative to solid wood. It's typically made with recycled plastic and recycled or virgin wood fibers. The plastic gives the decking rot resistance, while the wood gives it strength, UV-protection, and a pleasing texture and appearance. Both plastic and wood composite decking can be cut, milled, and fastened just like wood decking. They're also highly resistant to cracking, splitting, and fading, unlike solid wood. Some decking products are made with vinyl and offer similar durability to other plastic decking, but the potential health risks of PVC make it undesirable as a decking material (see The Great Vinyl Debate on page 78). For installation tips and more information on working with composite decking, turn to the project on pages 178 to 180.

Today's plastic and wood composite decking products come in a range of colors and textures and have a much more natural look and feel than many earlier versions.

Permeable Paving Options

If you're building a new patio or replacing your driveway, you can choose from a wide range of materials that offer strength, durability, and permeability. Patio surfaces laid over a sand-and-gravel base can be made with brick, stone, concrete pavers, adobe block, or even a loose material such as crushed stone, gravel, or river rock. You can also combine any of these materials to create custom designs or to provide different surfaces for different uses. Brick and stone can be especially green options if you use salvaged materials. The projects on pages 182 to 185 show you what's involved in laying several popular patio materials. The same installation steps and materials can be used for building walkways and garden paths.

Driveways must be stronger than patios, but many of the same materials can be used to create a beautiful and water-permeable surface. Concrete pavers and some types of brick are the most popular alternative materials for driveways, while homes in more natural or rural settings may have driveways of crushed stone or recycled concrete. Another option to consider is a turf block driveway. Turf blocks are strong concrete units with a web-like or grid structure that allows turf or ground cover plants to grow up through the blocks' cavities. The holes can also be filled with gravel and other loose materials. Due to the large size and strength requirements of driveways, most homeowners opt to have them installed by professionals.

Sand-set brick and other paving materials make for beautiful, long-lasting surfaces that let rainwater return to the ground where it belongs.

Turf block driveways and paths offer a distinctive, natural appearance by combining the rigidity of concrete and the softness and greenery of real plantings.

Pressure-Treated Lumber ▸

Any pressure-treated lumber you buy should carry a label or stamp indicating the type of chemical treatment used and the appropriate use of the lumber: either "Above ground" or "Ground contact." Use ground contact material for any pieces that will be buried or come within 12" of the ground.

Most structural lumber used outdoors is pressure-treated SPF (spruce/pine/fir). This means the wood has been permeated with a chemical treatment applied under pressure in a special facility. Pressure treatment makes wood species like pine, fir, larch, and other varieties highly resistant to rot from moisture and to bug infestation. In most areas, treated lumber is stronger, more plentiful, and less expensive than naturally rot-resistant species like redwood and cedar. For these reasons, treated lumber is preferred for structural members, such as the supporting posts and joists of a deck.

Prior to 2004, most pressure-treated lumber was treated with CCA (chromated copper arsenic). Due to concerns about chemicals—particularly arsenic—leaching out from the lumber, the EPA banned CCA-treated lumber for most residential applications, effective at the end of 2003. So if you buy pressure-treated material today

at your local lumberyard, what will you get? Most likely wood treated with ACQ (ammoniacal copper quarternary) or possibly CBA (copper boron azole), which have no arsenic or chromium and are considered safer than CCA. How safe are they? No one really knows yet. They haven't been in use long enough to support extensive testing in practical applications.

Given the lack of evidence surrounding the health risks of exposure to pressure-treated lumber, you may want to play it safe by avoiding its use in high-contact areas, such as deck railings, seats or benches, and tabletops. Also follow the EPA's recommendations for handling and disposing of treated lumber. Because ACQ and CBA treatments are corrosive to steel, use stainless steel or hot-dipped galvanized fasteners, or use the lumber manufacturer's recommended fasteners. Aluminum fasteners generally are not recommended.

Composite Decking

When it's time to replace worn wood decking, you can do yourself and the environment a favor by using wood-plastic composite (or solid plastic) decking instead of solid wood. Unlike traditional wood decking, plastic composite material doesn't need to be stained or sealed and won't flake or splinter as it ages. Composite decking can also be made with high percentages of recycled content and may be guaranteed for 25 years or more.

When choosing a new decking material, compare products for appearance, slip-resistance, texture, and durability. Many manufacturers also offer complete railing systems, as well as trim materials such as fascia boards for covering the visible parts of a deck's understructure. Wood composite materials cut and install much like conventional wood lumber, but it's important to follow the manufacturer's directions for fastening and gapping the members, as plastic expands and contracts somewhat with changes in outdoor temperature. Shown here are some general tips to follow when installing wood-composite decking. *Note: As of this writing, structurally rated composite lumber in not yet available commercially, but all indications suggest that it will hit the market in the very near future.*

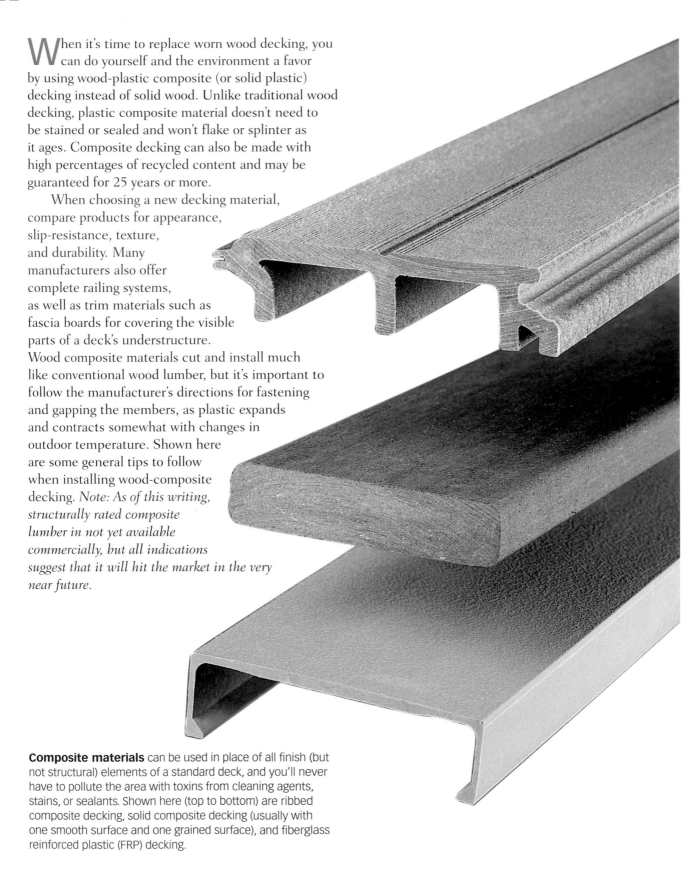

Composite materials can be used in place of all finish (but not structural) elements of a standard deck, and you'll never have to pollute the area with toxins from cleaning agents, stains, or sealants. Shown here (top to bottom) are ribbed composite decking, solid composite decking (usually with one smooth surface and one grained surface), and fiberglass reinforced plastic (FRP) decking.

How to Install Composite Decking

Lay composite decking as you would wood decking. Position with the factory crown up so water will run off, and space rows ⅛" to ¼" apart for drainage.

Predrill pilot holes at 75% of the diameter of the fasteners, but do not countersink. Composite materials allow fasteners to set themselves. Use spiral shank nails, hot-dipped galvanized ceramic coated screws, or stainless steel nails or deck screws.

Cut away for clarity

Alternate method: Attach composite decking with self-tapping composite screws. These specially designed screws require no pilot holes. If the decking "mushrooms" over the screw head, use a hammer to tap back in place.

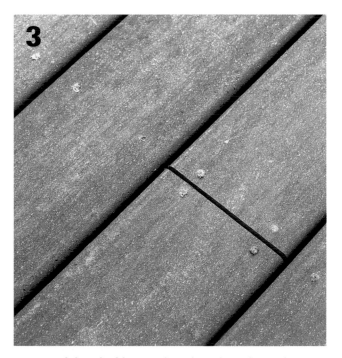

Lay remaining decking. For boards 16-ft. or shorter, leave a gap at deck ends and any butt joints, ¹⁄₁₆" for every 20°F difference between the temperature at the time of installation and the expected high temperature for the year.

How to Install Tongue & Groove Composite Decking

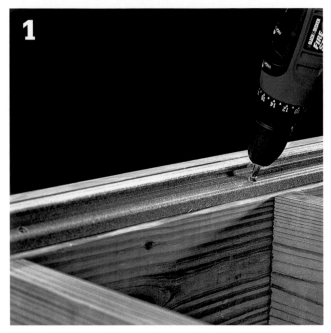

Position starter strip at far end of deck. Make sure it is straight and properly aligned. Attach with 2½" galvanized deck screws driven into the lower runner found under the lip of the starter strip.

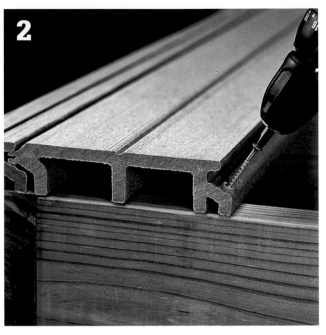

Fit tongue of a deck board into groove of starter strip. There will be approximately a ¼" gap between the deck board and the starter strip. Fasten the deck board to the joists with 2½" galvanized deck screws, working from the middle out to the sides of the deck.

Continue to add decking. To lay deck boards end-to-end, leave a ⅛" gap between them, and make sure any butt joints are centered over a joist.

Place final deck board and attach with 2½" galvanized deck screws driven through top of the deck board into the joist. If necessary, rip final board to size, then support the board with a length of 1 × 1 and attach both to the joist. Attach facing boards to conceal exposed ends.

Composite Fencing ▶

Composite (wood and resin) material is a good green choice for fence material (see Resources, page 237) for the same reasons it makes sense for decking and deck rails. The installation techniques vary a lot among manufacturers, but most composite fence systems are DIY-friendly. Like most, the Trex system seen here (See Resources, page 237) is supported by hollow post sleeves that fit over 4 × 4 treated wood posts that are set in concrete. The rails are reinforced with aluminum rails in this system so each section of fence can span up to 8 ft. without sagging. More inexpensive rails are reinforced with wood or require intermediate support from below. Most composite fence systems include an array of rail and post cap options, and some have optional matching gates available.

Fence posts are made by cladding 4 × 4 wood posts with a composite sleeve and setting it in concrete. This allows you to hang aluminum reinforced fence rails from the posts.

Interlocking composite fence panels are installed one at a time to create a board and batten effect.

Cap rails are attached to the rail hanger bracket with screws made for composite materials.

Permeable Patio Surfaces

Creating a new patio or walkway made of brick or concrete pavers, stone, or loose materials is a great do-it-yourself project that allows for design flexibility and an easy construction pace. These materials are preferable to impervious concrete and asphalt paving because they help keep landscape pollutants and rainwater out of public systems and return water to the ground to replenish aquifers.

A basic patio project begins with laying out the site and excavating the ground for a foundation of compacted gravel, followed by landscape fabric and a layer of sand for setting the paving material. Surfaces made with loose material, such as crushed stone or river rock, typically have a 2" compacted foundation layer over landscape fabric. This gets topped with a 1" to 2" layer of the surface material.

The main steps for preparing the site and installing various paving materials are shown here. Whatever paving surface you choose, be sure to grade the excavated ground so it's smooth and flat and slopes down and away from your house at a rate of ⅛" per foot.

PEEL-AWAY VIEW OF A PERMEABLE PATIO

Pavers

Sand

Water-permeable landscape fabric

Gravel

In a permeable patio, a gravel base provides stability while letting water pass through to the ground. A sand layer helps to level and secure paving materials and allows you to re-level the surface as needed. For a paving border, you can use a row of stone or pavers, or install plastic edging that can be covered with grass or other material.

Tips for Preparing a Site for Paving ▸

Low end

High end

Lay out the excavation site using stakes and mason's strings. Level the strings with a line level, then adjust the strings on the low side of the patio to establish the proper slope.

Add a 4" layer of compactible gravel, then tamp the base thoroughly with a hand tamp or rented plate compactor. Cover the base with landscape fabric, then install a border.

Add a layer of sand and use a long screed board set on pipes or side runners to smooth and level the surface. Brick and concrete pavers call for a 1" layer of sand; natural flagstone needs 2".

Install edging and fill in pavers. Although plastic landscape edging is used most often, try laying some of the pavers on edge or on-end to for a slightly greener solution.

Installing Paving Materials

Set paving materials into the sand layer according to your desired pattern. Brick and concrete pavers typically have spacing lugs on their side edges to create consistent gaps between the units.

Complete the installation by sweeping sand into the joints between paving units. Tamp the surface if recommended, then soak the patio with water to settle the sand. Repeat until the joints are full.

Installing Loose-Fill Patio Materials

Prepare the subbase as for pavers and install edging, preferably non plastic.

Set rows of pavers inside the excavation area in a pleasing pattern with plenty of space between rows.

Add surface material such as loose rock or gravel or even mulch between the rows of pavers. Tamp masonry materials with a hand tamper.

How to Install Sandset Flagstones

Arrange naturally shaped flagstones next to the patio site to complete most of the puzzle work before the installation. For best appearance, distribute small and large stones evenly to avoid a lopsided layout.

Place the stones in the sand bed and set them firmly with a rubber mallet.

Set a straightedge across sections of the stone to make sure the general surface is even.

Fill the joints with sand, packing with your hand. Spray the patio with water to settle the sand into the joints (inset).

Option: For planting between stones, fill the joints with a soil mixture suited to the type of plants you'll use.

Heating, Cooling & Ventilation

Heating and cooling systems are by far the biggest energy users in the average home. And while humans have been heating their dwellings in one way or another since the beginning of time, air conditioning has become standard only in the last half-century or so. Is this because we've just grown soft and simply refuse to tolerate hot weather? Well, yes. But more tellingly, it shows how our time indoors is increasingly spent in isolation from the natural world, making us more dependent upon mechanical "life support" to stay comfortable.

Not surprisingly, green philosophy aims to reverse this trend of isolation. In a green home, heating and cooling is more closely linked to natural patterns of sunlight and daily changes in outdoor air temperature. And when help from powered systems is required, as it almost always is, steps are taken to ensure equipment is working as efficiently as possible. By implementing some simple, low-cost solutions for reducing your home's heating and cooling loads, you'll get the most from your energy dollars. You'll also see how a back-to-basics approach is the best plan for a green future.

In this chapter:
- **Understanding Your Home's Circulatory System**
- **Cooling a Green Home**
- **Ceiling Fans**
- **Efficient Home Heating**
- **Programmable Thermostats**

Understanding Your Home's Circulatory System

Like the human body, a house relies on circulation to maintain comfortable temperatures. Your body circulates blood to regulate temperature, while your home circulates air. Therefore, thinking about airflow in and out of your home is the key to understanding heating and cooling systems.

Heating a home is a relatively simple process. The primary heat source—a furnace or boiler in most cases—burns fuel to heat air or water and sends it throughout the house to raise the temperature of the ambient air. The efficiency and effectiveness of the heating system depends primarily on how well the heat source converts fuel into heat and how well

the home retains the heated air. Proper circulation is important, too, because it makes sure the heat gets to the right places.

Keeping heat (and cold) inside your home is the main reason behind insulating, weatherizing, and installing high-performance windows. This is also the biggest step you can take toward improving your home's energy efficiency—and your comfort. The next most important step is making sure your heating system is working as well as it should. Even simple measures like regular maintenance and sealing ductwork can make a big difference in a system's performance.

The circulation of air through your home is critical to home health and system efficiency. The furnace and central air conditioner are the heart of the system, but ductwork, air exchangers, ventilation appliances, and supplementary heating plants all factor into the operation of the whole house.

To cool a home mechanically, you have to pull the hot air from the house, extract the heat and water vapor from the air, then pump the cooled air back in. With conventional air conditioners, this is accomplished with special refrigerants and a considerable amount of electricity. It is much like the process used in your car AC and your kitchen refrigerator. As with heating, a tight building envelope and properly tuned equipment are critical factors in determining a home's cooling efficiency.

Cooling a home naturally or with low-impact equipment such as window and ceiling fans is much simpler. During the day, you keep the hot air outside by closing up the windows and blocking direct sunlight with shades. As soon as the outdoor air temperature drops below the indoor temperature, you open the windows and flush the house with fresh air. The best part is, natural convection is working with you, as the hot air is already trying to get out and just needs some openings to do so. Cooling through convection is most effective in climates with relatively low humidity and relatively large changes in daily temperature.

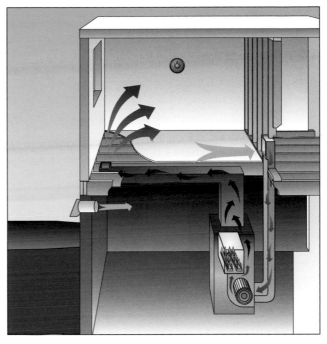

Forced-air heating systems (the most common type in American homes) blow heated air into living spaces, where it rises up toward the ceiling. As the air cools, it drops down and is drawn into return ducts and back to the furnace.

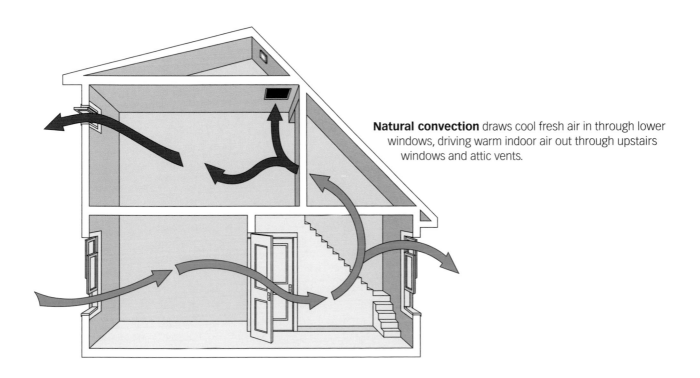

Natural convection draws cool fresh air in through lower windows, driving warm indoor air out through upstairs windows and attic vents.

Cooling a Green Home

Total reliance on electricity to cool homes is one area where modern architecture and living habits have gone awry. For centuries, homes were designed to suit the local climate, incorporating elements like verandas, overhangs, and breezeways to provide shade and promote natural cooling ventilation. As mechanical systems become standard features, architects and builders abandoned vernacular designs in favor of generic, hard-to-cool homes that, ironically, are ill-suited to virtually every climate. At the same time, homeowners have grown to demand instant, convenient comfort at all hours, and this is really possible only through artificial means.

Of course, air conditioning was only one factor in the dumbing down of conventional home design, but today it continues to create significant environmental problems. Excessive energy use during heat waves causes brownouts and blackouts in densely populated areas, while most air-conditioning equipment still uses ozone-depleting HCFC refrigerants. The Department of Energy reports that ⅔ of all homes in the U.S. have air conditioners, accounting for 5% of the nation's total electricity production. For each home with air conditioning, about two tons of carbon dioxide (a greenhouse gas) is released into the atmosphere every year.

Getting through the cooling season with little or no air conditioning is a good goal for any home but especially for a green one. Here are some tips and ideas for keeping the heat down without cranking up the AC:

Take advantage of nature. Few home improvements will lower your cooling energy consumption more than simply planting fast-growing shade trees around your house. The broad deciduous leaves of an elm, for example, provide cooling shade in the summer but gracefully go away in the fall so passive solar energy can help heat your house in the winter.

Preventing Heat Buildup

Your house warms up through a combination of indoor and outdoor heat sources. Reducing heat gain as needed on a daily basis makes natural cooling possible in many climates, and it lowers the demand for air conditioning in hot, humid areas.

The main sources of indoor heat are light fixtures, hot water, and appliances. Standard incandescent lightbulbs waste 90% to 95% of their energy in the form of heat, while only 5% to 10% is used to produce light. Switching to fluorescent bulbs throughout the house dramatically reduces heat gain through light fixtures (see page 207 for more information on choosing lighting products). Also, get into the habit of turning off the lights when they're not needed, and use focused task lighting for specific work areas in place of general room lighting.

Hot water from showering, bathing, dishwashing, and clothes washing adds heat and warm water vapor to your home's atmosphere. Whenever possible, run dishwashers and clothes washers during cooler times of the day, or use cold water for washing clothes. When showering or bathing, open bathroom windows and use a ventilation fan to get rid of heat and water vapor.

All electric appliances produce heat. The more energy-efficient a model is, the less waste heat it produces. When it's time to replace an appliance, choosing Energy Star models not only saves money on energy bills, it also helps minimize indoor heat gain. Cooking appliances and clothes dryers add significant amounts of heat to a home. During hot weather, plan meals to avoid using the oven or boiling water for long periods, and use the microwave or cook outdoors as much as possible. Run clothes dryers during cooler hours of the day, or better yet, dry laundry outside on a clothesline.

The main source of heat from outside the home is, of course, the sun. Solar heat gets into your house through convection—by heating up the walls and roof, through infiltration of heated outdoor air, and through direct radiation by shining through windows. Also, as outdoor elements and structures heat up during the day, they can radiate some of that heat into the home through infrared light. There are a number of steps you can take to minimize these ever-present heat sources.

Hot enough to bake a cake. Remember those toy ovens that bake a real, miniature cake? Their only heat source is a single incandescent lightbulb. Switching to a better light generating technology saves cooling energy as well as lighting energy.

Unload old appliances. Inefficient appliances, especially refrigerators, emit significant amounts of heat into the room. Waste heat can also be minimized by turning off computers, printers, and other electronics when not in use.

(continued)

COOLING WITH PLANTS

Trees, shrubs, grass, and other plantings lower the air temperature around a home through transpiration (the plant equivalent of sweating). Trees are also highly effective for shading walls, windows, and roofs. However, on the south-facing side of a house, it's usually better to use awnings to shade windows instead of trees. Because the sun passes more or less directly overhead in summer months, south-facing walls receive less exposure than east- and west-facing walls. Awnings block direct sunlight in summer but not in winter, when the sun is lower in the sky.

BLOCKING & REFLECTING SUNLIGHT

High-performance windows with low-E coatings reduce heat gain from sunlight. As for shading windows, light-blocking and insulated window coverings are reasonably effective, while exterior shades keep more of the sun's heat outside and reduce heat gained through conduction.

Roofs are exposed to the sun's hottest midday rays and can account for up to ⅔ of a home's solar heat gain. Many roofing manufacturers offer light-reflecting roofing to reduce heat absorption, as well as heat-reflective membranes (often called radiant barriers) that are installed underneath roofing materials. Clay tile and metal roofing help reduce heat gain because they install with an air space between the roofing and structural roof decking. But unless you're replacing your roof, the best ways to lower indoor temperatures is through attic and roof insulation and attic ventilation. Hot air that's trapped in the attic conducts heat down through ceiling surfaces. Insulation above the top-floor ceilings stops this heat migration, while attic ventilation helps rid the attic of hot air through natural convection.

Painting your exterior walls with light-colored paint helps reflect heat away from the house. Dark colors absorb more heat and can speed the deterioration of siding materials in addition to increasing solar heat gain inside the house. Insulation in exterior walls also helps reduce heat gain.

A solar-powered attic vent fan is one green option for cooling down your attic. Models are available for both roof and gable mounting; see www.airvent.com.

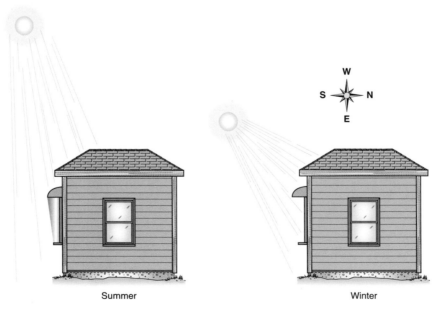

Summer

Winter

Awnings on south-facing windows minimize heat gain during summer but not in winter, when the lower angle of the sun's rays allows light to shine in under the awning.

COOLING WITH AIR CIRCULATION & VENTILATION

As people without air conditioning know, a home can be effectively cooled with windows and a little help from the wind and strategically placed fans. The key to cooling the whole house lies in flushing out the hot indoor air and replacing it with cooler outdoor air. During the day, when outdoor temperatures are as high or higher than the indoor temperature, you can help your body cool itself with air circulation provided by ceiling fans or freestanding fans.

The Chimney Effect. Because hot air rises, opening windows in the basement or lower levels of a house and windows in upper floors or the attic naturally draws cool up through the house, a process known as the chimney effect (see the illustration on page 194). Operable skylights or roof windows in an attic or cathedral ceiling are especially effective for inducing this effect. You can also speed this ventilation process with out-blowing fans in upper-level windows.

Windows & Window Fans. Rooms with windows on opposing or even adjacent walls can be ventilated much more quickly than rooms with only one window. This is due to the simple fact that air takes up space. In order to bring fresh outdoor air into a room, you have to get rid of an equal quantity of indoor air. When the same opening is used for both intake and exhaust, the exchange of air is greatly reduced (for the same reason, clearing the air in a bathroom with a vent fan is much faster if you leave the door ajar than if you close it completely).

It's important to plan for air exchange when cooling with windows and fans. Taking advantage of cool evening breezes is most effective when windows are open on both the windward and lee sides of the house. When the air outside is still, window fans can create the same effect. Place intake fans (blowing in) on the cooler side of the house (usually the east side or a side closest to a shaded part of the yard), and place exhaust fans (blowing out) on the opposite side; be sure to open all doors in between. Avoid working against prevailing winds by placing intake fans on the windward sides of the house.

Double-hung windows—in which the top and bottom sash open independently—create their own cross-ventilation (or stack ventilation) by pulling outdoor air in through the lower half and exhausting indoor air through the top. Doors with operable transom or awning windows above work the same way.

Reversible window fans offer convenience because you can change the direction of airflow without flipping the fan. For best results, window fans should cover as much of the opening as possible.

Whole-house Ventilation. The most effective way to night-flush a house with cool outdoor air is by using a whole-house fan. This is a powerful electric fan mounted horizontally into an upper-floor ceiling, typically in a hallway or other centrally located common area. When the fan is on, air is pulled in through open windows and sent into the attic where it escapes through gable or roof vents. This is the best way to ventilate a house because it draws from every open window at once and takes advantage of the chimney effect. It also drives accumulated heat from the attic.

Whole-house fans are not difficult or expensive to install, but you should consult an HVAC expert for help with sizing the fan and making sure your attic has enough vents for proper circulation. Also be sure to choose a fan with air-sealed louvers or a removable cover to prevent air infiltration during the heating season.

Another option for whole-house ventilation is to use an existing forced-air duct system to circulate fresh air to rooms and exhaust indoor air out through the attic. This type of system is typically powered by circulation equipment installed in the attic and draws fresh air through an intake port. Consult with a few local HVAC specialists to have your home and ductwork assessed for suitability for this type of system.

CEILING FANS

Ceiling fans are popular home fixtures throughout the world, a fact that speaks to their effectiveness in all types of climates. While ceiling fans don't actually lower the temperature in a room, they circulate air around your skin, which helps your body get rid of excess heat to cool you down. This also means that there's no point in leaving a ceiling fan running when no one is in the room.

Ceiling fans are effective in both air conditioned and naturally cooled homes. In fact, it's commonly estimated that running a ceiling fan while the air conditioning is on allows you to raise the thermostat by 4° F with no loss of comfort. This can yield substantial savings on monthly energy use and cooling costs (fans in general are quite energy-efficient, especially compared to air-conditioning equipment).

Most ceiling fans are reversible. In the summer, air is pulled up to the ceiling, where it travels out to the walls then down into the room to create general circulation. In winter, fans should be set on low speed blowing downward. This pushes heated air that would otherwise be trapped along the ceiling down into the living space. That's why rooms with high cathedral ceilings very often have ceiling fans. See the project on pages 196 to 197 for more information on choosing and installing a ceiling fan.

Whole-house fans quickly flush the house with outdoor air by pulling from open windows and sending air through a well-vented attic.

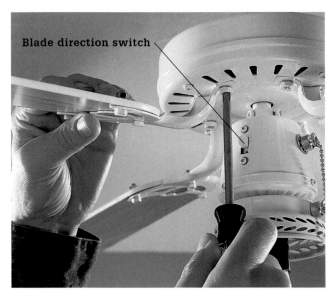

If you don't already have ceiling fans in your home, you'd be surprised at how much they can improve your comfort. Make sure to adjust your fans to draw warm air up in the summer and force warm air downward in the winter. *Tip: Test the blade screws for tightness every time you make an adjustment.*

Choosing a High-Efficiency Air Conditioner ▸

If you're not ready to go AC-free and it's time to replace your old unit, here's what to look for in a new energy-efficient model:

SEER OF 14 OR HIGHER
Central air conditioners are rated for efficiency by their seasonal energy efficiency ratio, or SEER. Federal minimums placed in 2006 mean all new central models have at least SEER 13, but better units are available at up to SEER 21.

EER OF 11 OR HIGHER
When shopping for a room air conditioner, look for models with an energy efficiency ratio (EER) of at least 11.

ADVANCED FAN FEATURES
Blower fans with variable speed can improve efficiency in hot, humid climates. Often, these have a humidistat that adjusts the fan speed based on humidity levels in the system. A fan-only switch allows you to ventilate the home during cooler hours without running AC. An auto-delay switch keeps a fan running for a few minutes after the compressor has shut off so residual cold is not wasted.

OZONE-FRIENDLY REFRIGERANT
Most standard air conditioners use an HCFC refrigerant (such as R-22), which contributes to the destruction of the ozone layer when released into the atmosphere. But several manufacturers have switched to HFC refrigerants (such as R-410A), which do not deplete the ozone.

However they will act as greenhouse gases if released into the air. CFC-free R-404 refrigerant is also available in a limited range of products.

ALTERNATIVES TO STANDARD COMPRESSOR SYSTEMS
If you're adding a new system, take a look at energy-efficient alternatives to standard compressor-based equipment. In dry climates, evaporative coolers, which use water instead of refrigerant to cool the air, can be much more efficient than standard systems. In mild climates, many homes rely on heat pumps (available in air-source types and geothermal types) for both cooling and heating

When choosing new equipment, be sure to consider lifetime operating cost. Energy-efficient air conditioners often have a higher initial point-of-purchase cost, but they more than make up for this over time because they use less electricity than standard models. For more information on choosing new air conditioners and HVAC contractors, visit the websites of Energy Star (www.energystar.gov) and the American Council for an Energy-Efficient Economy (www.aceee.org). It's also important to have the equipment installed and serviced by qualified professionals, because proper sizing and calibration of cooling systems are critical to their energy performance. Also check with your utility provider for available rebates and incentives for switching to high-efficiency cooling products.

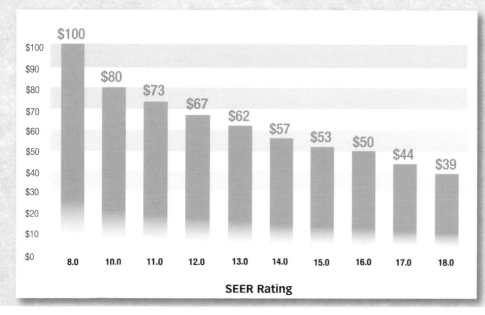

For every $100 spent to cool your home using an 8 SEER air conditioner, a 14 SEER air conditioner should cost you approximately $57. Actual savings will depend on the efficiency of your current system compared to the efficiency of a new system.

Source: Carrier Corporation

Ceiling Fans

Ceiling fans are available in several sizes and a huge range of styles, with or without integrated light fixtures. Consult manufacturers' literature for sizing recommendations. Rooms longer than 18 ft. generally require two fans. New fans with an Energy Star rating are typically 20% more energy-efficient than comparable standard models. Control options include pull-chain switches, wall switches with multiple speed settings, and remote control.

For optimal circulation, install your fan so the blades are seven to nine feet above the floor and 10" to 12" below the ceiling.

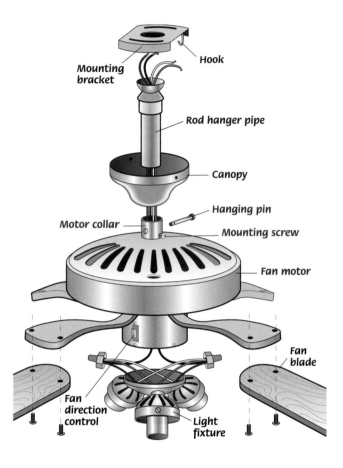

Tools & Materials ▸

Stepladder
Screwdrivers
Wire stripper
Pliers or
   adjustable wrench
Neon circuit tester
Hammer
Ceiling fan-light kit
2 × 4 lumber or
   adjustable ceiling
   fan cross brace
1½" and 3"
   wallboard screws

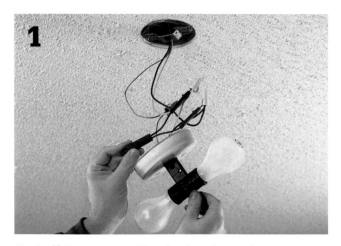

Shut off the power to the circuit at the service panel. Unscrew the existing fixture and carefully pull it away from the ceiling. Do not touch bare wires. Test for power by inserting the probes of a neon circuit tester into the wire connectors on the black and white wires. If the tester lights, return to the service panel and turn off the correct circuit. Disconnect the wire connectors and remove the old fixture.

Due to the added weight and vibration of a ceiling fan, you must determine whether the existing electrical box will provide adequate support. If you can access the box from the attic, check to see that it is metal, not plastic, and that it has a heavy-duty crossbrace rated for ceiling fans. If the box is not adequately braced, cut a 2 × 4 to fit between the joists and attach it with 3" screws. Attach a metal electrical box to the brace from below with at least three 1½" wallboard screws. Attach the fan mounting bracket to the box.

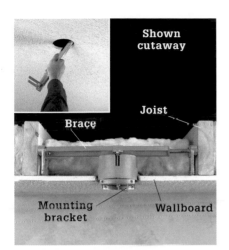

Variation: If the joists are inaccessible from above, remove the old box and install an adjustable ceiling fan brace through the rough opening in the ceiling. Insert the fan brace through the hole, adjust until it fits tightly between the joists, then attach the box with the included hardware. Make sure the lip of the box is flush with the ceiling wallboard before attaching the mounting bracket.

Run the wires from the top of the fan motor through the canopy and then through the rod hanger pipe. Slide the rod hanger pipe through the canopy and attach the pipe to the motor collar using the included hanging pin. Tighten the mounting screws firmly.

Hang the motor assembly by the hook on the mounting bracket. Connect the wires according to manufacturer's directions using wire connectors to join the fixture wires to the circuit wires in the box. Gather the wires together and tuck them inside the fan canopy. Lift the canopy and attach it to the mounting bracket.

Remote control variation: To install a remote control, fit the receiver inside the fan canopy. Follow the manufacturer's wiring diagram to wire the unit. The receiver has a set of three wires that connects to the corresponding wires from the fan motor and lights, and another set that connects to the two circuit wires from the electrical box.

Attach the fan blades one at a time with the included hardware. Follow the manufacturer's directions.

Connect the wiring for the fan's light fixture according to the manufacturer's directions. Tuck all wires into the switch housing and attach the fixture. Install lightbulbs and globes. Restore power and test the fan. If the fan vibrates excessively, check the manufacturer's documentation to adjust the balance. If the fan doesn't run at all, turn off the power and check the wiring connections.

Efficient Home Heating

In the average home, 52% of the energy used is devoted to space heating, which is probably the main reason why so many people can justify expensive upgrades like new windows. And good windows, along with adding insulation and stopping air leaks, are the most effective steps you can take in an existing home toward lowering heating costs and reducing your home's environmental impact.

All of these steps help minimize the amount of heated air that escapes your home, making your living spaces more comfortable with less applied heat. Thinking in the opposite direction, you can also add windows in strategic areas to bring in more solar heat during the day. A well-insulated home designed for passive solar heating may use only a fraction of the supplemental heat that a conventionally built home requires.

But even if you're not ready for a major remodel or big energy-saving improvements, there are several things you can do to reduce heat losses and enhance the performance of your heating system. The information here applies to the two most common types of home heating systems: forced-air (furnace) and hydronic (hot water). For a discussion of supplemental heating systems, including high-efficiency gas fireplaces and wood stoves, turn to pages 152-154.

Sealing & Insulating Ductwork

Often some of the biggest heat losses in forced-air systems are through duct joints and through the walls of ductwork in unheated parts of the home. Poorly sealed and unsealed joints can allow 15% to 20% of the heated supply air to leak into spaces where the heat can't be used, and they contribute to dust buildup in the duct network.

If you live in an older home, chances are the metal ductwork was not sealed, causing significant leakage at joints where straight duct runs meet bends, register boots, and other fittings. In the old days, HVAC contractors may have used standard duct tape to seal joints. Ironically, this all-purpose tape that's great for quick fixes throughout the house is unsuitable for ductwork: It dries out and can begin to fall off after just a few years. These days, the standard for sealing is duct mastic, a flexible, water-based adhesive that gets into the cracks of joints to create a complete air seal. You can apply duct mastic yourself following the manufacturer's directions.

Insulating ductwork in cold spaces stops heat from escaping through the walls of the ducts.

Ducts can also be sealed with UL-181 certified duct tape, which won't dry and flake off like standard duct tape but is generally less effective than mastic. Another option is to have an HVAC professional blow a latex aerosol into the ductwork, which seals gaps from the inside; for more information, visit www.aeroseal.com.

Most ducts in a forced-air system are made with thin metal that moves air efficiently but is highly heat-conductive. As heated air passes through supply (hot-air) ducts, 10% to 30% of the heat can be lost through conduction, and the losses are greatest where ducts run through unheated basements, crawlspaces,

and attics. Newer homes often have insulated supply ducts, while older homes often do not.

A simple solution for reducing this heat loss is to wrap the outsides of all supply ducts with an approved insulation and seal the seams with tape. In cold climates, insulation with R values of 5 to 8 (R-5 to R-8) is recommended. You can use foil-faced batt insulation (with the foil facing out) or use rigid insulation board, sealing the seams on either type with UL-181 duct tape. There are also vinyl-faced products made just for ductwork, which should be sealed following the manufacturer's recommendations.

Stop air leakage in duct joints by sealing them with a water-based duct mastic (See Resources, page 237). This is much more effective and long-lasting than standard duct tape.

Zone Heating

Zone heating involves various system controls to heat specific areas of the home more than others, rather than supplying full heat to all rooms at all times. With forced-air systems, zoning can be achieved with multiple thermostats that regulate hot-air supply with automatic duct dampers (a damper is a flap inside a duct that can be opened or closed incrementally to limit airflow as needed). A simpler method is to adjust dampers manually to restrict airflow to seldom-used spaces or to rooms that receive more passive solar heat during the day.

Most hydronic heating systems are set up with multiple zones. Each zone is controlled by a separate thermostat. If a system is poorly designed or doesn't supply heat where you want it most, you can have a plumber or HVAC professional modify the system to add zones or install supplemental heating units to specific areas. An example of the latter is a dedicated hot-water loop that feeds a small radiator or convector in a kitchen or remote room.

Programmable Thermostats

Programmable thermostats can reduce heating costs and energy use with most types of forced-air and hydronic systems. The main benefit of programmable thermostats is that they control your heating system automatically, so you'll never forget to lower the thermostat when you leave the house for the day. You can also set your thermostats to turn on the heat just before you get up in the morning and shortly before you go to bed at night.

Programmable thermostats that qualify for Energy Star meet strict government standards for energy efficiency and have at least four settings for regulating your heat during the week and on weekends. Installing a programmable thermostat is an easy do-it-yourself project that can save many homes hundreds of dollars a year or more in energy costs. See pages 202 to 205 for step-by-step instructions.

Advanced digital thermostats allow you to program specific temperature settings for each day of the week and have many other energy-saving features.

Maintaining Your Heating System ▶

Regular maintenance and periodic checkups on your heating system will improve its performance and efficiency and help extend the life of this expensive equipment. Some maintenance can be done by you, while other measures require professional equipment and expertise. Here are some things you can do yourself:

- Balance forced-air systems by identifying which ducts serve the various rooms of the house. Experiment with different damper settings until each space receives the desired amount of heat (see photo, below left).
- Inspect and/or replace your furnace's air filter monthly during the heating season. Better filters keep more dust out of your system—and your indoor air—but some high-efficiency filters may restrict airflow too much for some blower fans.
- Clean forced-air supply registers and grills on cold-air return ports regularly.
- Clean the fins on heating units (convectors) in hydronic systems. These use natural convection to heat the indoor air and don't work properly if airflow through the fins is restricted (see photo, below right)

Balancing a forced-air system: Label each duct for the area it serves, then mark the appropriate position for each damper. Dampers can be adjusted with levers or a screwdriver.

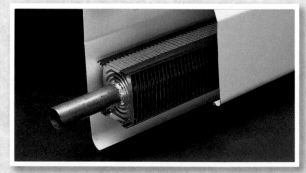

Baseboard and in-floor convectors in modern hydronic systems use thin, metal fins to transfer heat to the air. To clean these units, remove the front cover and carefully vacuum around the fins. Be careful not to bend or scratch the fins.

Choosing a New Furnace or Boiler

A well-maintained furnace can last 15 to 25 years, while boilers can last much longer. However, if your system is inefficient by design or due to its age, it may make sense financially to upgrade to a new high-efficiency unit. From an environmental standpoint, equipment upgrades almost always make sense. A good energy auditor (see pages 218 to 219) or HVAC technician should be able to advise you on the decision of whether to replace your old unit or whether to keep it and spend a little on modifications to improve its efficiency.

New home heating equipment is rated for efficiency by the annual fuel utilization efficiency, or AFUE, system. This is an accurate rating because it takes into account peak combustion efficiency as well as losses during start-up and cool-down times that occur during normal use. Today's best gas furnaces and boilers offer AFUE ratings upwards of 90%, some as high as 96%.

In addition to fuel efficiency, here are some features to look for in a new heating unit:

- Sealed combustion: This means the unit uses direct venting to the outdoors for both air intake and combustion exhaust. Sealed combustion eliminates the risk of backdrafting in negative pressure situations, and it doesn't draw heated indoor air for combustion, for additional energy savings.

- Condensing-type systems: Condensing furnaces and boilers are able to reclaim much of the waste heat from combustion that would otherwise go up the chimney. In conventional equipment, the temperature of exhaust air is around 400° F, while that of condensing units may be as low as 100° F. All of that reclaimed heat goes into your house instead of outside. *Note: Condensing units require specially lined exhaust piping that doesn't corrode due to the increased acidity in the unit's exhaust.*

- Variable speed and energy-efficient fan motor: Premium furnace models may feature an electronically controlled brushless DC motor (one brand name is ECM, for electronically commutated motor). These highly efficient motors automatically adjust their speed based on operating factors, such as heating and cooling requirements and duct pressure, and are most beneficial on systems that run for many hours of the day.

Choose a furnace that is at least 90% efficient and contains a condenser to reclaim heat from condensation in the exhaust pipe (called a condensing furnace).

Heat-Recovery & Energy-Recovery Ventilators ▸

In many of today's airtight homes, forced-air systems play an important role in circulating fresh outdoor air into the living space. During the heating season, replacing heated indoor air with cold outdoor air (and vice versa during the cooling season) reduces efficiency by making the furnace work harder to maintain temperature. Heat-recovery ventilators (HRV) can limit this specific heat loss by up to 90%.

HRVs capture the heat (or cold) from outgoing indoor air and transfer it via a heat exchanger to the incoming air. A similar type of system, called an energy-recovery ventilator (ERV), does the same thing as an HRV but also transfers water vapor to or from the indoor air to help maintain desirable levels of humidity. Most HRVs and ERVs are balanced, meaning the outgoing airflow is equal to the incoming flow. Systems are available with a range of flow capacities and features to suit different HVAC systems and climates.

Programmable Thermostats

Traditional furnace thermostats are low-voltage models that do a simple, but necessary, job. They sense changes in the house air temperature—and when it's too low, the thermostat turns on the heat; when it's too high, the thermostat turns off the heat. For many years this was all we needed to make our homes comfortable and no one gave much thought to improving this performance. Then, fuel shortages and high energy costs made everyone interested in lowering the heating fuel bill.

One innovation that has advanced this effort is the programmable thermostat. This provided more control over furnaces and, as a result, reduced energy consumption. If everyone in the house is gone during the day, there's no reason to keep the heat at 68 or 70 degrees or more. And when everyone goes to sleep at night, these thermostats turn down the heat automatically and turn it back on before anyone gets up. Different models that offer different levels of control are available. Generally, the more capability a unit has, the more it costs. While there is variety in what the units can do, most are easy to install, as shown here.

Tools & Materials ▸

Screwdrivers
Masking tape
Programmable thermostat

Replacing a manual thermostat with a programmable model is a relatively simple job that can have a big payback on heating and cooling energy savings.

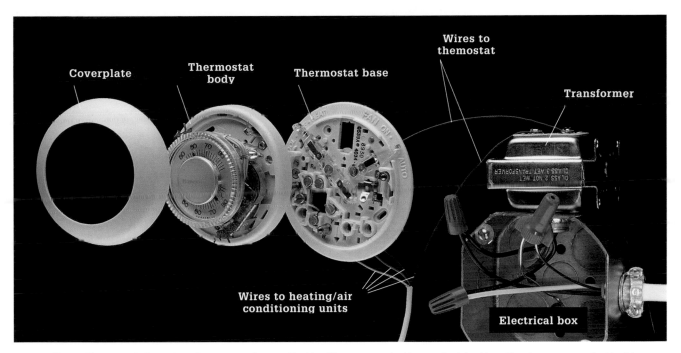

Coverplate

Thermostat body

Thermostat base

Wires to themostat

Transformer

Wires to heating/air conditioning units

Electrical box

Low-voltage thermostat system has a transformer that is either connected to an electrical junction box or mounted inside a furnace access panel. Very thin wires (18 to 22 gauge) send current to the thermostat. The thermostat constantly monitors room temperatures, and sends electrical signals to the heating/cooling unit through additional wires. The number of wires connected to the thermostat varies from two to six, depending on the type of heating/air conditioning system. In the common four-wire system shown above, power is supplied to the thermostat through a single wire attached to screw terminal R. Wires attached to other screw terminals relay signals to the furnace heating unit, the air-conditioning unit, and the blower unit. Before removing a thermostat, make sure to label each wire to identify its screw terminal location.

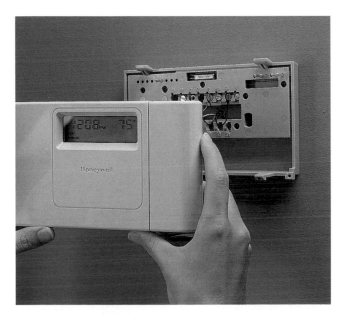

Programmable thermostats contain sophisticated circuitry that allows you to set the heating and cooling systems in your house to adjust automatically at set times of day.

Check Before You Buy ▶

When buying a new thermostat, make sure the new unit is compatible with your heating/air-conditioning system. For reference, bring the brand names and model numbers of the old thermostat, the furnace, and the central air-conditioning unit to the store and provide the information to the sales assistant.

How to Upgrade a Thermostat

Start by removing the existing thermostat. Turn off the power to the furnace at the main service panel. Then, remove the thermostat cover.

The body of the thermostat is held to a wall plate with screws. Remove these screws and pull the body away from the wall plate. Set the body aside.

The low-voltage wires that power the thermostat are held by screw terminals to the mounting plate. Do not remove the wires until you label them with tape, according to the letter printed on the terminal to which each wire is attached.

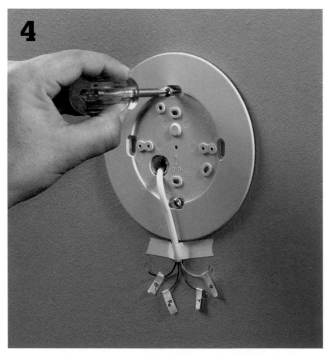

Once all the wires are labeled and removed from the mounting plate, tape the cable that holds these wires to the wall to keep it from falling back into the wall. Then unscrew the mounting plate and set it aside (see sidebar, next page).

5

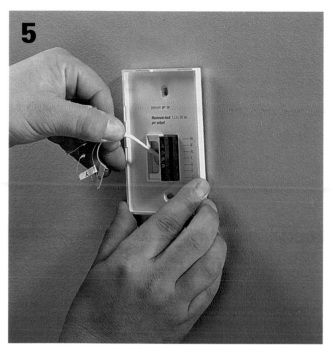

Position the new thermostat base on the wall and guide the wires through the central opening. Screw the base to the wall.

6

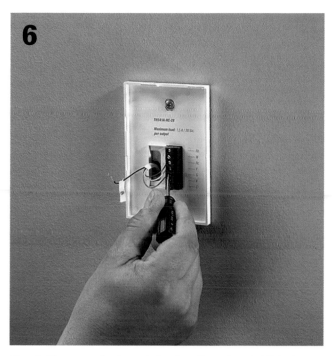

Check the manufacturer's instructions to establish the correct terminal for each low-voltage wire. Then connect the wires to these terminals, making sure each screw is secure.

7

These thermostats require batteries to store the programs so they won't disappear if the electric power goes out in a storm. Make sure to install these batteries before you snap the thermostat cover in place. Then program the new unit to fit your needs and turn on the power to the furnace.

Mercury Thermostats ▸

Older thermostats (and even a few still being made today) often contained one or more small vials of mercury totaling 3 to 4 grams in weight. Because mercury is a highly toxic metal that can cause nerve damage in humans, along with other environmental problems, DO NOT dispose of an old mercury thermostat with your household waste. Instead, bring it to a hazardous waste disposal site or a mercury recycling site, if your area has one (check with your local solid waste disposal agency). The best way to determine if your old thermostat contains mercury is simply to remove the cover and look for the small glass vials or ampules containing the silverish mercury substance. If you are unsure, it is always better to be safe and keep the device in question out of the normal waste stream.

Green Lighting

If Thomas Edison were alive today, he might be surprised to find that most homes are still lighted with essentially the same device he helped to develop in the 1800s. Being a forward-thinking, industrious person, surely he would question why the modern world continued to favor a product that functioned at no better than 10% efficiency. And we of the modern world would have no good explanation for our Fecklessness, except perhaps to say, "Well, at least lightbulbs are cheap." Unfortunately, regular lightbulbs aren't even cheap when you consider their operating cost, which is about three times higher than it needs to be.

Now, if Edison were to visit a green home, he would find, at the very least, some technologically improved lightbulbs and more than likely a thoughtful lighting plan that provides the homeowners with all the lighting they need in just the right places. He might discover innovations like motion detectors and timer switches that control lights automatically, and he would marvel at outdoor fixtures that are fed not by the power grid but by the sun (Eureka!).

But barring the unlikely event of being visited by famous inventors of the past, there are still plenty of reasons to improve the efficiency and quality of lighting in our homes. It's certainly the easiest green step we can take, and if everyone gets involved, the environmental benefits can be enormous.

In this chapter:

- New Fluorescents
- Fluorescent Light Fixtures
- Tubular Skylights

New Fluorescents

By now, everyone is familiar with compact fluorescent lamps (CFLs), those odd pigtailed lightbulbs that are taking the world by storm. If you experimented with them when they first hit the market 10 or 15 years ago, there's a good chance you didn't buy very many of them due to their high cost and the poor quality of light they produced (not to mention the irritating delay from switch-on to lights-on). But that's all changed. Today's instant-on CFLs cost only a fraction of what early versions did, their light quality has improved considerably so it's now much more like the familiar glow of incandescent bulbs, and they are available in a much greater range of shapes and sizes. *For the record*: The lighting industry uses the term "lamp" instead of "bulb" because not all light devices are bulb-shaped. Here the terms are used interchangeably.

If you make only one green improvement in your home, it should be to swap out the incandescent bulbs in your most-used light fixtures with CFLs. The reason for this is obvious when you look at the numbers: CFLs use ⅔ to ¾ less electricity than incandescent bulbs, and they last about eight to 10 times longer. Over the life of a CFL bulb, that translates to a savings of over $30 for a light that's on for two hours a day to over $60 for a light that's on for four hours a day—and that's for just one lightbulb.

On a national scale, the energy savings with CFLs is even more enlightening. According to the Energy Star website: "If every American home replaced just one lightbulb with an Energy Star qualified bulb, we would save enough energy to light more than 3 million homes for a year, more than $600 million in annual energy costs, and prevent greenhouse gases equivalent to the emissions of more than 800,000 cars." To argue with numbers like that, you would have to be a pretty dim bulb indeed.

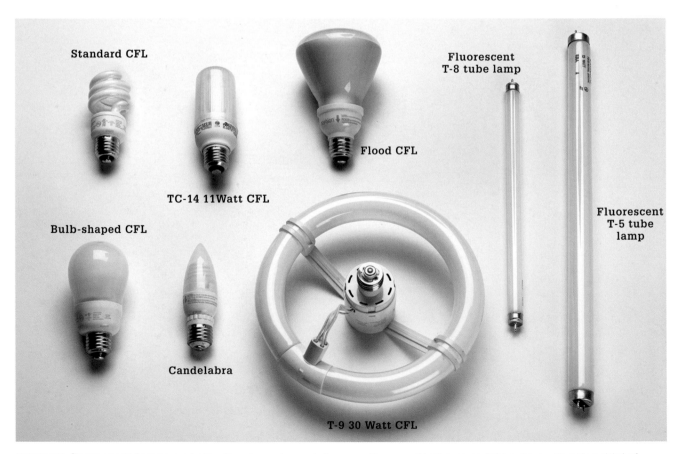

Standard CFL

TC-14 11Watt CFL

Bulb-shaped CFL

Candelabra

Flood CFL

Fluorescent T-8 tube lamp

Fluorescent T-5 tube lamp

T-9 30 Watt CFL

Compact fluorescent lamps are better than incandescents because they provide the same light output with only a third of the wattage. Depending on the type, CLFs can be used with standard incandescent fixtures, fluorescent fixtures, and those with dimmer switches.

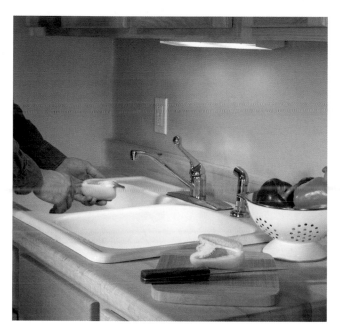

Kitchen and workroom task lighting is a perfect application for today's compact fluorescent tube fixtures.

Innovations in lighting aren't limited to the bulbs. Lighting manufacturers are increasingly blending creative design with fluorescent technology and environmentally friendly fixture materials.

The other big advantage of CFLs is that they burn much cooler than standard incandescent bulbs, which lose 90% to 95% percent of their energy in heat, making them far better heaters than light producers. All of that waste heat puts unnecessary stress on your cooling system and makes it harder to cool your home naturally. The cooler operating temperature of CFLs also makes them superior to halogen lights, which get very hot and are only about ½ as efficient as fluorescents. The waste heat from halogen fixtures can pose a safety hazard, too, especially with torchiere-type floor lamps. If you don't believe it, try putting your hand close to a halogen bulb that's been on for a while (just don't touch it).

So now that you've been convinced to make the switch to CFLs (assuming you needed convincing), what about the light fixtures that don't use standard, screw-in bulbs? Fluorescent tube fixtures, the kind typically used only in utility areas, such as the garage or laundry room, now are available in a wide range of styles and with light quality that makes them suitable for many more applications. Better fixtures (and all CFLs) use electronic ballasts, so the lights start up instantly, and there's none of the annoying humming that plagues magnetic-ballast fixtures. New tube fixtures are also much more efficient and contain fewer toxic materials than older versions.

Streamlined, cool-running fluorescent tube fixtures are ideal for providing focused task lighting in the kitchen (see pages 52 to 53) and in home offices and study areas. For overhead lighting in workrooms, you can easily replace inadequate standard fixtures or old tube fixtures with new electronic ballast units that use T-8 lamps. T-8 lamps use less electricity than standard T-12 tubes, and they put out about 27% more light per watt.

If you'd like to replace standard fixtures in your living spaces or outdoors, consider new fluorescent units with integral ballasts. These are made for CFLs that don't need a ballast for each bulb (like regular CFLs do), which cuts down on production resources. Ballasts in dedicated CFL fixtures can last up to 50,000 hours or more (and are often replaceable), while the bulbs are often cheaper than standard CFLs with integral ballasts. Many types of CFL fixtures offer multiple light settings and dimmer capability. See the projects on pages 212 to 213 for step-by-step instructions on installing CFL and fluorescent tube fixtures.

Tips for Effective & Efficient Lighting ▸

During the day, the best way to illuminate a house is, of course, with natural light. Properly placed windows and skylights bring in huge amounts of free light every day of the year among other obvious benefits. But that's a big subject on its own. Alternatively, for areas that are impractical for window or skylight installations, you might consider adding a solar tube skylight (or "light tube") for natural, no-cost lighting; see pages 214 to 215.

Getting back to artificial lighting, here are some tips for cutting energy use without compromising on the quality of your indoor and outdoor lighting:

- Provide brighter, more focused lighting for tasks instead of raising the levels of overhead or background lights.
- When planning lighting for rooms that need a lot of light, such as the kitchen, start with a bright, central overhead fixture rather than loading up on background or accent lighting (see page 207 for more information on kitchen lighting).
- Install dimmer switches for better control on appropriate fixtures. Dimmers allow you to set the right mood with different light levels and also help save energy during times when you don't need full lighting.
- If you leave some lights on for security when you're away from home, use timers to save energy and create a more realistic impression that you're home.

- Replace standard outdoor flood lamps with outdoor-rated CFLs. Wattages of 9 to 18 watts are recommended for reducing glare and improving nighttime visibility.
- Use solar-powered fixtures for landscape and other outdoor lighting. These are free to operate and can be installed anywhere because they don't have to be wired to a house circuit. Virtually every type of popular outdoor fixture is available in a solar version, including path and driveway lights, patio lights, floods and spotlights, and utility lights for outbuildings.
- Control outdoor lights with timers, photocells, or motion-sensors so lights go on only when they're needed.
- When using incandescent bulbs, remember that a single high-wattage bulb is more efficient than multiple low-wattage bulbs. For example, a 100-watt bulb produces the same light as two 60-watt bulbs or three 40-watt bulbs. *Note: Never exceed a fixture's maximum wattage rating.*
- Replace incandescent nightlights with super-low-wattage LED lights or fluorescent fixtures. LED nightlights can use less than 0.5 watt and may never need to be replaced.
- Turn off the lights when you leave the room. This familiar parental reminder seems to have been lost on many of today's homeowners. It's time to get back into the habit of basic conservation.

Choosing Fluorescent Lights

When shopping for fluorescent bulbs or tubes, choose products based on their type (size, shape, with or without integral ballast, etc.), wattage and light output, and color quality. Lamps earning the Energy Star label meet minimum government requirements for lamp life, light output, and energy use.

TYPE

For use in standard incandescent light fixtures (and fixtures with a dimmer or 3-way switching), you need screw-in bulbs with integral ballasts. Use the manufacturer's recommended bulb type for CFL fixtures. For outdoor fixtures, choose outdoor-rated or cold-start CFLs. In general, fluorescent bulbs are available for most fixtures.

WATTAGE & LIGHT OUTPUT

Wattage is the amount of energy used by a lightbulb, but most people think of this as brightness. However, the true measure of light output is lumens, which may or may not be listed on a product's packaging. If it's not, wattage is the next best indicator. To make things easier for consumers, bulb packages usually state the equivalent wattage of CFL to match the light output of a comparable incandescent bulb. The ratio is approximately 1-to-3; for example: A 13-watt to 15-watt CFL replaces a 60-watt incandescent; an 18-watt to 25-watt CFL replaces a 70-watt incandescent; a 23-watt to 30-watt CFL replaces a 100-watt incandescent

COLOR

The general quality or look of a bulb's light is indicated in its temperature value, or correlated color temperature (CCT), which is measured in degrees kelvin (K):

- For a warm, yellowish glow similar to incandescent light, choose a bulb in the 2,700K to 3,000K range. These are often described as "soft white."
- For brighter, cooler light that's closer to the glow of daylight, look for 4,100K or higher color temperatures. These may be described as "bright white," "cool white," or "natural."

For reading lamps and study areas, you might consider buying a full spectrum bulb, which is designed to mimic the full spectrum of sunlight. This makes reading easier and helps reduce eye strain.

If you can't find the right bulb in your local store, you can probably order it online. General retailers typically carry a very limited range of lighting products, and they mostly stock economy-quality bulbs. A quick Internet search or a visit to a local lighting dealer will give you a better idea of what's available. Also visit the Energy Star website (www.energystar.gov) and click on "Lighting" for more information on choosing and using CFLs.

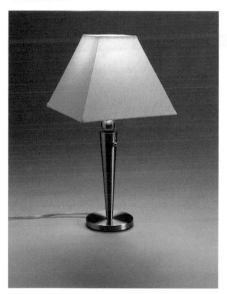  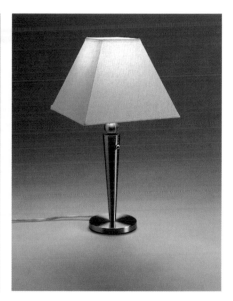

A comparison of three different lamp products in the same fixture: a lower-temperature lamp (left), a higher-temperature lamp (middle), and a full-spectrum lamp (right).

Tip: Recycle Used Fluorescent Bulbs & Ballasts ▶

CFLs and tubes that you buy today contain mercury, the same highly toxic stuff used in old thermometers and thermostats. The amount of mercury in a CFL is about 5 milligrams, which is around 1/100 of the amount found in older thermometers, but it's enough to warrant careful handling to prevent breakage and to recycle the bulbs rather than throw them in the landfill.

Contact your local solid waste authority to learn about where to recycle used CFLs. You can also check online at www.epa.gov/bulbrecycling or www.earth911.org to find recycling centers in your area. Some states prohibit disposal of CFLs in curbside trash pickup.

If you're replacing an old fluorescent tube fixture, be sure to recycle it. Old fixtures contain large amounts of PCB (polychlorinated biphenyl, a highly toxic chemical that was banned in the 1970s) and mercury.

The mercury in CFLs is inside the glass tubing. If you break a bulb, don't vacuum it up. Instead, with gloves on, remove the fragments using a piece of stiff paper, then carefully pick up the white powder with a damp paper towel or wet wipe. Dispose of everything within doubled and sealed plastic bags, and recycle or discard it according to local regulations.

Fluorescent Light Fixtures

Replacing old incandescent lights with energy-efficient fluorescent fixtures is an easy do-it-yourself job. Fluorescent fixtures connect to household (120-volt) circuits just like standard fixtures. Be sure to shut off the power to the circuit at the service panel (breaker box) and test the circuit wires with a neon circuit tester before removing the old fixture wires. Simply turning off the wall switch doesn't ensure that all circuit wires to the electrical box will be without power. Connect the new fixture following the manufacturer's wiring diagram.

How to Remove Light Fixtures

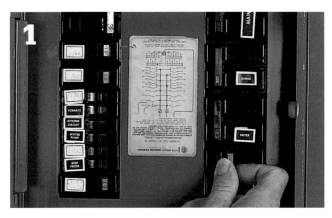

Shut off the power to the fixture's circuit by flipping the appropriate breaker switch (or removing the fuse) at your home's main service panel.

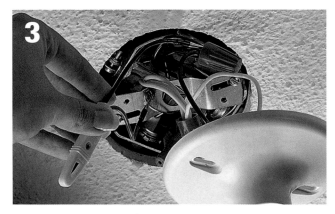

Remove all bulbs from the old fixture. Remove the fixture base or coverplate. Be careful not to touch any wires or sockets until you've tested the circuit for power (Step 3).

Test the circuit wires for power using a neon circuit tester. Touch one probe of the tester to a grounding screw while touching the other probe to the bare ends of each of the circuit wires. If the tester lights up, return to the service panel and shut off the correct circuit.

When you are sure the power is off, remove the circuit wires from the screw terminals on the fixture base, or unscrew the wire connectors to remove the fixture's wire leads.

How to Install an Exterior CFL Fixture

Remove the old light fixture following the steps on page 212. With the power off, inspect the bare-metal ends of the circuit wires. If the ends are nicked or misshapen, cut off the bare end and strip about ½" of the wire insulation using a wire stripper.

With a helper supporting the new fixture, connect the black fixture lead to the black (hot) circuit wire using the appropriate size of wire connector. Connect the white fixture lead to the white (neutral) circuit wire. Connect the green (ground) fixture lead to the circuit's bare copper grounding wire or to the grounding screw on the electrical box if it's a grounded metal box.

Carefully tuck the wires into the electrical box, then mount the fixture to the box using the provided screws. Install the appropriate CFL bulb as directed, then restore power to the circuit to test the fixture.

Tip ▸

To install an interior fluorescent tube fixture, mount the fixture cabinet to the ceiling or wall using the appropriate wall anchors. Make the wiring connections as directed, then install the fixture's internal cover to enclose the wiring before installing the lamps.

Tubular Skylights

Any interior room can be brightened with a tubular skylight. Tubular skylights are quite energy-efficient and are relatively easy to install, with no complicated framing involved.

The design of tubular skylights varies among manufacturers, with some using solid plastic reflecting tubes and others using flexible tubing. Various diameters are also available. Measure the distance between the framing members in your attic before purchasing your skylight, to be sure it will fit.

This project shows the installation of a tubular skylight on a sloped, asphalt-shingled roof. Consult the dealer or manufacturer for installation procedures on other roof types.

Tools & Materials ▸

Pencil	Utility knife
Drill	Chalk
Tape measure	Tubular skylight kit
Wallboard saw	Stiff wire
Reciprocating saw	2" roofing nails or
or jigsaw	flashing screws
Pry bar	Roofing cement
Screwdriver	
Hammer	
Wire cutters	

How to Install a Tubular Skylight

Drill a pilot hole through the ceiling at the approximate location for your skylight. Push a stiff wire up into the attic to help locate the hole. In the attic, make sure the space around the hole is clear of any insulation. Drill a second hole through the ceiling at the centerpoint between two joists.

Center the ceiling ring frame over the hole and trace around it with a pencil. Carefully cut along the pencil line with a wallboard saw or reciprocating saw. Save the wallboard ceiling cutout to use as your roof-hole pattern. Attach the ceiling frame ring around the hole with the included screws.

In the attic, choose the most direct route for the tubing to reach the roof. Find the center between the appropriate rafters and drive a nail up through the roof sheathing and shingles.

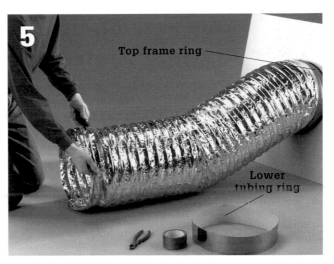

Use the wallboard ceiling cutout, centered over the nail hole, as a template for the roof opening. Trace the cutout onto the roof with chalk. Drill a starter hole to insert the reciprocating saw blade, then cut out the hole in the roof. Pry up the lower portion of the shingles above the hole. Remove any staples or nails around the hole edge.

Pull the tubing over the top frame ring. Bend the frame tabs out through the tubing, keeping two or three rings of the tubing wire above the tabs. Wrap the junction three times around with the included PVC tape. Then, in the attic, measure from the roof to the ceiling. Stretch out the tubing and cut it to length with a utility knife and wire cutters. Pull the loose end of tubing over the lower ring and wrap it three times with PVC tape.

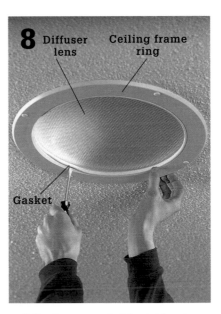

Lower the tubing through the roof hole and slide the flashing into place with the upper portion of the flashing underneath the existing shingles. This is easier with two people, one on the roof and one in the attic.

Secure the flashing to the roof with 2" roofing nails or flashing screws. Seal under the shingles and over all nail heads with roofing cement. Attach the skylight dome and venting to the frame with the included screws.

Pull the lower end of the tubing down through the ceiling hole. Attach the lower tubing ring to the ceiling frame ring and fasten it with screws. Attach the gasket to the diffuser lens and work the gasket around the perimeter of the ceiling frame. Repack any insulation around the tubing in the attic.

The Thermal Envelope

In builders' parlance, *thermal envelope* describes the insulated barrier that separates the inside of a home from the outdoors. This includes the wall and roof structures and finishes, the insulation, the windows and doors, and every building material designed to stop drafts, like weatherstripping and caulk. To the average homeowner, however, this complex thermal system (and its overall effectiveness) boils down to two things: comfort and energy bills.

The greatest energy losses in most homes come from heated air escaping through the thermal envelope. And in hot climates, keeping warm air out can be just as important. Therefore, improving the thermal performance of an existing home starts with a thorough investigation to assess insulation levels, locate possible air leaks, and identify other potential problems such as poor ventilation. You can do some basic sleuthing yourself, but a better option is to hire a professional to perform a complete energy audit.

In this chapter:

- The Good Kind of Audit
- Insulating & Air-Sealing Your Home
- Energy-Efficient Windows

The Good Kind of Audit

If the word *audit* conjures a frightening image of a dour, gray-suited official from the IRS knocking at your door, don't worry; an energy audit is quite a different thing. Energy auditors are trained professionals who use special equipment and techniques to assess the energy performance of a home. In essence, they tell you where your energy dollars are going and offer suggestions for changes to lower your consumption and trim monthly utility bills.

Speaking of utility bills, your energy auditor will probably ask to see a year's worth of them, to look for usage patterns and possibly aberrations that indicate system problems or, more likely, energy-wasting habits. But perhaps the most valuable service provided by energy auditors is in finding out where your house is leaking air and where it needs more insulation. To do this, auditors use a blower door and may use an infrared camera. A blower door seals over an exterior door opening and has a fan that blows out, creating negative pressure (like a vacuum) inside the house.

Energy auditors use blower doors and other specialized equipment to find where homes are leaking air and where they can benefit most from added insulation and other energy improvements.

With the system running, an auditor uses monitoring equipment to pinpoint the major air leaks throughout the house.

An infrared camera, or thermo imaging, tells an auditor where heat is escaping through the walls and other surfaces of a house. For example, if your home's builder neglected to insulate the walls behind your kitchen cabinets (a bizarre yet all-too-common occurrence), it will show up as a dark area on the infrared image. Thermo imaging can also reveal places where insulation was installed improperly or where it has settled over the years, leaving gaps and uninsulated spaces in framing cavities.

In addition to visual and instrument tests on the thermal envelope, an auditor will check your heating and cooling systems for proper operation, temperature settings, potential air leaks, etc. Hot water heaters, major household appliances, and lighting are also considered for their role in the overall energy picture.

After the assessment, your energy auditor can recommend ways for getting the most energy bang for your improvement buck. An experienced auditor can also tell you what's appropriate for your house and the local climate, such as the right types of insulation to use and what you might do to seal or insulate a basement or crawlspace.

If you're planning to invest significant amounts of time and money into energy improvements, an energy audit is essential. You don't want to spend $15,000 to replace your old, leaky windows, when you could save just as much energy by adding $500 worth of insulation to your attic. Or you might want to do both, to double your energy savings. Even if your improvement plans are modest, an energy audit can quickly pay for itself with the knowledge you gain about your house and your living habits.

To find a qualified energy auditor, check with your state energy office and your utility company. They may employ auditors or can direct you to resources for finding them. Some community and municipal energy and conservation programs offer low-cost or subsidized energy audit services. You can also look in the phone book under Energy Management & Conservation Consultants.

An infrared photo can be a valuable tool for tracking down air leaks and identifying the most important improvements you'll need to make to your thermal envelope.

Insulating & Air-Sealing Your Home

Insulation helps keep your home warm (or cool) by slowing the transfer of heat through walls, ceilings, and other surfaces. Most of this transfer occurs through a process of conduction, where the heat travels between molecules in solid objects or in air. Dense materials, like brick and wood, conduct heat better than porous materials, like insulation.

The other process of out-going heat transfer is convection, where heated air is quickly ushered from the warm indoors to the cold outdoors (heat is always drawn to cold, regardless of the means of transfer). Through convection, air leaks compromise your home's thermal envelope in two ways: They allow conditioned air to escape to the outdoors; and they reduce the effectiveness of insulation by compromising its air-trapping qualities.

Windows transfer heat through conduction (via the glass and frame materials), through convection (via air leaks around the sash and framed opening), and through radiation (on light and heat waves passing through the glass). That's why high-performance windows are designed to deal with all three types of heat transfer. New windows are discussed later in this section.

So now you can see how buttoning up your house involves a combination of sealing air leaks and adding insulation where it's needed most.

Stopping Air Leaks

If you've opted for an energy audit, you should have a good idea of where your thermal envelope needs help. If you're doing your own investigative work, here are some prime places to look for leaks:

- worn or missing weatherstripping around windows and doors
- spaces between window and door frames and the structural wall framing
- pipe, vent, and cable penetrations through the roof and exterior walls
- seals where masonry chimneys pass between floors and through the roof
- fireplace dampers
- electrical boxes in exterior walls
- attic access openings (doors or hatches in conditioned living spaces should be insulated on the attic side and sealed with a gasket material)
- standard recessed "can" light fixtures
- the top of foundation walls, where the masonry meets the wood framing (sill plate)

There are a number of products available for sealing air leaks around the home. For sealing around windows and doors, choose a high-quality weatherstripping that's right for each application. Expanding foam sealants are great for sealing large gaps around plumbing pipes and other exterior penetrations. These are commonly available in polyurethane and latex polymer types. Be sure to read the product information carefully, as foams vary in a range of properties, such as heat and fire ratings, UV and water resistance, and expandability.

Careful weatherstripping significantly reduces air leakage around older windows and doors.

Stop air leakage around electrical boxes with foam gaskets or by caulking around the edges of the boxes.

If your windows and doors feel drafty around the interior molding (casing), there may be no insulation between the unit's frame and the wall studs and headers. Remove the casing for an inspection. Fill empty gaps with loosely packed fiberglass insulation or with a low-pressure or mild-expanding foam sealant. Packing too much insulation into the voids or using a high-expanding foam can force the jambs inward, causing the door or window to stick. Replace the casing, then caulk and touch up paint to seal the trim to the surrounding wall surfaces.

High-quality caulk is good for sealing small gaps (up to about ¼" wide) both inside and outside the house. For interior applications, use a paintable caulk that you can paint to match nearby surfaces, or choose a caulk color that will blend in. For exterior applications, use a siliconized latex or acrylic latex caulk rated for exterior use. Most of these are paintable and offer better UV resistance than polyurethane caulks.

Fill uninsulated voids around window and door jambs with minimal expanding foam sealant or loosely packed insulation.

Use a high-quality exterior caulk to seal around exterior wall penetrations, exterior window and door trim, and along the sill plate atop foundation walls.

Insulation

Insulation improvements in existing homes are typically limited to the attic and the basement or crawlspace. Because the walls are already covered and finished, adding insulation there requires replacing the interior or exterior surfaces. However, if you've determined through an energy audit that your walls are uninsulated or have severely compromised insulation (due to settling or other factors), you can have a professional insulator fill the empty wall cavities with blown-in insulation.

Attic insulation is critical to thermal performance for several reasons. Insulation along attic floors (typically in the ceiling framing above the home's top floor) keeps heated air in the living spaces below during the heating season, and it keeps hot attic air from transferring to the living spaces during warmer months. This thermal barrier is especially important in winter, because the chimney effect (see page 193) naturally moves hot air up to upper-floor ceilings where it can easily escape into the attic through conduction or be drawn through air leaks in the ceiling surface. Also, excess heat in an attic space warms up the roof, leading to ice dams in snowy climates.

Most homes, even old ones, have some insulation in their attic. Depending on how much is there,

it might be beneficial to add more insulation, and it's always a good idea to fill in where insulation is insufficient. Adding a blanket of unfaced fiberglass insulation is a common upgrade that homeowners can do themselves. If your attic is vented through soffit vents (under the eaves), make sure the insulation doesn't block airflow underneath the roof deck. If necessary, install insulation baffles to create an air channel above the insulation (see photo, below).

Insulating an unfinished crawlspace or basement is recommended for most homes and climates. If the space is unheated, it's usually best to insulate between the floor joists to keep heated air inside the first-floor living spaces. Fiberglass batts are used most often for this application, but you may prefer to use an alternative batt material. If the batts are faced, position the facing toward the living space.

Be sure to insulate any water piping that may be susceptible to freezing in cold weather (see page 38). It's also a good idea to cover bare dirt floors in crawlspaces with a layer of 6-mil polyethylene sheeting to prevent ground moisture from migrating into the space. Check with your local building department for specific insulation and installation recommendations for your area.

Fiberglass batts are affordable and are still the easiest insulation products for DIYers to install. Here, a second layer of fiberglass insulation is being installed perpendicular to the ceiling joists (attic floor joists) to supplement the attic blanket.

FIP insulation (Foamed In Place) is a relatively new product that normally is installed only by a crew of professionals. The sticky foam is sprayed into the wall cavity and then trimmed flush with the studs after it expands and dries.

Know Your Insulation ▶

The thermal performance of every type of insulation is shown in its value of resistivity, or R-value. The higher the R-value, the better the insulation is at slowing heat transfer through conduction. Residential building codes specify recommended R-value minimums for all areas of a home's thermal envelope. For help with choosing the right type of insulation for your home, consult with your local building department or a qualified energy auditor or insulation professional. Keep in mind that proper installation is essential for achieving the rated R-value of any insulation product.

Here is an overview of the most common types of insulation available:

SPRAYED-FOAM INSULATION

Sprayed-foam, or foamed-in-place, insulation (see photo, previous page) is commonly made with polyurethane foam, while some products are cement-based and some are formulated with soybean oil instead of petroleum products. In existing homes, spray-foam insulation can be used to fill wall cavities through holes in the interior or exterior wall finish. This must be done by a certified professional installer. Avoid polyurethane foams made with ozone-depleting HCFC blowing agents.

COTTON

Cotton insulation is often considered a "natural" alternative to traditional fiberglass. It's made primarily from recycled cotton textiles, such as denim, which are treated with borate for insect and moisture resistance and with non-toxic flame retardants. Cotton insulation products include batts, rolls, and loose-fill forms for blow-in applications.

CELLULOSE

Cellulose is a popular green insulation option for several blow-in applications. It's made primarily from recycled newspaper treated with non-toxic borate and/or ammonium sulfate flame retardants. Damp-spray forms (right) are the standard for new construction, while dry, loose-fill versions are used for blow-in applications in attics and for filling wall cavities in existing homes.

Damp-spray cellulose

FIBERGLASS

By far the most common types of insulation found in American homes are fiberglass batts and rolls. These come in precut strips made to fit between studs, floor joists, rafters, and ceiling joists or truss members. Fiberglass batts are available with or without

Faced fiberglass batts

facings of kraft paper or foil, which serve as a vapor barrier to keep the moisture of hot air out of the framed structure. Vapor barriers are typically installed on the warm-in-winter side of the wall or ceiling. Batts are also available encased in plastic, to contain the glass fibers and eliminate the itchy discomfort of installation. Another form of fiberglass insulation is a loose-fill product used by professionals for blow-in applications in attics.

Conventional forms of fiberglass insulation are made with phenol-formaldehyde binders (see page 235), but now many manufacturers offer formaldehyde-free products for improved indoor air quality. Look for insulation with Greenguard

Unfaced formaldehyde-free

certification (from the Greenguard Environmental Institute) for low emissions.

RIGID FOAM BOARD

Rigid foam panels are widely used to insulate foundation walls and roofs over cathedral ceilings (which often don't have sufficient framing depth for other types of insulation). Two common types are expanded polystyrene (EPS) and polyisocyanurate

(ISO, or "polyiso"). A third type of rigid panel, extruded polystyrene (XPS) is commonly made with HCFC (ozone-depleting) blowing agents and is therefore a less-green option.

High-Performance Windows ▸

Due to their inherent thermal weaknesses and their ability to bring in heat, windows play a disproportionately large role in a home's thermal envelope. Windows can account for a third of the total heat loss in a home and, conversely, most of its heat gain. In other words, in the winter they let out too much heat and in summer they let in too much. Fortunately, building science has made great strides in solving this conundrum, and today's best windows are over twice as efficient as those from 25 years ago.

But does that mean that every green home should have only the latest, most efficient windows available? From an energy standpoint, that would be ideal. But there are other factors at play. Namely, your budget and the fact that the energy savings of new windows can be largely offset by shortcomings elsewhere in the thermal envelope. If you're considering new windows strictly for the energy savings (which can be significant, no doubt), you should have an energy audit done first, to determine just how much the windows will save you as opposed to other, less expensive and less resource-intensive, improvements.

Of course, new windows come with many other great features in addition to energy efficiency, such as easy cleaning and low-maintenance materials and finishes, so there are plenty of reasons to buy them. Here, the discussion will focus on energy performance, which is the biggest differentiator between green and not-so-green windows. If your current window frames and trim are in good condition, you might also consider replacement inserts instead of total window replacement. The project on pages 226 to 227 gives you an overview of how to install replacement windows.

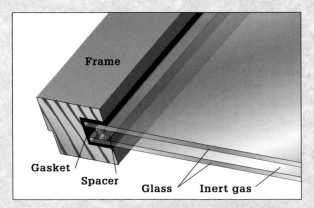

Multiple glazing, gas fill, and low-e coatings are the main technological advances that make today's windows much more energy-efficient than older single-pane windows.

PERFORMANCE FEATURES TO CONSIDER

Regardless of the type, style, or size of window you get, you should be able to choose from a range of high-tech features to tailor the windows' performance to suit your home and climate.

GLAZING

All energy-efficient windows have at least two panes of glass to create an insulating dead-air space within the glazing. Triple- and quadruple-glazed windows are also available, both of which may use a thin film of plastic in place of glass for one or more of the panes. Double-glazed windows insulate almost twice as well as single-glazed units.

GAS FILL

Instead of a sealed air space between glazing panes, manufacturers often fill the space with a low-conductivity gas, which insulates better than air. Argon is the standard gas fill, while krypton or argon-krypton mixtures offer even better performance.

EDGE SPACERS

The spacer material used between multiple layers of glazing is critical to a window's performance and longevity. Spacers separate the glazing and seal in the air or gas fill between the panes. If this seal breaks, the air or gas escapes and fresh air and water vapor are allowed inside, leading to condensation (windows fogging from the inside) and greatly reducing the insulating quality of multiple panes. Common spacer materials include metal (aluminum or steel), silicone foam, butyl rubber, and vinyl. Because metal is a good heat conductor (bad for windows), these spacers should have a thermal break to minimize heat loss. Be sure to ask manufacturers about their warranties against seal failure, as a broken seal usually means the glazing must be replaced.

LOW-E & OTHER COATINGS

A low-e, or low-emmisivity, coating is a super-thin, transparent metal film that lets light and heat in through the window but restricts heat going out. The same technology can be used to keep heat out of a house in warmer climates where cooling is more important than heating.

Tinted glazing is another way to reduce solar heat gain through windows. Better tinted glass and tinting films cut down the heat with less darkening of the window for greater visibility.

PERFORMANCE RATINGS

The primary industry authority that establishes performance ratings on new windows is the National Fenestration Rating Council (NFRC), a nonprofit group made up of window manufacturers, government agencies, and building trade associations. Look to the official NFRC label to compare performance ratings of various products and manufacturers. The two most important energy factors to consider are U-factor and solar heat gain coefficient (SHGC).

U-FACTOR

U-factor is a measure of how well a window insulates between hot and cold areas. NFRC tests for U-factor take into account the entire window—the glass, the glazing edges, and the window frame. The lower the U-factor, the better the window is at keeping heat in, or out of, a home.

SOLAR HEAT GAIN COEFFICIENT

SHGC is a measure of how much solar heat a window lets in. Generally, homes in cold climates should have windows with high SHGC, while homes in hot climates are better with lower SHGC. However, you may decide to fine-tune your windows' heat gain based on each window's location in your home.

ADDITIONAL PERFORMANCE RATINGS

Two other factors that may or may not be included on NFRC labels are visible transmittance and air leakage. The visible transmittance rating indicates how much light is allowed through a window. Clear-glass windows with minimal frame structures have higher visible transmittance ratings than tinted windows and those with more framing per glass area.

Air leakage is pretty self-explanatory. It's a measure of how much air can get through the window at joints where the sash meets the frame and other points of air infiltration. A non-operable picture window will have lower air leakage rating than a double-hung or slider window.

Choosing the best windows for your home and climate involves balancing the various performance features and ratings, which can get pretty confusing. To help consumers make informed choices, the Energy Star website includes a wealth of information on selecting windows for different weather zones. You can also find a list of manufacturers with Energy Star-qualified products, plus help with finding out about tax credits for purchasing high-performance windows. See the Tip below for additional resources on choosing new windows.

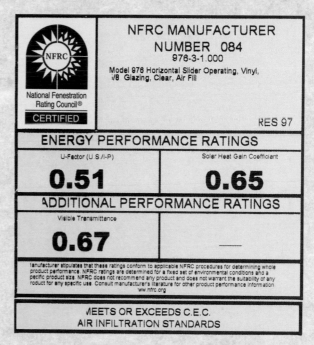

Official NFRC labels carry the "CERTIFIED" NFRC logo and include a description of the window or product line.

Tip: Resources for Window Information ▸

- Energy Star: www.energystar.gov
- NFRC: www.nfrc.org
- Efficient Windows Collaborative: www.efficientwindows.org
- American Architectural Manufacturers Association: www.aamanet.org
- Home Energy Magazine: www.homeenergy.org

Energy-Efficient Windows

Replacement window inserts can be a great money-saving alternative to complete ("prime") window replacement. Inserts are custom-made to fit into your old window jamb frames. This means you don't have to replace your old jambs, trim, and interior and exterior wall surfaces surrounding the windows. With proper installation, inserts can offer virtually the same levels of energy performance as new windows.

The following is an overview of how to install a new replacement window in an existing window frame (often called "pocket window" replacement). Installation procedures are very specific to each product, so be sure to follow the manufacturer's directions for all measuring, ordering, and installation steps. To ensure optimal energy performance, make sure your old window frames are properly insulated and air-sealed, particularly the spaces between the window frame and the structural wall framing.

Tools & Materials ▸

Putty knife	Safety glasses
Pry bar	Caulk gun
Utility knife	Replacement insert window
Screwdrivers	Wood shims
Level	Backer rod
Drill	Exterior paintable caulk

Replacement inserts give you all the performance benefits of new windows without the expense or disruption of complete window replacements.

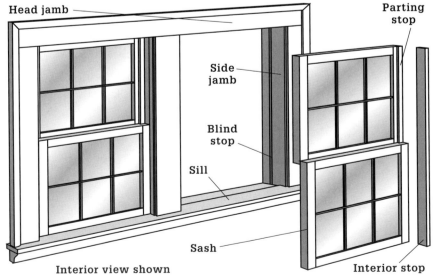

Interior view shown

Head jamb · Side jamb · Blind stop · Sill · Sash · Parting stop · Interior stop

When removing old windows, score the paint along the interior stop and any interior molding at the side and head jambs, then remove carefully using a stiff putty knife or a pry bar. If the stop or molding is difficult to remove, use a wood chisel. Be careful not to damage the blind stop. Make sure to inspect the jambs, blind stop, and sills for signs of water damage. Repair or replace any damaged or rotted members before installing the replacement insert. Also, clean the opening of any dirt, debris, or excess old paint.

How to Install Replacement Inserts

Take three measurements for both the height and width, and use the smallest dimensions for ordering. For the height, measure between the head jamb and sill at both side jambs and in the middle, and for the width, between the side jambs at the top, middle, and bottom. Make sure to measure from the jambs and not the blind or parting stops.

To remove old windows, use a putty knife or pry bar to carefully pry the interior stop and molding at the jambs (see illustration, page 226). Cut the sash cords and let the weights fall into the weight cavity, then remove the lower sash. Next, remove the parting stop and upper sash; be careful not to damage the blind stop. Finally, remove the sash cord pulleys and fill the weight cavity with insulation.

Install the sill angle at the bottom of the insert on the exterior side. Attach the head expander to the top of the unit, placing insulation in between the two. Apply a bead of caulk along both the sill angle and the head expander.

Apply caulk to the inside edges of the blind stop, then lift the insert into the opening with the bottom, inside edge on the sill. Tilt the top into the opening until the entire unit is tight against the blind stop. Make sure the sill angle remains in place, flush with the sill. Check the insert for plumb, level, and square using a level and tape measure. Use wood shims to make adjustments.

Remove the sash stops and place shims behind the screw mounting holes, located at the top-inside and bottom-outside jamb pockets. Drill pilot holes and install the installation screws. Recheck the insert for square and adjust the installation screws as needed, then snap the sash stops back in place. If necessary, align the sash and jamb by tightening the adjustment screws located near the center of the lower sash side jambs. Finally, push the head expander against the jamb and secure with the provided screws.

On the interior side, replace any molding, then seal any gaps between the molding and insert using an exterior-grade, paintable caulk. Fill large gaps with backer rope before caulking. Refinish wood frames as desired. On the exterior side, caulk any gaps between the insert frame and the blind stop, sill, and brick molding. Also fill any old screw holes from storm windows or screens.

APPENDIX: Solar for the Home

When NASA scientists of the 1950s needed a revolutionary source of power for their spacecraft, they had to look and think beyond the earth. Their challenge was monumental, yet their solution poetically simple: They would find a way to tap into the most abundant, most accessible, and most reliable source of energy in the universe—the sun.

Producing your own electricity with photovoltaics, or PV, is certainly one of the most exciting and rewarding ways of going green. And in addition to electrical power, homeowners everywhere are using the sun to heat water for their showers, heating systems, and even swimming pools. The economic benefits can be significant, and when you consider that supplying the average home with conventional power creates over three tons of carbon emissions each year (over twice that of the average car), the environmental benefits of pollution-free, solar energy are nothing to squint at.

This appendix introduces you to the most popular solar options for supplementing your existing systems or even declaring energy independence by taking your home "off the grid." As solar technology continues its journey from the space program to suburban rooftops and beyond, anyone serious about climbing aboard will find a vibrant new marketplace that's more than ready to help.

Made with lightweight materials and highly durable materials, today's low-profile solar panels are ideal for discreet rooftop installation.

New solar products have made it easier to be green in urban locations. Here, slim solar panels are secured to a homeowner's balcony in the city.

Solar for Electricity

Residential PV systems supply electricity directly to a home through solar panels mounted on the roof or elsewhere. These are essentially the same systems that pioneering homeowners installed back in the 1970s, except in those days panels were less efficient and much more expensive—to the tune of over $300 per watt in setup costs compared to around $9 per watt today (and people in many areas can cut that number in half with renewable energy rebates and tax credits).

Here's how PV power works: A solar panel is made up of small solar cells, each containing a thin slice of a silicon, the same stuff used widely in the computer industry. Silicon is an abundant natural resource extracted from the earth's crust. It has semi-conductive properties, so that when light strikes the positive side of the slice, electrons try to move to the negative side. By connecting the two sides with a wire, you create an electrical circuit and a means for harnessing this electrical activity.

Solar cells are grouped together and connected by wires to create a module, or panel. Modules can be installed in a series to create a solar "array." The size of an array, as well as the quality of the semiconductor material, determines its power output.

The electricity produced by solar cells is DC, or direct current, which is what most batteries produce and what battery-powered devices run on. Most household appliances and light fixtures run on AC, or alternating current, electricity. Therefore, PV systems include an inverter that converts the DC power from the panels to AC power for use in the home. It's all the same to your appliances, and they run just as well on solar-generated power as on standard utility power.

GRID-CONNECTED & OFF-THE-GRID SYSTEMS

Home PV systems can be designed to connect to the local utility network (the power grid) or to supply the home with all of its electricity without grid support. There are advantages and disadvantages to each configuration.

In a grid-connected setup, the utility system serves as a backup to supply power when household demand exceeds the solar system's capacity or during the hours when the sun is down. This obviates the need for batteries or a generator for backup and makes

Being off the grid means no electric bill, no concerns about rate hikes, and no utility-based power outages.

Solar cells: building blocks for a future of clean energy.

grid-connected systems simpler and less expensive than off-the-grid systems. One of the best advantages of grid connection is that when the solar system's output exceeds the house's demand, it delivers power back to the grid and you (may) get credit for every watt produced. This is called net-metering and is guaranteed by law in many states; however, not every state requires utility companies to offer it, and not all companies offer the same payback. Some simply let the meter roll backwards, essentially giving you full retail value for the power, while others buy back power at the utility's standard production price—much less than what they charge consumers.

The main drawbacks of being tied to the grid are that you may still have to pay service charges for the utility connection even if your net consumption

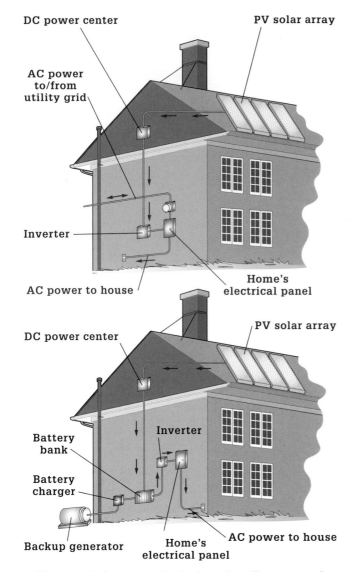

Labels for top diagram:
- DC power center
- AC power to/from utility grid
- PV solar array
- Inverter
- AC power to house
- Home's electrical panel

Labels for bottom diagram:
- DC power center
- PV solar array
- Battery bank
- Battery charger
- Inverter
- Backup generator
- Home's electrical panel
- AC power to house

Grid-connected systems (top) rely on the utility company for supplemental and backup energy. Off-the-grid systems (bottom) are self-sufficient and must use batteries for energy storage and a generator (usually gas-powered) for backup supply.

is zero, and you're still vulnerable to power outages at times when you're drawing from the grid. But the convenience of grid backup combined with the lower cost and reduced maintenance of grid-tied systems makes them the most popular choice among homeowners in developed areas.

Off-the-grid, or stand-alone, systems serve as the sole supply of electricity for a home. They include a large enough panel array to meet the average daily demand of the household. During the day, excess power is stored in a bank of batteries for use when the sun is down or when extended cloud cover results in low output. Most stand-alone systems also have a gas-powered generator as a separate, emergency backup.

For anyone building a new home in an undeveloped area, installing a complete solar system to provide your own power can be less expensive than having the utility company run a line out to the house (beyond a quarter-mile or so, new lines can be very costly). There are some maintenance costs, namely in battery replacement, but it's possible to save a lot of money in the long run, and never having to pay a single electric bill is deeply satisfying to off-the-grid homeowners.

As mentioned, off-the-grid systems are a little more complicated than grid-tied setups. There are the batteries to care for, and power levels have to be monitored to prevent excessive battery run-down and to know when generator backup is required. To minimize power demands, off-the-grid homes tend to be highly energy-efficient. Using super-efficient appliances and taking smaller steps like connecting electronics to power strips that can be switched off to prevent small but cumulative energy losses from devices running in "standby" mode enables homeowners to get by with smaller, less expensive solar arrays. If you're interested in taking your home off the grid, talk with as many experts and off-the-grid homeowners as you can. Their experiences can teach you invaluable lessons for successful energy independence.

SOLAR PANEL PRODUCTS

PV modules come in a range of types for different applications and power needs. The workhorse of the group is the glass- or plastic-covered rigid panel that can be mounted to the roof of a house or other structure, on an exterior wall, or on the ground at various distances from the house. Panel arrays can also be mounted onto solar-powered tracking systems that follow the sun for increased productivity.

Rigid modules, sometimes called framed modules, are designed to withstand all types of weather, including hail, snow, and extreme winds, and manufacturers typically offer warrantees of 20 to 25 years. Common module sizes range in width from about 2 ft. to 4 ft. and in length from 2 ft. to 6 ft. Smaller modules may weigh less than 10 pounds, while large panels may be 30 to 50 pounds each.

In addition to variations in size, shape, wattage rating, and other specifications, standard PV modules can be made with two different types of silicon cells. Single crystalline cells contain a higher grade of silicon and offer the best efficiency of sunlight-to-electricity conversion—typically around 10% to 14%.

Multicrystalline, or polycrystalline, cells are made with a less exacting and thus cheaper manufacturing process. Solar conversion of these is slightly less than single crystalline, at around 10% to 12%, but warrantees on panels may be comparable. All solar cells degrade slowly over time. Standard single crystalline and multicrystalline cells typically lose 0.25% to 0.5% of their conversion efficiency each year.

This fiber-cement shingle roof features an integrated array of shingles laminated with thin-film PV modules.

Mounting solar arrays on the ground offers greater flexibility in placement when rooftop installation is impractical or prohibited by local building codes or homeowners associations.

AMORPHOUS SOLAR CELLS

Another group of solar products are made with amorphous, or thin-film, technology in which non-crystalline silicon is deposited onto substrates, such as glass or stainless steel. Some substrates are flexible, allowing for a range of versatile products, including self-adhesive strips that can be rolled out and adhered to metal roofing and thin solar modules that install just like traditional roof shingles. Amorphous modules typically offer lower efficiency—around 5% to 7%—and a somewhat faster degradation of 1% or more per year.

THE ECONOMICS OF GOING SOLAR

While the environmental benefits of solar electricity are obvious and irrefutable, most people looking into adding a new solar system need to examine the personal financial implications of doing so. PV systems cost only a small fraction of what they did 30 years ago, but they're still quite expensive. For example, a three-kilowatt system capable of supplying most or all of the electricity for a typical green home can easily cost $30,000 (before rebates and credits) and take 20 to 25 years to pay for itself in reduced energy bills. An off-the-grid system will cost even more. Nevertheless, depending on the many factors at play, going solar can be a sound investment with a potentially high rate of return.

One way to consider solar as an investment is to think of it as paying for a couple of decades' worth of electricity bills in advance. Thanks to the long warrantees offered by manufacturers and the reliability of today's systems, the costs of maintenance on a system are predictably low. This means that most of your total expense goes toward the initial setup of the system. If you divide the setup cost (after rebates and credits) by the number of kilowatt hours (kWh) the system will produce over its estimated lifetime, you'll

Installing solar panels over an arbor, pergola, or other overhead structure can create a unique architectural element. Here, panels over an arbor provide shade for a patio space while generating electricity for the house.

come up with a per-kWh price that you can compare against your current utility rate. Keep in mind that your solar rate, as it were, is locked in, while utility rates are almost certain to rise over the lifetime of your system.

Now, about those rebates and credits: In many areas, homeowners going solar can receive sizable rebates through state, local, or utility-sponsored programs, in addition to federal tax credits, as applicable. All told, these financial incentives can add up to 50% or more of the total setup cost of a new PV system. To find out about what incentives are available through any of these sources, check out the Database of State Incentives for Renewables & Efficiency, online at www.dsireusa.org. Established solar businesses in any given area are also very well informed about incentives available to local residents.

Here are some of the factors that tend to affect the cost of a PV system, its effectiveness or efficiency, and the homeowner's return on investment:

- The house and geographic location—how much sun reaches the house; the roof's slope and roofing material
- Electric utility rates and net-metering rates
- Increased home value—PV systems and other energy-saving upgrades can increase a home's resale value (often without raising the property value used for tax assessment)
- Loan rate, if the system is financed

With so many factors to consider, getting to the bottom line can be complicated. Full-service solar companies will perform a cost/benefit analysis to help potential customers make a decision based on the financial picture. Of course, you should always check their numbers and scrutinize any variables used. You can also learn a lot by talking to other homeowners in your area who have had similar systems installed. Are they getting the return they expected? Have their systems been reliable and low-maintenance? Would they change anything given the chance to do it over?

WORKING WITH SOLAR PROFESSIONALS

Companies that provide solar equipment and system design, installation, and maintenance services are rising in number every year. A few of these were around during the lean years of the 1980s and '90s, but many more have sprouted up in the last decade or so. In any case, this is now a highly competitive industry, so you can, and should, expect great service at competitive prices.

The reputation and reliability of your local solar provider are important considerations, but perhaps more important is the stability of the original equipment manufacturers (OEMs) who produce the main parts of your system and who carry those long warrantees. Many of these are large, well-established companies with expertise in energy and/or electronics, so it's a good bet they'll be around in 20 or 25 years to honor their product warrantees. Always discuss warrantees carefully with your solar provider.

At present, the solar industry really isn't set up for do-it-yourself system design and installation. Professional installation may run you around 15% of the total system cost—quite a low rate for the home improvement industry—and that amount is subject to rebates and credits, which are based on installed system prices.

Before giving you a quote for the system package, a solar provider will want to know about your home, what type of roofing you have and what the southern exposure is like. To ballpark the size of system you'll need, they'll probably look at your utility bills from the past year and ask how much power you want to get from solar: Will it cover all household demand or just a portion of it? You may have to pay a fee to cover the provider's legwork required for working up an accurate quote.

Services likely to be included in a provider's system package are:

- complete system design and installation
- guarantees on workmanship/installation
- obtaining building/electrical permits
- coordinating hookup with utility company
- obtaining rebates and credits
- help with OEM warrantee claims
- lifetime technical support

Another thing to be aware of when comparing various providers' quotes, and in talking to other customers, is the actual output of a panel or array as opposed to its STC (or "name plate") wattage rating. Industry sources say the actual useable power of a system is typically about 75% of the rated power. This means that if your home needs three kilowatts of power your system should be rated for four kilowatts.

Solar for Hot Water & Heating

The science behind solar water heating is quite simple: If you've ever turned on a garden hose that's been left out in the sun (only to get extremely hot water when you expected cold), you pretty much get how it works. In a basic solar hot water system, water or an antifreeze fluid is circulated through rooftop collector units, then down into the house (or swimming pool) where it feeds a system to supply domestic hot water or to supplement space heating equipment.

Solar hot water systems are used in many different climates and are inexpensive and reliable enough to yield relatively quick financial returns in addition to long-term environmental benefits. For most homes, the solar system is used in conjunction with conventional heating equipment, such as a hot water heater or boiler, providing preheated water to the system to reduce its net energy use. On average, solar heaters for domestic hot water are most cost-effective when they supply around 70% of a home's hot water. Solar systems supplementing heating equipment are most cost-effective when designed to offset 40% to 80% of the home's annual demand.

TYPES OF HOT WATER SYSTEMS

The basic setup of a solar hot water system includes one or more collectors, a storage tank, various control devices, and a network of piping. Indirect systems circulate the same water or fluid through a continuous pipe loop and transfer heat via a heat exchanger. Direct systems run fresh water through the collector's piping and into the home for direct use.

Systems are also defined by their means of circulation: active heaters use an electric pump (which may be solar-powered) to move the water or fluid mechanically; passive heaters move water without the use of pumps, usually through the natural process of thermosyphoning: as the water in the collector heats up, it rises up into a storage tank while cold water refills the collector tubes.

Solar heaters for domestic hot water may include a separate storage tank that feeds preheated water into a standard tank-style hot water heater or a tankless on-demand heater (see pages 105 to 107). The water heater can then boost the temperature of the water for use, as needed. In other systems, solar-heated water is fed directly into a single hot water tank, which typically contains its own conventional heat source.

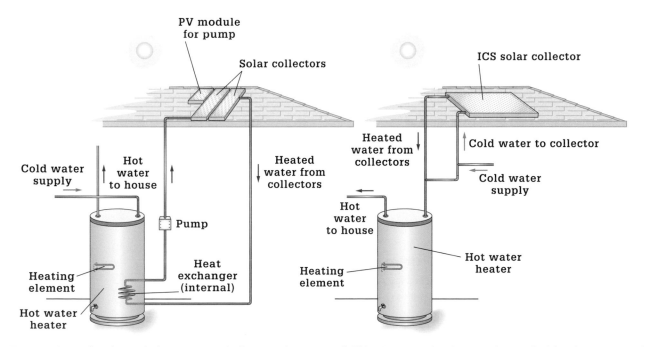

Two systems for domestic hot water: An indirect, active system (left) heats water via a heat exchanger inside a hot water tank and uses a pump to circulate fluid to and from the solar collectors. A direct, passive system (right) heats the same water that gets used in the house and relies on natural processes for circulation.

TYPES OF COLLECTORS

Solar collectors for rooftops and other installations come in a few different varieties. The most widely used type in residential systems is the flat-plate collector, which is essentially a heat-absorbing box filled with winding tubes that carry the water or antifreeze solution for heating. Evacuated tube collectors are made up of parallel rows of glass tubes, each containing a smaller, inner tube that carries the heat transfer fluid. The air space between the inner and outer tubes is vacuumed out (evacuated) to reduce heat loss through convection and conduction. And a third type of collector that's becoming more popular for residential systems is made from plastic polymers (see sidebar, right).

To help consumers and building professionals make informed decisions about solar water systems, there are two groups that provide unbiased performance ratings for different types of solar collectors and hot water systems:

Solar Rating and Certification Corporation

The SRCC is a nonprofit group of solar industry professionals, government energy experts, and consumer advocates. They evaluate and certify solar equipment through their OG-300 program. This group also provides performance estimates for solar products in various climates. Performance ratings and other information are available online at www.solar-rating.org.

Florida Solar Energy Center The FSEC is the Florida state energy research institute. Among its many roles in the solar industry, the FSEC conducts tests to compare the efficiency and economics of flat-plate solar collectors. The institute's website (www.fsec.ucf.edu) includes a list of tested products (by manufacturer), plus numerous educational tools for consumers thinking about going solar.

GETTING STARTED WITH SOLAR HOT WATER

Choosing the right system for your home involves many factors, including the local climate, the orientation of your house, your average hot water or heating needs, and the existing systems and how they will integrate with the solar equipment. For help with assessing your situation, consult with local solar providers—experienced professionals who design and install the types of systems you're interested

in. Local pros know best how to design systems for the prevailing conditions and are up to date on the financial incentives available to local residents. For additional considerations when choosing a solar provider or contractor, see Working with Solar Professionals, on page 232.

DIY Solar ▸

Solar water heating has long been available to homeowners wanting to reduce their energy bills, but until recently the systems have never been designed for do-it-yourself installation. One product changing that is the lightweight polymer solar collector. While standard copper or glass tube collectors are housed in heavy rigid panels that must be hoisted onto rooftops with a crane or a small crew, polymer collectors weigh less than ½-lb. per square foot and can easily be installed by two people. They're also flexible and can be rolled up for efficient shipping and transport. Another feature of easy-install solar hot water kits is flexible PEX tubing, which replaces the rigid copper or plastic piping found on standard systems; flexible tubing is much simpler to install and is easy to route around framing and other obstructions.

The collector shown here can be laid right over standard roofing shingles and mounted with straps and screws. Installation typically takes less than a day.

Glossary

Active solar—Solar equipment or system that has a mechanical device, like a pump or fan.

Blowing agent—Chemical compound that creates air pockets in foam insulation. Traditional agents with ozone-depleting HCFCs and CFCs have been removed from the market, with the exception of extruded polystyrene (XPS).

Btu—British thermal unit; the amount of heat energy required to raise the temperature of one pound of water 1°F. See also: Therm

Carbon dioxide (CO2)—A colorless gas produced by combustion, respiration of animals, and decay of animal and vegetable matter. A primary greenhouse gas, CO2 is absorbed from the air by plants through photosynthesis.

Carbon monoxide (CO)—A colorless, odorless, highly toxic gas resulting from incomplete carbon combustion.

Certified wood—Certified by a third-party organization to come from responsibly managed forests and involve sustainable production methods. See also: Forest Stewardship Council (FSC).

Conduction—The molecule-to-molecule transfer of heat through a material.

Convection—The transfer of heat via fluid, air, or refrigerant.

Daylighting—The use of sunlight to illuminate interior spaces.

Deconstruction—Disassembly of a structure in order to salvage all re-usable materials.

Energy Star—Program sponsored by the U.S. Dept. of Energy and the U.S. EPA that awards Energy Star labels to the most energy-efficient products. Energy Star products are typically 10% to 30% more efficient than their conventional counterparts.

Engineered wood—Wood product made with wood fibers, chips, or thin layers bound with adhesive. Engineered wood is a resource-efficient alternative to solid lumber for a variety of structural and finish applications.

Embodied energy—Total energy required to produce a product or material. Includes growing, harvesting, or mining raw materials; fabrication and installation of the finished product; and all transportation throughout the process. Commonly used as a measure of a product's environmental impact.

Forest Stewardship Council (FSC)—Independent, non-profit organization that sets standards for sustainable forestry and wood harvesting and production practices. The FSC and its approved third-party certifiers monitor wood products from the forest to point of sale.

Formaldehyde—Toxic organic gas commonly used in the manufacture of adhesives, binders, and preservatives. Formaldehyde is a known carcinogen.

Gray water—Household waste water from sources such as dishwashers, clothes washers, showers, baths, and bathroom sinks. May include fresh water from kitchen sinks but does not include food waste or waste from toilets (black water) or other sewage.

Greenhouse gas—Any of a variety of heat-trapping gasses that absorb infrared radiation from the sun and are believed to contribute to global warming. The primary greenhouse gases are carbon dioxide and water vapor. Other types include methane, nitrogen oxides, and ozone.

Ground-level ozone (O3)—Primary element of smog. Created by a chemical reaction when nitrogen oxides and volatile organic compounds (VOCs) combine in sunlight. Sources of nitrogen oxides and VOCs include electric power plants, motor vehicles, and chemical solvents. Ground-level ozone contributes to a number of human health problems and widespread damage to the ecosystem. It has the same chemical structure as the protective layer of ozone in the earth's stratosphere.

Hydrochlorofluorocarbon (HCFC)—When released into the atmosphere, Hydrogenated chlorofluorocarbon (chemical compound used in refrigerants and as a blowing agent for plastic foam and insulation) damage the ozone layer protecting Earth from solar radiation. CFCs are far more damaging to the ozone layer than HCFCs and were banned by the EPA in 1997.

Kilowatt-hour (kWh)—A measure of electrical power consumption. A 100-watt light bulb burning for 10 hours uses one kilowatt-hour (1kWh) of electricity. One kilowatt equals 1,000 watts.

Offgassing (outgassing)—Release of vapors or volatile chemicals into the air. Common sources include: paints, stains, adhesives, home furnishings, and various building materials.

Old-growth—Natural forests of mature trees or the trees or timber from such forests. In general, old-growth forests are biologically diverse and are not touched by logging operations.

Passive solar—Heating the interior of a home by collecting and storing heat from the sun. This solar system does not require mechanical equipment for operation.

Phenol-formaldehyde—Formaldehyde-based binder (adhesive) made with phenolic resins, used to manufacture exterior-grade plywood and fiberglass insulation. Typically offgas lower levels of formaldehyde than urea-formaldehyde binders.

Post-consumer—Recycled goods from discarded consumer products, such as newspapers and beverage containers.

Post-industrial—Recycled content from manufacturing processes.

Polyvinyl chloride (PVC, vinyl)—Thermoplastic polymer used in construction and household products. Green experts recommend not to use PVC products due to health concerns affiliated with the manufacture, use, and destruction of PVC.

R-value—Measure of resistance to heat conduction, used as a performance rating for insulation. A higher R-value results in better insulation.

Radiation—Transfer of heat via electromagnetic waves moving through space (air). The sun warms objects via radiation.

Renewable energy—Electricity or thermal energy produced from solar, wind, hydropower, or biomass resources.

Renewable resource—Materials that are quickly and efficiently replenished.

Sustainable—Practices and methods that support long-term implementation without causing excessive damage or permanent depletion of resources.

Thermal envelope (building envelope)—House exterior that protects the structure and interior from moisture, cold, heat, and air infiltration. Includes exterior walls, roofing, foundation, windows, doors, and insulation.

Therm—Quantity of heat equal to 100,000 Btu. Used as a measure of natural gas household consumption. See: Btu.

Thermal mass—Ability to absorb and store heat. Materials with high thermal mass, such as concrete, store solar heat during the day, then release it as the temperature drops.

Urea-formaldehyde—Formaldehyde-based binder often used in plywood and other sheet goods. They typically offgas higher levels of formaldehyde than phenol-formaldehyde binders.

Volatile Organic Compound (VOC)—A class of chemical compounds that readily volatize (turn to vapor) at room temperature. VOCs occur naturally and during the production of products such as paints, stains, adhesives, caulks, and household furnishings. When released into sunlit air, VOCs contribute to ground-level ozone (smog). Direct exposure to VOCs can cause short- and long-term reactions, including nausea, headache, and eye irritation.

Metric Conversion Chart

Lumber Dimensions

Nominal - U.S.	Actual - U.S. (in inches)	Metric	Nominal - U.S.	Actual - U.S. (in inches)	Metric
1 × 2	¾ × 1½	19 × 38 mm	1½ × 4	1¼ × 3½	32 × 89 mm
1 × 3	¾ × 2½	19 × 64 mm	1½ × 6	1¼ × 5½	32 × 140 mm
1 × 4	¾ × 3½	19 × 89 mm	1½ × 8	1¼ × 7¼	32 × 184 mm
1 × 5	¾ × 4½	19 × 114 mm	1½ × 10	1¼ × 9¼	32 × 235 mm
1 × 6	¾ × 5½	19 × 140 mm	1½ × 12	1¼ × 11¼	32 × 286 mm
1 × 7	¾ × 6¼	19 × 159 mm	2 × 4	1½ × 3½	38 × 89 mm
1 × 8	¾ × 7¼	19 × 184 mm	2 × 6	1½ × 5½	38 × 140 mm
1 × 10	¾ × 9¼	19 × 235 mm	2 × 8	1½ × 7¼	38 × 184 mm
1 × 12	¾ × 11¼	19 × 286 mm	2 × 10	1½ × 9¼	38 × 235 mm
1¼ × 4	1 × 3½	25 × 89 mm	2 × 12	1½ × 11¼	38 × 286 mm
1¼ × 6	1 × 5½	25 × 140 mm	3 × 6	2½ × 5½	64 × 140 mm
1¼ × 8	1 × 7¼	25 × 184 mm	4 × 4	3½ × 3½	89 × 89 mm
1¼ × 10	1 × 9¼	25 × 235 mm	4 × 6	3½ × 5½	89 × 140 mm
1¼ × 12	1 × 11¼	25 × 286 mm			

Metric Conversions

To Convert:	To:	Multiply by:	To Convert:	To:	Multiply by:
Inches	Millimeters	25.4	Millimeters	Inches	0.039
Inches	Centimeters	25.4	Centimeters	Inches	0.394
Feet	Meters	0.305	Meters	Feet	3.28
Yards	Meters	0.914	Meters	Yards	1.09
Square inches	Square centimeters	6.45	Square centimeters	Square inches	0.155
Square feet	Square meters	0.093	Square meters	Square feet	10.8
Square yards	Square meters	0.836	Square meters	Square yards	1.2
Ounces	Milliliters	30.0	Milliliters	Ounces	.033
Pints (U.S.)	Liters	0.473 (Imp. 0.568)	Liters	Pints (U.S.)	2.114 (Imp. 1.76)
Quarts (U.S.)	Liters	0.946 (Imp. 1.136)	Liters	Quarts (U.S.)	1.057 (Imp. 0.88)
Gallons (U.S.)	Liters	3.785 (Imp. 4.546)	Liters	Gallons (U.S.)	0.264 (Imp. 0.22)
Ounces	Grams	28.4	Grams	Ounces	0.035
Pounds	Kilograms	0.454	Kilograms	Pounds	2.2

Photographers

Carolyn Bates
p. 12, 17, 130, 216

Collinstock, LLC, photo by Greg Premru
p. 76

Fotolia / www.fotolia.com
p.168 (top) © Olga D. van de Veer

Garden Picture Library
p. 174 Ron Sutherland

Tony Giammarino
p. 55 (top)

Tria Giovanni
p. 80

istock / www.istock.com
p. 8 Paul Vasarhelyi, 9, 10, 25, 37, 95
  (lower left), 104 Tomas Bercic, 112,
134 Brad Killer, 164 (left) Ann Abejon,
165 (left) Jan Paul Schrage, 165 (right)
Warren Brooks, 167, 168 (lower), 169,
175, 191 (right), 209 (right), 226 (lower)
Alan Tobey, 227 (top) Jim Pruitt, 228
(lower), 229 (top)

Dency Kane
www.dencykane.com
p. 169 (lower)

Douglas Keister
p. 7 (top), 54

Karen Melvin
p.63 (left)

Andrea Rugg
p. 16, 22, 56, 206

Roger Turk / Northlight Photography
p. 49 (left), 63 (right)

Brian Vanden Brink
p. 6, 162

Jessie Walker
p. 164 (right), 176 (left), 190, 228 (top)

Scott Zimmerman
p. 4, 118, 160, 186

Resources

AAir Vent, Inc.
800 AIR VENT
www.airvent.com
p. 192

The American Institute of Achitects
800 AIA 3837
www.aia.org
p.15

Alcoa
www.alcoa.com
p. 11 (lower)

A. O. Smith
www.hotwater.com
p. 108

Atlantis Energy
Sun Slates
916 438 2930
www.atlantispv.com
p. 229 (lower), 231 (top right)

Black & Decker
800 544 6986
p. 166

Bricor
800 624 7228
www.bricor.com
p. 101 (lower right & left)

Buderus / Bosch
600 552 1100
www.buderus.net
www.bbtna.com
p. 105 (left), 107

Bulbrite Industries
201 531 5900
www.bulbrite.com

Carrier Corp.
www.corp.carrier.com
p.195

Central Fiber Corp.
800 654 6117
www.centralfiber.com
p. 222 (right)

Dawn Solar
Solar water heating systems
866 338 2018
p. 106 (lower)

Diamond Cabinets
www.diamond2.com
p. 59 (top), 61 (right)

Eco-Friendly Flooring
866 250 3273
www.ecofriendlyflooring.com
p. 75 (lower), 79 (right)

Ecotimber
888 801 0855
www.ecotimber.com
p. 74, 75 (top)

The Energy Conservatory
www.energyconservatory.com
p. 218

Energy Star
www.energystar.gov
p. 21 (right), 200 (top) Honeywell / Energy Star

Envirosink®
888 663 4950
www.envirosink.com
p.34, 39

FLOR
Recycled carpet tiles
www.flor.com
p. 142-145

Gaggenau
877 4GAGGENAU
www.gaggenau.com
p. 24 (top)

General Electric
p. 20 (right), 23, 26, 29, 36 (lower), 42

Green Leaf Cabinetry
877 422 2463
www.greenleafcabinetry.com

H20 Kits
888 H20 KITS
www.h2okits.com

Hakatai Enterprises, Inc.
888 667 2429
www.hakatai.com
p. 45, 129

Hamilton beach
p. 24 (lower)

Heliocol
800 79 SOLAR
www.heliocol.com
p. 7 (lower)

Henkel
www.henkel.com
p. 11 (middle)

Honeywell
http://yourhome.honeywell.com

Hot2O
530 332 2100
www.fafco.com
p. 106 (top), p.234

IceStone
718 624 4900
www.icestone.biz
p. 64 (top), 79 (middle)

Ikea
610 834 0180
www.ikea-usa.com
p. 18, 125 (lower left), 209 (right)

Kohler
www.kohler.com
p. 51, 82, 84, 85, 86, 87 (top), 95 (top), 100,
    125 (lower right)

Lennox
800 953 6669
www.lennox.com
p. 201 (lower)

National Association of Home Builders
    (NAHB)
www.nahb.org
The nation's leading organization of
    professional home builders educates
    members and consumers on a broad
    range of green building issues. The
    NAHB's Model Green Home Building
    Guidelines formed the basis of the
    National Green Building Standard, used
    by home builders when designing and
    building a green home. Information
    about the standard and the companion
    NAHB National Green Building Program is
    available at the Association's website.

Namasté Solar / Atlantis Energy
303 447 0300
www.namastesolar.com
p. 231 (left top and lower)

Natural Area Rugs
www.naturalarearugs.com
p. 140

Neil Kelly Cabinets
www.neilkellycabinets.com
p. 48, 79 (left)

New England Classic
888 460 6324
www.newenglandclassic.com
p. 138 (lower)

Niagra Conservation
Earth™ Massage 1.5 gpm Showerhead
800 831 8383
www.niagra
p. 101 (top)

Oasis Montana
www.eco-fridge.com
p. 20

Paperstone
360 538 9815
www.paperstoneproducts.com
p. 64 (lower)

Room and Board
800 301 9720
www.roomandboard.com
p. 77, 132

Shetka Stone
p. 13

Solatube International, Inc.
888 765 2882
www.solatube.com

Sun-Mar Corp.
888 341 0782
www.sun-mar.com
p.87 (lower)

Teragren
Fine bamboo flooring, panels & veneer
800 929 6333
www.teragren.com
p146-151

Tremron Group
800 567 1480
www.tremron.com
p.176 (right)

TREX
800 289 8739
www.trex.com
p. 181

The United States Green
    Building Council (USGBC)
Non-profit composed of leaders from
    every sector of the building industry
    working to promote buildings that are
    environmentally responsible, profitable,
    and healthy places to live and work.
202 828 7422
www.usgbc.org
P.14

Urban Homes, NY
www.uhny.com
p. 49 (right)

Vermont Castings
800 668 5323
www.vermontcastings.com
p. 152-153

Wilsonart
www.wilsonart.com
p. 62

Index

Also From CREATIVE PUBLISHING international

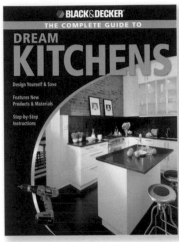
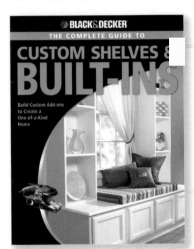
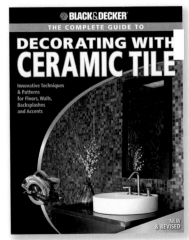